THE
INQUISITION

THE INQUISITION

THE HAMMER OF HERESY

EDWARD BURMAN

SUTTON PUBLISHING

This book was first published by The Aquarian Press in 1984

This edition first published in 2004 by
Sutton Publishing Limited · Phoenix Mill
Thrupp · Stroud · Gloucestershire · GL5 2BU

British Library Cataloguing in Publication Data
A catalogue record for this book is available from the British
Library

ISBN 0 7509 3722 X

Printed and bound in Great Britain by
J.H. Haynes & Co. Ltd, Sparkford.

Contents

For
Martin Booth

Preface

In the popular imagination, the Inquisition is synonymous with terror, nocturnal arrest and torture. Its fictional evocation pervades Edgar Allan Poe's story *The Pit and the Pendulum,* with its chilling description of the pendulum torture, and it has thus contributed to the genre of horror stories; opera lovers recall Don Alhambra del Bolero, the Grand Inquisitor of Gilbert and Sullivan's *The Gondoliers,* or the terrifying ending of Verdi's *Don Carlo*; readers of poetry remember the lines from Tennyson's poem *The Revenge:*

> I should count myself the coward if I left them, my Lord
>   Howard,
> To these Inquisition dogs and the devildoms of Spain.

More recently, the Monty Python team has used the same potent images of terror to comic effect.

But the Inquisition, or Holy Office, is something infinitely more complex and fascinating than these images and stereotypes might suggest, and its history over the past seven hundred years provides an intriguing alternative viewpoint for reflection on the modern history of Europe. The aim of this book is to present an overall interpretation of the Inquisition from its origins in the early thirteenth century to its lingering influences today. This necessarily entails a synthesis of previous research rather than the study of primary sources, and has been carried out mainly on the basis of materials published since the middle of the nineteenth century. But while using secondary sources, reference has been made as often as possible to primary materials printed in them and to editions of manuscripts, rather than to the ready-made conclusions of earlier writers.

Books and articles have appeared in all the major European languages, but none has substantially altered the skeletal history set out by nineteenth-century scholars. Many works have been weakened on the one hand, by a desire to justify the work of the Inquisition, or, on the other, to use it as a weapon for attacking the present-day Catholic Church; such propagandistic and heavily biased books often distort the truth, although some of them are hoards of otherwise inaccessible material. Recent scholarly research has concentrated on specialist areas and periods, enabling parts of the early historiography to be improved upon. In particular, there have been great changes in the fields of medieval heresy and witchcraft studies.

This book attempts to synthesize such materials up to the present, basing what might otherwise be an unwieldy structure on a hypothetical framework consisting of two essential moments in the history of the Inquisition: the gradual establishment of the tribunal in response to heretical movements in the thirteenth century, and its dramatic reflowering three hundred years later – with ramifications in the Spanish Inquisition, the Counter-Reformation and the Witchcraft Trials. This structure is as strictly as possible chronological, and ideally the book should be used in conjunction with good general histories of the two main periods, since they are far too complex for even brief outlines to be given in a short survey of the Inquisition. The cases of important individuals, such as Joan of Arc and Galileo, or historically important events, such as the trial of the Knights Templar, have been treated exclusively from the point of view of their significance in the history of the Inquisition.

Some works cited in the text but otherwise of no direct relevance to the history of the Inquisition have been given their full titles and bibliographical references in footnotes or chapter references. Otherwise, short titles are always given; the full titles will be found in the Select Bibliography. Quotations from foreign language sources have been translated by the author.

EDWARD BURMAN
La Vascuccia
1 August 1984

PART ONE: THE MEDIEVAL INQUISITION

1. Genesis

The launching of the First Crusade by Pope Urban II in 1096 may be considered the inauguration of an era of warfare, economic change and social upheaval that radically altered medieval Europe. Between the middle of the eleventh century and the departure of crusading armies participating in this long-awaited attempt to reconquer Jerusalem, the outlook for Western Europe had changed in almost every conceivable way. R. W. Southern has summarized the essential transformations: 'The secular ruler had been demoted from his position of quasi-sacerdotal splendour, the pope had assumed a new power of intervention and direction in both spiritual and secular affairs, the Benedictine Rule had lost its monopoly in the religious life, an entirely new impulse had been given to law and theology, and several important steps had been taken towards understanding and even controlling the physical world.'[1]

Behind this transformation was a sudden acceleration in the rate of economic development, which was given a further impulse as the creation of the Latin Kingdom of Jerusalem opened a closed feudal society to new trading routes. But these routes also served to forge a direct link with Eastern heresy: ideas flowed with merchandise, leading to that spectacular increase in heretical movements that was one of the most distinctive features of twelfth-century Europe.[2] An increasing flood of heresies from about 1150 forced the papacy to devise a protective response and means of repression. Thus, towards the end of that century, the Church introduced a series of tentative measures that were to culminate in the foundation of the ecclesiastical tribunal known as the Inquisition.

Background of Heresy

These heresies took root quickly in fertile soil, prepared at least in part by the moral laxity and corruption of the clergy – whose behaviour did not serve as an adequate model for a laity in search of moral and spiritual guidance at such a tumultuous period of change. The Council of Evreux (1195) mentions indulgences being sold by clergy, and bishops selling holy oil and relics; the Council of Avignon (1209) cites an example of a priest gambling for penances with dice, and others opening taverns with the clerical collar as an inn sign; the Council of Paris (1209) forbade the faithful to attend masses celebrated by married priests and concubinaries, and also mentions nuns organizing parties and wandering in the streets at night. Hunting, gambling and heavy drinking were rife, while those in both male and female religious orders took lovers – as the canons of the Fourth Lateran Council implied by cracking down on such practices. Contact with the East was thought to have introduced the habit of taking concubines amongst the French nobility, and luxuries such as perfumes, silk, ivory, and gold or silver ornaments were considered to encourage covetousness and immorality. While the Church held that Troubadour love poetry was decadent, and the tradition of courtly love a form of wanton paganism, her own clergy were scarcely better. Innocent III's opening address to the Fourth Lateran Council affirmed that the corruption of the people derived from that of the clergy.[3]

Yet the word 'heresy' is used more or less loosely to cover a wide variety of phenomena. Some so-called heretical movements were simply expressions of disgust at the excesses of the clergy and the wealth of the Church, while at the same time 'the feudal society of Christian Europe came into conflict with social groups which it could not assimilate, and whose defence of their own identity was seen, at first, as "heresy"'.[4] The Inquisition came into being to eradicate far more serious heresies than these: clearly defined and organized groups of people propagating ideas that represented more than simple opposition to the Church, and which threatened the basis of medieval society.

Heresy may be defined as 'a theological opinion or doctrine held in opposition to the "catholic" or orthodox doctrine of the Catholic Church'.* In a sense it could therefore arise only when there existed a body of orthodox doctrine: at the end of the twelfth century there was no such body and thus no legislation against heresy. It was not until a full century later that St Thomas Aquinas – whose writings sustain the basis of Catholic doctrine still today – could describe heresy as 'a sin which merits not only excommunication but also death'.[5] Before Aquinas the definition given above would have been impossible, and the *Summa contra Gentiles* and the *Summa Theologica* are as much an outcome of the Church's response to this outburst of heresy as the Inquisition itself.

The increase in heresy was in direct proportion to the increased power of the Church, which reached its zenith during the pontificate of Innocent III (1198-1216) – the first and most important of the great series of 'lawyer-popes' who dominated the thirteenth century. But the revival of Roman Law that marked the partial reconquest of Roman order, and provided the juridical basis for the new power of the papacy, also entailed the revival of its antithesis: pagan beliefs and opposition to orthodoxy.[6] It has been argued that the real cause of heretical movements in such proliferation was not doctrinal difference, but protest against a secularized Church.[7]

The modern concept of papal power and universal control of the Church is something that only began to emerge in the years from 1140 to 1150. The papacy slowly became a centralized, law-providing bureaucracy whose power extended into every sphere of everyday human life: '. . . it gave laymen a discipline which was clear-cut but not onerous; it laid down rules and conditions for all the main occasions and areas of the Christian life – baptism, confirmation, confession, communion, penance, marriage, religious instruction and religious duties, alms, usury, last wills and testaments, the last rites, burial, graveyards, prayers and masses for the dead. With similar clarity and completeness it dealt with all the incidents of clerical life – dress, education, ordination, duties, status, crimes and punishments.'[8] This passage gives some idea of the oppressive

---

*OED. The touchstone of Tertullian in *De praescriptione haereticorum*, one of the earliest Christian works on heresy (*c.* AD 200), was whether a new doctrine could be traced back to the Apostles.

secularization that provoked strong reactions, and led people to seek protection under such secular lords as Frederick II of Swabia rather than the Pope.

The climax of the activity occurred during the pontificate of Innocent III, although even within the Church, St Bernard of Clairvaux (1090-1153) had already recognized the dangers of legalistic bureaucratization, and the corresponding alienation of the papacy from its spiritual function.[9] It is natural that this degree of control and surveillance appeared asphyxiating to some, and created resistance; it is equally natural that this legalistic machinery should sooner or later be concentrated on the problem of heresy as the Church perceived it.

By 1200, two years after Innocent became Pope, there were two principal heretical traditions, which were to become the targets of the Inquisition in the first phase of its existence. The first, and most dangerous from the Church's point of view, was the dualism of the Cathars; the second, which the Inquisition never succeeded in exterminating and which survives to this day, was that of the Waldensians, or 'poor men of Lyons'.

Cathars

In a sense the Cathars were not Christian heretics at all, since they denied the fundamental tenet of Christianity: they did not believe in a single God, but in a good God who had created the immaterial world and an evil God who had created the material world. Thus they belonged to the dualist tradition deriving ultimately from the dualism of Zoroaster and early Christian gnostic sects. It was perhaps this fact – the threat of a genuine cultural alternative with ancient lineage – that generated terror in the minds of the Popes and nurtured such a violent reaction against the Cathars.

Dualism represents one of the great challenges of monotheistic religions: the problem of evil. John Hick has presented the dilemma in the following terms:

> If God is perfectly loving, he must wish to avoid evil; and if he is all-powerful, he must be able to abolish evil. But evil exists; therefore God cannot be both omnipotent and perfectly loving.[10]

This formulation echoes the kind of questions which the thirteenth-century Italian inquisitor Moneta puts into the mouths of heretics in his *Adversus Catharos et Valdenses*: 'How can the fire that burns the houses of poor and holy men be created by God? How can the God who sends suffering to good men be good himself?'[11] Although theologians, notably St Augustine, had attempted to solve this dilemma to the satisfaction of the faithful, the ancient prejudice that matter is evil persisted and was the fundamental impulse behind movements advocating poverty that flourished in the twelfth and thirteenth centuries. It is easy to understand how the simplicity of Cathar doctrine, and the manifestly incorrupt behaviour of the *perfecti*, or initiated priests, could appeal to men and women plagued by such doubt and disgusted by the wealth and power of the Church.

By the beginning of the thirteenth century the Cathars in France and Italy appear to have been organized into dioceses, each with a bishop supported by a *filius maior*, a *filius minor* and a deacon. The bishop presided over his congregation of *perfecti* and uninitiated believers in evident opposition to the diocesan organization of the Church. Cathar doctrine and rites were based upon five basic ceremonies: the *salutatio*, which consisted in an embrace and kiss when a believer met a *perfectus*; the *melioramentum*, in which a believer paid homage to a *perfectus* and asked him to intercede for God's forgiveness; the *apparellamentum*, a monthly confession in front of other believers; the *consolamentum*, or initiation ceremony for *perfecti* (carried out after a year of trial, and reserved to only a few members of the Cathar 'Church'); and the *endura*, a controversial suicide rite that was usually undergone at the moment of death from illness.* The rite that was fundamental to many of these ceremonies was the recitation of the Lord's Prayer over bread that was then distributed among the believers. It seems that only the *perfecti*, who formed a small proportion of the Cathar 'Church', followed its doctrines in the fullest sense; it must have required enormous strength of will and courage to perform the missionary and preaching work under their conditions of life.

---

*Information on doctrines is taken from the *Manuel de l'Inquisiteur* of Bernard Gui, Part V, and the survey of Cathar ritual in Manselli, *L'Eresia del male*, pp. 231-41. See also the 'Vocabulaire Occitan du Catharisme' in Nelli, *La Philosophie du Catharisme*, pp. 191-199, and Douais, *Les Albigeois*, pp. 224-265.

Perfecti attained eternal life by means of three 'seals': the *signaculum oris,* which implied total abstinence from impure food – meat, eggs, milk and cheese; the *signaculum manus,* which forbade the killing of any living thing; and the *signaculum sinus,* which barred all forms of sexual relationship.[12] These 'seals' were held to assist the spirit in its battle against matter, and were complemented by three weekly fasts of bread and water, plus three annual fasts of forty days each. The *perfectus* represented God on earth and was the only element of light in the battle against Satan; thus his life was a mirror and model for the believers and symbolized the life of God. All this, Manselli explains, 'justifies the veneration with which the *perfecti* were surrounded, and the care with which they were attended, guarded and protected'.[13] Again, it is easy to see how these *perfecti,* who travelled in pairs along the major routes of Western Europe, at the same time appealed to the people and irritated the Church.

But Catharism also represented a potentially devastating political threat to the Popes. In their search for spiritual perfection the Cathars were led to reject orthodox Christianity as assigning too much value to the flesh, and too little power to the spirit. They argued that the Church had compromised with the Devil: in the words of John Passmore, the Church 'had succumbed to the temptations of wealth and worldly power; it had failed to insist with sufficient force on celibacy, as a pre-requisite of salvation'.[14] Beyond the evident spiritual threat represented by the *perfecti,* the Church also feared the Cathars' penetrating criticisms of the accretion of wealth and worldly power.

It is now generally accepted that the Cathars were a Western branch of the Bogomils,[15] and there is ample evidence that the Bogomils sent missionaries into the West with the specific task of converting European Christians to their own, dualist, doctrines.[16] Bogomil, a priest at the time of Tsar Peter (927-969) had been spokesman of the peasants against that tsar's oppression, and his dualist church had quickly spread throughout Eastern Europe. The *Gesta Francorum* suggests that crusaders from southern Italy were converted by Bogomils in Macedonia,[17] while Anselm of Alexandria concluded that French crusaders had been converted by the Bogomils of Constantinople and had then disseminated the heresy when they returned home.[18] It is evident that this heresy appears in areas where crusaders had been recruited for the Second Crusade – Flanders, Champagne, Loire, the Rhineland – and that the rapid growth of Catharism in Western Europe coincides with the date of the return from that Crusade.

By the end of the twelfth century the highest concentration of Cathars in Western Europe was in south-west France, in the area of Toulouse, Agen and Albi – from which town the French Cathars took their name.* It was the Albigensians who provoked the violent reaction of Innocent III that was to lead irrevocably to the creation of the Inquisition.

Waldensians

The Waldensians were a sect of Christian fundamentalists who were first known as the 'Poor Men of Lyons', but later adopted the name of their founder, Peter Waldo (or Valdès). They have often been described as representatives of a kind of evangelical Christianity that preceded the Protestant Reformation. One of the reasons for their great success was their use of a French translation of the Gospels made by Waldo himself, which formed the basis of their teaching.[19] They explicitly condemned and combatted the corruption and accretions of the Church in the centuries since its foundation, going back to a simplified form of worship that rejected the authority of the priesthood and such elements of orthodox worship as infant baptism, the veneration of saints and martyrs, and the necessity of huge and expensive edifices in which to worship. They have recently been described as 'a would-be reform movement drawn into heresy by the inadequacies of ecclesiastical authority'.[20]§

Their history, and Waldo's own fate, become ironic when seen against the light of later events. Waldo was excommuni-

---

*Christine Thouzellier has shown in a detailed argument how Albigensian is a misnomer 'implying a value judgement' that gives a perjorative overtone to a town loyal to both bishop and king. Toulouse was the real centre, *mater haeresis*, of this form of Catharism (cf. *Hérésie et Hérétiques*, pp. 223-262).

Manselli observes that Pierre de Vaux-Cernay, contemporary writer, distinguished carefully between *albigenses* (the heretics) and *albienses* (the people of Albi) (cf. *L'Eresia del Male*, p. 304, note).

§Norman Cohn has illustrated the later process of "demonization" of the Waldensians (*Europe's Inner Demons*, pp. 32–42.)

cated by Lucius III in 1184, while only twenty years later a Bull
of Innocent III, which is considered to be the document of the
foundation of the Mendicant Orders and was issued on 19
November 1206, urged the clergy to imitate Christ's poverty and
vagrant preaching in much the same terms as Waldo had used. It
seems to have been a quirk of chance that Waldo was
condemned while Francis was encouraged – for the Waldensians were not heretical in the same sense as the dualist Cathars.
Dominicans and Franciscans were allowed to come into being
because Innocent III's far-sightedness enabled him to perceive
their potential value as a task force in an anti-heretical crusade.

The fact that two men of similar ideas and aspirations should
find themselves judged in such radically different ways by
history is symptomatic of the great unrest and uncertainty
prevalent at the end of the twelfth century. In the manuals and
trial documents of the Inquisition, the Waldensians are
constantly put on the same plane as the Cathars, while other
minor heresies or sects are associated with both of them almost
at random; but there is really little comparison between them.

In practice, however, they were allowed greater freedom of
movement than the Cathars. They were allowed to retreat to the
valleys of Piemonte and the southern cities of Apulia, where they
still flourish today. In Bohemia, they paved the way for the later
reformist heresy of John Hus, and were adopted by Protestant
apologists of the sixteenth century as predecessors of the
Reformation.

Magic, Impiety and Ignorance

Heresy was the external threat, encroaching on the power of
Rome by means of Bogomil missionaries,* returning crusaders,
and the spreading Cathar and Waldensian Churches. Yet
deep-rooted superstitions, a widespread lack of faith and the
ignorance of both clergy and laity also contributed to the crisis of
the Church at Rome in the late twelfth century – and caused
several attempts at reform, which were crystallized in the canons
of the Fourth Lateran Council of 1215.

Keith Thomas has demonstrated the fundamental importance

---

*Bulgarian delegates attended the Cathar Council at Saint-Félix de Caraman, near
Toulouse, in 1167.

of magic in the medieval Church, and how the Church found itself with the tradition that the 'working of miracles was the most efficacious means of demonstrating its monopoly of the truth'.[21] Local patron saints with strong territorial associations gave hagiolatry an almost totemic character, but 'the worship of saints in general depended upon the belief that the holy men and women of the past had not merely exemplified an ideal code of moral conduct, but could still employ supernatural power to relieve the adversities of their followers upon earth'.[22] Rituals and formulas of blessing utilized the idea of exorcism, using ceremonies with the sprinkling of water, talismans and relics to protect houses and land – or to relieve the problems of everyday life.

The sacraments were essential to this magical use of Christian faith. The host was held to turn literally into flesh and blood, while those who took it away from the church were believed to possess magical powers. Henry Lea cites a case where a Jew of Segovia accepted a host from the sacristan of San Fagun as security for a loan – thus providing testimony of the magical significance and value of the host.[23] Richard Kieckhefer gives the example of a woman who kissed her husband while holding a host in her mouth, 'so as to gain his love'.[24] The possession of a host was commonly believed to provide immunity to drowning. Important ceremonies such as baptism and confirmation were undergone in the belief that they would somehow confer greater power: Thomas cites the case of a Norfolk woman who had been 'bishopped' seven times because she found that it helped her rheumatism.[25] The assimilation of pagan feasts and traditions into the Church brought with it surviving pagan beliefs. Thomas gives the example, which will serve as a parallel, of the Ceûra tribe of Zambia and Malawi, who perceive conversion to Christianity as an alternative means to achieving material success.

In the twelfth century, when many Christians only heard a sermon when their bishop chose to visit the area, this frontier zone between magic and religion – between the lingering influence of local superstitions and the central power of the Church – must have been very difficult to hold in focus. Although intercession in the case of a natural disaster was not explicitly guaranteed by the Church, as a sorcerer might seek to guarantee a cure, there can be little doubt that the unspoken power of the Church became associated in the minds of semi-literate worshippers with the powers of the sorcerer. Moreover, there is ample evidence that many people in the Middle Ages considered Christ himself as a kind of sorcerer.*

It would be wrong to imagine the whole of medieval Western Europe as uniformly believing in a single faith and a single doctrine; what is often described as an age of faith was permeated by impiety. Alexander Murray has analysed the sermons of mendicant friars travelling and preaching in Italy during the thirteenth century, and has drawn the conclusion – surprising at first sight – that 'substantial sections of thirteenth-century society hardly attended church at all'.[26] Even the clergy, according to Humbertus de Romanis, 'scarcely come to church'. Similarly, when Blessed Giordano of Rivalto, a Dominican preacher, suggested to a woman that she should take her daughter to church at least on feast days, she replied: 'It is not the custom.'[27]

This widespread impiety was reinforced by frequent statements of religious doubt. The modern idea that in the late Middle Ages there was no such doubt – that all men believed in the basic tenets of Christian faith – does not bear careful examination. Since the times of Peter Abelard (1079-1142), who in his *Dialectica* had considered the problem of truth in terms of the relation between faith and reason, an undercurrent of rationalism had been developing in Western thought. At a lower intellectual level, there were frequent manifestations of attitudes that were 'largely inspired by respect for the needs of reason and common sense'; such respect was based on 'a consciousness of the value of human personality, and a search for coherence which could provide a firm link between the duties of religious faith and man's practical behaviour'.[28]

Concepts such as the Virgin Birth and the Resurrection caused as many problems and doubts then as in later periods, especially for peasants whose lives were based on the tangible facts of everyday life – and a practical empiricism that produced a fundamentally sceptical view of the world. Such concepts

---

*Such a belief is supported by the passage in Luke 11:15: 'But some of them said, "He casts out demons by Be-el'-zebul, the prince of demons".' Arnobius of Sicca, teacher of Lactantius, asserts that the Gentiles considered Christ as a magus (*Adversus Nationes*, Book 1). Christianity is indeed 'a religion founded upon, and authenticated by, miraculous occurrences' (Anglo, *Evident Authority and Authoritative Evidence*, p. 9).

could only be understood in terms of supernatural or magical phenomena. It would appear that although the Church presided over the external lives of all men through the sacraments, at a profounder level it had much less influence than is often imagined.

Obviously this presence of magic, impiety and ignorance was a serious obstacle to strengthening the position of the Church, and created ideal conditions for heresy to flourish. It was with the threefold intention of reforming the Church, reconquering the holy city of Jerusalem and suppressing heresy that Innocent III convoked the Fourth Lateran Council in 1215. From this Council, as we shall see, derived not only the orthodox dogma that still forms the basis of Catholic doctrine, but also the mechanisms that soon led to the establishment of the Inquisition. Once there was a clearly defined dogma, then a police force of some kind could be set up to sustain it.

Towards the Inquisition

It has been suggested that a shift from reluctant tolerance of heresy to persecution occurred between 1163 and 1184,[29] although an important element in shaping future thought was St Augustine, 'whose attitude changed from tolerance to advocacy of "righteous persecution", conducted with secular assistance'.[30] As late as 1162, Pope Alexander had refused to sentence some Cathars sent to him by the Archbishop of Reims, because 'it was better to pardon the guilty than to take the lives of the innocent'.[31]

Half-hearted attempts had been made to stem the increasing flood of heresy, but the first sign of an official policy developing was Pope Lucius III's Bull *Ad abolendam* of 1184, which ordered bishops to 'make inquisition' for heresy. It has been described as the first attempt to deal with heresy 'from a supra-national point of view'.[32] But busy bishops who rarely had time to visit their dioceses could not perform this function satisfactorily, so that this 'episcopal inquisition' was almost totally ineffective. It was with the beginning of the pontificate of Innocent III in 1198 that a co-ordinated policy was conceived.

Innocent III (1160-1216; Pope 1198-1216) came to the Holy See with exceptional intellectual gifts and an extreme spirituality that had been expressed in his earlier book *De Contemptu Mundi*, in which the contempt for the world was directed against the sins of pride and sensuality. Later judgements of harshness against the man who could write the following advice to the Archbishop of Narbonne seem unjust: 'The prudent surgeon, to cure a serious wound, first uses bitter medicaments, but once the sick person reaches the moment of convalescence, he completes the cure with the help of sweet unguents.'[33] This attitude to dealing with heresy in the diocese of Narbonne must be borne in mind when formulating judgements against the progenitor of the Inquisition; yet the care and anguish in the early years of his pontificate, evident from his vast correspondence, must be set against the more notorious Albigensian Crusade. This apparent contradiction was conditioned by the fact that when Innocent accepted the papal crown, he had immediately to face two of the greatest ever threats to the papacy.

Each of these threats engendered fear: first, the imminent threat of encroaching Islam, especially after the fall of Jerusalem in 1187 and the death of the Holy Roman Emperor Henry VI the year before Innocent's election; second, heresy – particularly the Cathars in southern France, but also the prophetic powers of Joachim da Fiore (d. 1202), then at his prime. The reform of the Church and the liberation of the Holy Land remained the two main objectives of Innocent's policies throughout his pontificate.* Already in the year of his election he called for the execution of relapsed heretics when excommunication was ineffective. He also proposed the use of such weapons as exile, confiscation, and removal from official posts against heretics; these were to remain part of the Inquisition's armoury of punishments, but for the most part Innocent did not go beyond the 1184 Bull of Lucius III at this stage. As the 'principal advocate of the theocratic ideal',[34] his efforts were mainly directed towards the consolidation and increase of papal power.

Amidst constant legal and diplomatic activity, however, two events occurred that were to shape the future battle against heresy: the founding of the Mendicant Orders, and the Albigensian Crusade.

As early as 1204, Innocent III had invited the Cistercians to leave their cloisters for the purpose of preaching against heresy.

---

*For instance, they were reasserted in the Bull of 12 April 1213 convoking bishops to the Fourth Lateran Council.

Some of them went to preach against Cathar *perfecti* in the province of Narbonne, but it was evident that their training did not prepare them for such a task; their lives had been devoted to prayer, meditation, and the hard physical work involved in setting up monasteries in the frontier zones of Christian Europe.

Fate suggested a more suitable model in the presence near Toulouse of Diego, Bishop of Osman, and his companion Dominic Guzman – who had already obtained some success preaching against the Cathars on his way home to Spain from Denmark. It was said that in 1203 he had converted an innkeeper in Toulouse after an entire night of debate.[35] Then, while visiting Citeaux and Montpellier three years later, Dominic met Innocent's delegates engaged in the task of attempting to convert some Cathars, and he suggested 'poor preaching' as a means of counteracting the aura of spirituality surrounding the *perfecti*. The Pope's Bull of 17 November 1206, in which he spoke of the need to imitate Christ's poverty and 'to go humbly in search of heretics and lead them out of error', is considered to be the document of foundation of the Mendicant Orders.[36] Thus the primary function of Dominic and his early followers was to *preach* against heresy; but, as Maisonneuve has observed, 'preaching tends naturally towards inquisition'.[37]

In 1210, the same Pope gave oral permission to Francis Bernadone of Assisi (1181/2-1226) to found a preaching order, but it was only to preach on moral issues and had no precise Rule – whereas Dominic's methods had been sanctioned by Innocent three years before. It was in this way that the Church embraced teaching in the name of the 'poor Christ', approving of Dominic and Francis while accusing similarly motivated men of heresy. The two Orders were to play an essential role in the eradication of Catharism during the second half of the thirteenth century, both as preachers and as inquisitors.

For the moment, a quicker, military solution suggested itself, and led to some of the strangest episodes in the history of the Church. The idea of using force against the heretics had already been mooted when in 1207 Innocent invited Philip Augustus of France to proceed against the Albigensians; by offering the same crusader indulgences as for travelling to the Holy Land – the forgiveness of past sins, and the martyr's palm in the case of death in the field – the Pope had effectively applied the idea of a crusade to the situation in Languedoc. But the spark that set off the so-called Albigensian Crusade was the murder in January 1208 of Peter of Castelnau, a Cistercian and a papal legate; the reason for such a violent reaction on the part of Innocent III may lie in Manselli's affirmation that Peter was more than a mere legate – he was 'an *alter ego* of the pope, and like him worthy of maximum consideration and respect'.[38]

Great secular lords such as the Duke of Burgundy, the Count of Nevers and the Count of Saint-Pol saw that it was an ideal opportunity to gain the material and spiritual benefits of a crusade without the necessity of an arduous and time-consuming journey. They also knew that they would be attacking a 'society in an advanced stage of disintegration which still clung to the husk of a civilization that had all but disappeared'.[39] The largely mercenary troops defending Languedoc were no match for the stronger northern armies, and lack of co-ordination and common intent between Raymond, Viscount of Béziers, and Raymond VI of Toulouse contributed to the easy victories of Burgundy, Nevers, and Saint-Pol.

At Béziers, 7,000 people were massacred and the cathedral destroyed – a victory that gave the attackers a psychological advantage for the rest of the campaign; but what was intended as a forty-day punitive expedition dragged on for twenty years, and set the seal of approval on later violence. Strictly speaking, the 'Crusade' ended in 1209 when the three great lords left the field to Simon of Montfort, but it remains difficult to reconcile the ferocity of that year with the concept of crusading as an act of love – as an action based on profound Christian charity.* Perhaps worse still, the Albigensian Crusade had the effect of scattering the Cathars even further through Europe, into Bohemia, Poland, and especially south into northern and central Italy – where they represented a more direct threat to the power of the clergy in many important cities. Ironically, perhaps, the Crusade rendered the work of the Mendicant Orders more difficult, and created a necessity for a more pervasive and efficient organization.

The chief monument of Innocent III's pontificate was the Lateran Council, which opened in Rome on 1 November 1215 with the presence of over four hundred bishops and eight hundred abbots, together with the representatives of most of the

---

*Cf. Jonathan Riley-Smith, *Crusading as an Act of Love*, p. 177.

rulers of Western Christendom.* 'It issued a detailed formulation of orthodox belief, which not merely reiterated the traditional faith of the church, but also listed, clause by clause, the ways in which that faith was erroneously interpreted by heretics, particularly by Cathars. The Council also imposed on all adult Catholics of both sexes the obligation of making confession to their parish priests and receiving Holy Communion once a year at Easter-tide.'[40]

This Council represented the peak of legislative activity in the medieval Church,§ and synthesized Innocent's two main objectives: a crusade was planned to depart for the Holy Land on 1 June 1217, and the third Canon issued by the Council was specifically devoted to the suppression of heresy.

Canon 3 repeated the provisions for confiscation, removal from public office, and excommunication for relapsed heretics. But it added important new clauses: heretics found guilty were to be handed over to the secular arm for punishment (which was not specified); feudal lords were expected to expel heretics from their lands; bishops were to force the faithful to denounce any heretics known to them, and then to call the heretics before a special episcopal tribunal; finally, the sanctions of canon law were to be applied to heretics. Furthermore, in clear reference to the failure of earlier attempts to establish an episcopal inquisition, bishops who were lax in their duties would be removed from their posts. Thus Pope Innocent III, who had opened his papal career by advising the Archbishop of Narbonne to cure heretics as a surgeon cures the sick, was forced by exceptional circumstances – and perhaps by the lesson learned from the obvious failure of the Albigensian Crusade – to adopt harsher measures in the battle against heresy.

The provisions embodied in the canons of the Fourth Lateran Council have been said to represent 'a first sketch of the Inquisition, with the sole difference being that the Inquisitors are not religious belonging to a congregation specifically

---

*Innocent was terrorized by the then widely held view that the symbolic 666 years of the beast of the Apocalypse was about to come; Islam, with its conquests of Christian lands, was seen as bringing about this vision. Cf. Michele Maccarrone, *Studi su Innocenzo III*, Padua: Editrice Antenore, 1972, p. 100.

§See the excellent chart in Southern, *Western Society and the Church*, p. 107, which shows clearly how six of the ten major councils between 650 and 1350 took place in the relatively short period from 1123 to 1274.

charged to preach to and punish heretics'.[41] But it is important to recall that Innocent III never expressly recommended the death penalty for heretics, and that in this sense he was more judicious than secular rulers who had condoned the burning of heretics for at least two hundred years. At his death in 1216, the Inquisition did not yet exist.*

*It is worth noting that an Inquisition, miḥna, existed in Islam during the reign of al-Ma'mūn (813-833). Its task was to obtain public declarations of faith in the Qur'ān as the created speech of God. Cf. *Bell's Introduction to the Qur'ān*, Montgomery Watt (ed.), Edinburgh University Press, 1970, p. 171.

2. Foundation

There is no precise date for the foundation of the Inquisition, but it may safely be stated that it came into being during the first six years of the pontificate of Gregory IX – between 1227 and 1233.*

To 'make inquisition' was not, however, a new procedure. Since the early Middle Ages the episcopal courts used three distinct forms of action in criminal cases, based upon civil law: *accusatio*, *denunciatio*, and *inquisitio*, the last of which usually resulted in the lightest penalties.[1] The method of *inquisitio* was later adopted by secular rulers and became the standard procedure against heretics after the Council of Verona in 1184. In fact, after the previous forms of inquisition – the episcopal and the legatine – this new papal, or monastic, inquisition caused resentment amongst the bishops, while the 'pronounced theocratic Rulers, such as those of France, Aragon, partly of Germany, Bohemia, Hungary, facilitated the work of the papal Inquisition in every way'.[2]

*Most of these years have been cited for the foundation date of the Inquisition. Maisonneuve, *Études*, p. 253, gives 1227 – when the first monastic inquisition was created in Tuscany; Guiraud, *Medieval Inquisition*, p. 59, and Lea, *Inquisition of the Middle Ages*, vol. I, p. 359, both give the 1229 Council of Toulouse; Douais, *L'Inquisition*, pp. 132-5, suggests the 1231 Bull, *Excommunicamus;* Coulton, *Inquisition and Liberty*, p. 113, and Molinier, *L'Inquisition*, pp. xv-xvi, both cite the entrusting of this work to the Dominicans in 1233; Vacandard, *L'Inquisition*, p. 146, suggests the Bull to French bishops of 1233 to be the effective start of the Inquisition.

It is this almost random genesis and acceptance of the Inquisition that renders its early history complex. Its predominantly local character, and dependence on the temperament and personal power of inquisitors, are evident from the beginning in the sporadic bursts of fanaticism and cruelty that mark the first two decades of its operation. This zeal is usually attributable to individuals rather than to the institution – especially in those early years when the inquisitors themselves were often uncertain about their precise function and mode of operation. Legislation was built up as slowly and as haphazardly as the organization itself; it is perhaps this fact which conferred upon the Inquisition throughout its history that element of arbitrariness which Charles Molinier indicated as its essential characteristic.[3]

The fundamental papal Bulls will serve as a structure to survey the first chaotic twenty years of the Inquisition's existence.

Excommunicamus et anathematisamus (February 1231)

From the moment of his election to the Holy See in March 1227, Gregory IX had dedicated his energy to the fight against heresy, perhaps prompted by the Spanish canonist Raymond of Peñafort. He was himself an intellectual and canonist like his uncle Innocent III, who had created him Cardinal in 1198 and assigned to him a series of important tasks. Gregory was pervaded by the new spirit which the Mendicant Orders had introduced into the Church, having been a personal friend of both St Dominic and St Francis – and the chief patron of the Franciscans in the Roman Curia during the pontificate of his uncle. Above all, he was noted for his firm, intransigent and sometimes irascible character: one of his first actions as Pope was to excommunicate the Emperor Frederick II of Swabia, whom he had earlier sustained, and in 1229 he introduced new and harsher terms into the negotiations that were finally to resolve the crisis created in France by the long-drawn-out Albigensian Crusade.

In the same year, the Council of Toulouse set up a special court of permanent judges to search out and try heretics. But although twenty of the forty-five articles of that Council dealt with the problem of heresy, it did not yet create a new and specific institution for this work. The local bishop remained the final judge, and had the power to commute sentences.[4]

An ominous step was taken two years later, when Gregory included in his register the 1224 constitution of Frederick II, which permitted the burning at the stake of heretics. This constitution had been prepared as a letter to the imperial legate in Lombardy, the Bishop of Magdeburg, perhaps to appease the then Pope, Honorius III.[5] But already at the 1184 Council of Verona, and in the 1215 Lateran Council, the papacy had established the *animadversio debita* – an ambiguous formula which allowed the secular power to decide penalties for heresy, but in practice meant the stake. The inclusion of Frederick's constitution in the papal register had the effect of rendering this previously ambiguous penalty explicit.[6]

Finally, in February 1231, Gregory IX took a decisive step when he issued the constitution *Excommunicamus,* which provided detailed legislation for the punishment of heretics. Its provisions included:

1. The surrender of heretics to the secular arm for *animadversio debita.*

2. The excommunication of all Cathars, Waldensians, other heretics, and their defenders, followers, friends, and even those who do not denounce heretics they might know to the authorities.

3. Suspected heretics who did not submit to 'canonical expurgation'* within a year of being suspected automatically became heretics.

4. Four clauses became law from that date:
    (a) life imprisonment for impenitent heretics (already in the eleventh canon of the Council of Toulouse);
    (b) the right to appeal was denied;
    (c) suspected heretics could not be defended by lawyers;§
    (d) children of heretics were to be excluded from ecclesiastical appointments to the second generation.

5. The exhumation of unpunished heretics.

6. The demolition of the homes of convicted heretics.[7]

Purgatio canonica was a procedure in which the accused swore innocence with the support of friends and neighbours (*compurgatores*), and was in use until the end of the thirteenth century.

§This clause, shocking to modern eyes, has a certain logic behind it, since for a lawyer to defend a heretic would be tantamount to admitting that he was himself a heretic.

Thus in renewing and reinforcing previous dispositions, Gregory provided judges with an important weapon for the suppression of heresy; but as the result of uncertainty these provisions were not immediately utilized to the full. It was only with the same Pope's entrusting of this work to the Mendicant Orders founded by St Dominic and St Francis that they were thoroughly exploited.

Yet it is important to emphasize that Gregory IX, himself a man of moral integrity and faith, considered the suppression of heresy to be an integral part of pastoral care. It was for this reason that he saw in the friars the ideal combination of gifts: they were

> trained in theology and therefore qualified to identify heretics; but they were also trained in pastoral work and knew how to talk to ordinary people, which most professional theologians did not. The orders had attracted some of the best intellects among the younger generation of men trained in the universities. The friars were all vowed to personal and corporate poverty and were likely to be impervious to bribes; their orders were directly under the authority of the pope, *nullo medio;* and the friars, unlike earlier inquisitors, could engage in the work of the inquisition on a full-time basis.[8]

The enthusiasm with which some of them took to this new task, and the ease with which they were able to contradict the above statement by their action in succeeding decades, represent one of the most astonishing aspects of the history of the tribunal – and one of the most curious episodes in the history of the Church. The following passage from the *Annals of Worms* shows how both Orders had spontaneously joined the activity of the episcopal inquisition as early as 1227; the chronicler's surprise indicates how exceptional such an event must have seemed even to him: 'What an astonishing thing! A certain number of Dominicans and Franciscans totally attached themselves to them. They accepted a mandate from those who have no mandate from the Holy See themselves, and like them burned heretics . . .'[9]

Brief case histories of individual inquisitors from three countries, Germany, France and Italy, will best serve to illustrate this disorganized and highly idiosyncratic phase of the Inquisition's history, which was marked by sporadic outbreaks of extreme violence tempered by periods of relative calm and inactivity. It is the inquisitor rather than the Inquisition who counts during these first twenty years.

Conrad of Marburg

One of the most notorious of the early inquisitors was Conrad of Marburg, who had already been persuaded to work in the Albigensian Crusade by Innocent III. His results there were marked by a series of bloody massacres, but Conrad's position constantly improved until in 1225 he became confessor to St Elizabeth of Thuringia, wife of the Landgrave Louis IV of Thuringia. Even as her confessor, he managed to gain further notoriety for the physical brutality with which he treated St Elizabeth.[10]

Gregory IX had already employed Conrad as an episcopal inquisitor on papal licence in 1227, and it has recently been suggested that his role as inquisitor does not belong to the history of the Inquisition in the full sense of the term.[11] But when religious discord in the Rhineland required the presence of an inquisitor in 1231, it was again to Conrad of Marburg that Gregory turned, in clear demonstration of his belief that Conrad was the man best suited to suppress supposed outbreaks of Luciferism there.*

His success was dubious, and the Archbishop of Mainz complained to the Pope that Conrad had been forcing innocent people to confess by threatening them with the stake.[12] But his efforts were supported by Gregory even in the face of these criticisms, and this fact suggests an intriguing hypothesis: it is likely that Gregory IX had known Conrad personally during two periods spent in Germany as papal legate for Innocent III; it seems in any case likely that he would at least have heard of this zealous man, who had served his uncle in southern France. Whatever the truth of such a hypothesis, Gregory entrusted this secular priest with the task of exterminating heresy, denouncing clerical marriage, and reforming the German monasteries, in a Bull of 11 October 1231 that was later repeated in France and Italy: *Ille humani generis.*

This Bull is of great interest because it provides the first sketch of the procedure that later became standard for

---

*These presumed Luciferans were in fact Waldensians who Conrad himself had accused of devil-worship.

inquisitors, and in the following year Conrad actually became
the first man to bear the title of *Inquisitor haereticae pravitatis*, or
'inquisitor into heretical depravity', which remained thenceforth
the official denomination used in papal letters and Bulls.[13] In
this letter, Gregory IX wrote:

> When you arrive in a town, you will summon the prelates, clergy and
> people, and you will preach a solemn sermon: then you will assume
> several discreet persons as assistants and begin your enquiry into the
> beliefs of heretics and suspects with diligent care (they will already
> have been denounced). Those who, after examination, are
> recognized as guilty or suspected of heresy must promise to obey the
> orders of the Church absolutely; if they do not, you should proceed
> against them, following the statutes that we have recently
> promulgated against the heretics.[14]

The statutes to which the Pope refers were those of the Bull
Excommunicamus, promulgated eight months earlier.

Conrad chose Dominicans and Franciscans as his assistants,
and launched himself against the so-called Luciferans with such
enthusiasm that appeals against his savagery were made to the
Pope, as we have seen. No evidence of any proceedings by
Conrad survives, and it would appear that he went straight
ahead with coercive measures without bothering with the
formality of trials. With the help of Friar Conrad of Tor and
Jean le Borgne, he burned heretics with such frenzy that
contemporary chroniclers say that even the king and bishops of
the Rhineland feared for their lives while he was at work.[15]
Terror reigned in Germany, but this terror was equally of the
avidity of the inquisitors: it seems that when Conrad eventually
turned his interest to Count Henry of Sayn in 1233, it was the
Count's immense wealth that had excited his envy.

On 25 June 1233, a council comprising King Henry, the
Archbishop, bishops, clergy and Conrad of Marburg met at
Mainz to discuss the charges of heresy brought against Count
Henry – who was himself present. The council declared him to
be innocent, but Conrad refused to accept such a decision and
demanded that it be reversed. He departed from Mainz without
his demands being met, and in an apparent reprisal was
assassinated on the road near the town of his birth five days
later, together with his faithful Franciscan follower Gerhard.

Robert le Bougre

When Robert le Bougre, a Dominican and ex-heretic as his
name implies,* was empowered on the same terms to extirpate
heresy in Burgundy on 19 April 1233, he applied himself to his
task with enthusiasm at least equalling that of Conrad of
Marburg. So efficient was he that he earned the epithet *Malleus
Haereticorum* – the Hammer of Heretics.§ His violent activity
stands out even against the regular burnings and massacres that
characterized France in the first half of the thirteenth century,
and already in 1234 protests from the French bishops against his
work forced Gregory to order the suspension of Robert's
activity.

Yet the Cathar threat perturbed Gregory, and Robert le
Bougre was soon reinstated with even greater powers than
before as Inquisitor-General for the whole of France. His
method was to arrange a public confrontation with suspects
rather than the more usual private trial, after which heretics and
suspects who recanted were sentenced to public penance –
'while those who refused to do so were adjudged guilty and were
burnt'.[16] One of his most notorious spectacles took place at
Douai on 2 March 1236: in the presence of the bishops of Arras,
Cambrai and Tournai, and Joan, Countess of Flanders, with a
group of Flemish noblemen – as if he were an entrepreneur
offering a show – Robert burnt ten heretics in the town
square.[17]

But the climax of his brief career as inquisitor came three
years later at Mont-Wimer in Champagne, where a large crowd
of suspected heretics had been summoned. There, in the
presence of the bishops of Orléans, Troyes, Meaux, Verdun and
Langres, Robert le Bougre carried out a detailed interrogation
of the assembled heretics. On 13 May 1239 – with the
above-named bishops and the King of Navarre in attendance –
183 Cathars were publicly burned at the stake in what a
contemporary chronicler, Alberic des Trois-Fontaines, described as a 'holocaust, very great and pleasing to God'.[18]

---

*From Latin *bulgarus* (Bulgarian), through Old French *bougre*, derives modern English
bugger – not far from its original sense of 'heretic'.

§The same epithet was applied to many other inquisitors later. Among the earliest were
Bernard of Caux, inquisitor in Languedoc, and the Franciscan inquisitor Antonio of
Padua (unrelated to the homonymous saint). Much later, Cardinal Robert Bellarmine,
inquisitor of Galileo, was officially designated 'Hammer of Heretics', in the necrology of
the Holy Office (Redondi, *Galileo Eretico*, p. 5).

Robert le Bougre's inquisitorial zeal, as one can easily imagine, struck fear into the minds of people of all ranks and religious convictions throughout France,* and it has been suggested on the basis of a statement by Matthew Paris that he 'infatuated' his victims and thereby exercised some form of hypnotic control over them; it has also been argued that he was 'a homicidal maniac'.[19] Yet, as can be seen in the above examples, he never acted alone. Even the largest and most horrific of his actions, at Mont-Wimer, was attended and presumably condoned by an archbishop, several bishops, and a secular ruler. And Alberic's obvious approval might well be an accurate reflection of general opinion about the executions at Douai and Mont-Wimer. Moreover, Robert's travel and trial expenses were borne by the King of France, who also guaranteed his safety during his movements within the realm and financed the imprisonment of the heretics that he tried.[20]

Robert le Bougre cannot therefore bear the entire responsibility for his actions. What seems nearer to the truth is that a strange combination of zeal and demagogic power led him to find heresy in innocent people, and enabled him to convince others of their guilt.[21] The results would appear to justify Coulton's assertion that history 'affords few plainer examples of the demoralising effects of absolute power upon fairly ordinary men'.[22]

His contemporaries recognized this fact: he was removed from office and imprisoned for life by his own Order, the Dominicans. It could be argued that his zeal did at least have the effect of eliminating Catharism from northern France, and driving the Cathars south into Languedoc and Lombardy. But it is salutary to remember Haskins's observation that 'the wide prevalence of heresy in the South and the drastic measures which were found necessary for its extermination were to a certain extent abnormal, and are apt to create a false impression of the conditions which called the papal Inquisition into existence'.[23]

The real point to emphasize is that there were no *normal* conditions, and therefore no normal or coherent response. Even the most savage episodes of mass murder were often the signs of

*Popular resentment against inquisitors is vividly recorded in the *Chronicle* of William Pelhisson, Dominican friar at Toulouse. Cf. Wakefield, *Heresy, Crusade, and Inquisition*, pp. 207-36, for an English translation of this fascinating document.

real weakness in the Inquisition, symptoms of its disorganization. When over two hundred Cathars were burnt after the famous siege of Montségur in 1244, for instance, the Inquisition was only marginally involved – although the siege had been stimulated by the assassination of William Arnaud, the inquisitor at Toulouse. As Bernard Hamilton has suggested, this murder was parallel in the unexpected immediacy of its effect to the assassination of Peter of Castelnau nearly thirty years earlier.[24] Neither the Albigensian Crusade nor the taking of Montségur was the consequence of a plan or papal programme, and both cases illustrate the random and idiosyncratic nature of official reaction to heresy in those years. They also illustrate in an ironic way the weakness of the Church: a papal legate and a papal inquisitor could be easily disposed of without qualms by secular rulers – who certainly never anticipated the exaggerated reaction.

And, as we have seen, the Cathars represented a concrete challenge to the Church in Rome and the theocratic ambitions of thirteenth-century Popes. Only the fear of losing power acquired over a period of a thousand years can satisfactorily explain such violent reactions. The career of Robert le Bougre can be understood in terms of identification with such a fear.

Peter of Verona (St Peter Martyr)

Similar confusion and irony surrounds the assassination of the Italian inquisitor Peter of Verona, when again a single murder was to have unanticipated consequences.

Peter was born of Cathar parents in Verona about 1205 and studied at the University of Bologna – where he met and became friendly with St Dominic. About 1221 he entered the Dominican Order. In 1233 he was appointed inquisitor in Lombardy, where his work was much facilitated by the Archbishop of Milan and by Oldrado di Trission, the *Podestà* or Governor.[25] He was successful in his work as inquisitor and was made Dominican prior of Asti in 1240 and of Piacenza in 1241. It has often been asserted that the successful launching of the Italian Inquisition was entirely due to Peter of Verona.[26]

At that time in Italy the greatest problem of heresy was to be found in Florence, where anti-Church noblemen acting with the implicit backing of the Emperor Frederick II – then excommunicated by Pope Gregory IX – opposed the activities of the Inquisition. Their strength and success were such that for many years the expression 'Ghibelline', meaning a supporter of the Emperor, was almost synonymous with 'heretic'. Thus in Italy the work of the Inquisition was from the first complicated by the presence of political considerations, and Luigi Fumi has shown in a study of rebels and heretics in nearby Umbria how closely intermeshed were heresy and purely secular rebellion. Umbria, like Tuscany, had its own Cathar diocese with a bishop and missionary *perfecti* who travelled south into the Kingdom of Naples – stronghold of Frederick II – in search of potenial converts.[27]

In 1244, Peter of Verona, bolstered by his great success in northern Italy, was sent to Florence. There, his presence was soon felt. He invented the technique of founding pseudo-military confraternities loosely based on the crusading orders to combat heresy and assist the Inquisition. For example, the *Società de' Capitani di Santa Maria* was founded by orthodox noblemen (that is, Guelphs loyal to the papal faction) to protect Dominican inquisitors against all potential hazards.[28] This and other confraternities turned the fight against heresy into a bloody political battle, with what Hamilton has called 'Catholic gangs' roaming the streets of Florence with the blessing of the Church.[29] The efficiency of this method was soon appreciated in other Italian cities, and there was a proliferation of similar confraternities known as the *Crocesegnati* because of the red cross which was conspicuous on the white doublets they wore – in evident reference to the crusaders.

Peter's enormous success both in Lombardy and Florence obviously created many enemies. In 1252, while returning to Milan from Como with a companion named Dominic, he was attacked near the town of Barlassina by a group of Cathars who bludgeoned him to death with an axe. Tradition says that at the moment of death he managed to write 'I believe in God' with his own blood. In a sign of papal support for inquisitors and the Inquisition, Pope Innocent IV – who had worked actively against heresy since the beginning of his pontificate ten years earlier – canonized Peter in 1253, and made him the patron saint of inquisitors.*

*In 1586, Sixtus V designated Peter as the second head of the Inquisition after St Dominic, and as its first martyr. There was a widespread cult in his favour in the thirteenth and fourteenth centuries. Fra Angelico, also a Dominican, included him in a

Peter's death on 6 April seems to have provoked an immediate and violent reaction on the part of Innocent IV, who announced perhaps the most terrible of all Bulls in the history of the Inquisition on 15 May 1252, *Ad Extirpanda*.

Ad Extirpanda

Innocent IV, like his predecessors in the great line of lawyer-popes, Innocent III and Gregory IX, was a master of canon law, and even wrote a famous commentary on it. His pontificate was dominated by the final stage of the long struggle for power between Frederick II and the papacy. After Frederick's death in 1250, the political situation in Italy changed dramatically and a rapid succession of Bulls to the Dominican provincials gave fresh momentum to the Inquisition. It was also at this point that the Franciscans became involved as inquisitors on a large scale. This frenetic activity of Innocent IV culminated with the Bull *Ad Extirpanda*, 'to extirpate', which 'sought to render the civil power completely subservient to the Inquisition, and prescribed the extirpation of heresy as the chief duty of the State'.[30]

Ad Extirpanda effectively established a police state in Italy and is noteworthy for having introduced the use of torture into inquisitorial procedure, and for explicitly condoning burning alive at the stake for relapsed heretics. Resistance amongst secular lords was overcome by a brilliant diplomatic manoeuvre: Innocent incorporated the *Sicilian Constitutions* of 1239 into a subsidiary Bull, *Cum adversus haereticam*, thus turning Frederick II's legislation against the heretics and Ghibellines that the Emperor had previously protected.[31] This terrible weapon provided for:

1. torture as a means of obtaining confessions;

2. the death penalty at the stake;

3. a police force at the service of the Office of the Faith (that is, the Inquisition);

fresco in the cloister of the monastery of St Mark in Florence; Titian painted a large and important canvas of his martyrdom in the church of SS Giovanni and Paolo in Venice. This painting was destroyed by fire in 1867, but a seventeenth-century copy can still be seen; the original was described in detail by Vasari in his 'Life of Titian' (see Vasari, *Lives of the Artist*, Penguin, 1965, p. 450).

4. the preaching of a crusade against heretics in Italy with the same indulgences and privileges as in a crusade to the Holy Land;*

5. the extension of the principle of confiscation to the heirs of heretics.

Later Bulls served to refine this legislation, and it is interesting to see amendments being made constantly in response to specific demands or problems that arose in the work of inquisitors: personal letters written by the Pope carry the force of Bulls.[32] But Innocent IV had, with this single stroke, instituted a system of repression that was then honed by Alexander IV (1254-1261), Urban IV (1261-1265), and Clement IV (1265-1268), himself an ex-inquisitor, and finally codified by Boniface VIII in the *Liber Sextus* of 1298.§ The provisions of the Bull were accorded theological respectability by St Thomas Aquinas in his *Summa Theologica*.†

Super Extirpatione (30 March 1254)

In 1246 Innocent IV had officially called upon the Franciscans to join the Dominicans in the work of the Inquisition. As individuals, they had been closely involved from the beginning; we have already met Gerhard, follower of Conrad of Marburg, and it seems that Blessed Pietro d'Arcagnano was an inquisitor in Milan as early as 1234.[33] But, perhaps pressed by necessity and seeking fresh impetus in the Inquisition, Innocent IV divided Italy into two inquisitorial provinces with the Bull *Super Extirpatione*: the Franciscans were to have central and north-east Italy (mainly Tuscany, Umbria and the Veneto), while the Dominicans presided over the remainder of the country.[34]

---

*For example, in April 1253 Innocent ordered the Dominicans of the Roman province to preach a crusade against the heretics of Lombardy and Tuscany. Padua was sacked by these 'crusaders' (cf. Lea, *Inquisition in the Middle Ages*, vol. ii, pp. 226-7).

§Church law was contained in five books of bulls and decrees edited by Raymond of Peñafort in 1234. Book V was called *De Haereticus*, and contained the principal constitutions of the Inquisition. All the later bulls, including those of Innocent IV, were added by Boniface VIII in 1298. Hence its title, the 'sixth book'.

†Cf. *Summa Theologica*, II-II, quaestio 11, arts. 3 ad 4.

Europe was divided as follows: the Franciscans were to have as their province Eastern France south of the Loire, Poland, Dalmatia, Bohemia, Croatia, Serbia, Hungary, Jerusalem and the Holy Land; the Dominicans were to have Northern France, Western France south of the Loire, Germany and Austria. Together, they would operate in Aragón, Navarre, Burgundy and Italy.

Thus, with satisfactory legislation, a new organization and enthusiastic papal backing, the Inquisition was ready to start work on a grand scale shortly after the mid-point of the thirteenth century.

3. Manuals and Inquisitors

The examples of Conrad of Marburg, Robert le Bougre and Peter of Verona illustrate a further deficiency of the Inquisition at this early stage of its history: the lack of precise, pragmatic instructions for the use of new or inexperienced inquisitors. This deficiency was slowly and haphazardly overcome by a series of manuals for inquisitors which began to circulate in the 1240s and continued well into the seventeenth century in Spain.

The most important early manuals were the *Directory*, written by St Raymond of Peñafort for the inquisitors of Barcelona in 1242, and the *Processus inquisitionis*, written in 1244 by Bernard of Caux and John of St Pierre for the inquisitors of Narbonne. Since the writing of manuals was essentially a matter of compilation of existing materials together with fresh additions, later manuals derived from these models. The more famous manuals, such as Bernard Gui's *Practica officii inquisitionis heretice pravitatis* of 1323-4 and Nicholas Eymerich's *Directorium inquisitorum* of about 1360, were elaborated from these short and precise instructions; such celebrated works as the *Malleus Maleficarum* of 1488, and late Spanish texts such as the *Instrucciones del Sancto Oficio*, published in Madrid in 1627, were further elaborations written in response to specific needs. But their tone and function remained the same.

In this chapter we shall examine and compare the two earliest manuals, which are much shorter and can easily be summarized while maintaining a clear idea of their structure and tone; the later and better known compilations of Bernard Gui and Nicholas Eymerich will be used as sources for details of penances, punishments and other features in later chapters.

Raymond of Peñafort's *Directory*[1]

The genesis of this untitled manuscript illustrates one of the difficulties faced in the organization of the Inquisition in the thirteenth century. When instructions to 'make inquisition' into local heretics reached the diocese of Barcelona in 1242, that city was temporarily without a bishop and the clergy were uncertain how to set about this new task. A group of jurists formulated a series of written questions addressed to the Bishop of Tarragona, Pierre d'Albalat, who in turn charged Raymond of Peñafort to reply. No better person could have been given the task than the canonist who had helped Gregory IX formulate the Bulls concerning the Inquisition. In answer to such precise questions as: what was to be the form of abjuration? how were they to recognize heretics? and should repentant heretics be delivered to the secular arm?, Raymond of Peñafort provided unequivocable formulas and sentences.[2]

The *Directory* is divided into ten sections, which already in 1242 abound in the special vocabulary that was to become characteristic of inquisitors – both in manuals and in trial transcripts. Titles and some key words and phrases will be given in Latin to give some flavour of these early manuals. The sections are as follows:

1. *Qui dicantur heretici, qui suspecti, et sic de singulis* (Who should be declared heretics, who suspects, and so for others).

This section provides a straightforward definition of heretics: people who listen to the sermons of Cathars (*Insabbatati**), and those who believe the Cathars to be good men (*bonos homines*). It also gives a longer list of suspected heretics: *celatores*, hiders, or those who see heretics but do not report them; *occultatores*,

---

*The nomenclature of heretics is often confusing, and often local. Reviglio della Venera gives the following Italian synonyms for Cathars: *paterini, poplicani, bulgari, turlupini, speronisti, insabbatati, ribaldi, gazzari, pisti, pangeni, bonhommes, tisserands* (*L'Inquisizione medioevale*, p. 15). In France, the *Perfecti* were also known as *Amis de Dieu, Consolés, Consolateurs, Paraclets* and even *Bons chrétiens* (Douais, *Les Albigeois*, p. 249).

concealers, who make a pact not to reveal the presence of heretics; *receptatores*, receivers, who actually conceal heretics within their homes; *defensores*, defenders, who defend the heretics in any way. Most important of all is the category of *fautores*, or factors, which later came to mean simply defenders in a general sense; the *fautores* include all the above categories and anyone who in any way gives assistance or provides favours to the *Insabbatati*. The final category is that of the *relapsos*, people who have relapsed or returned to heretical practices after having abjured them.

2. *Sentencia autem contra fautores formabitur ut infra* (The sentence against *fautores* is formed as below).

This section provides a module of a sentence for the use of inquisitors. It states that those who are clearly shown by the inquisitors to be *fautores* will be judged excommunicate and suspected of heresy. Furthermore, if the suspect who has been excommunicated does not manage to absolve the suspicion against him within a year, and does not perform the necessary penances within that year, he will be condemned as a heretic.

3. *De hereticis dogmatizantibus relapsis in credentiam quid sit agendum* (Of dogmatized heretics relapsed into their faith . . .).

If, after being captured, heretics refuse to repent, they are to be handed over to the secular arm (*judicio seculari*); this is the formula for consignment of heretics to the civil authorities for imprisonment or burning at the stake. It is the formula which has enabled apologists of the Inquisition to maintain that the tribunal never actually punished or burned its prisoners.

The section continues: if heretics are willing to abjure, the judge can inflict the penalties of canon law; heretics who return to their beliefs after abjuration will be condemned to life imprisonment (*ad perpetuum carcerem*); whoever gives the Cathar kiss (*osculum Insabbatato*), or knows a Cathar, or prays with them or hides with them, and listens to their preaching and believes them to be good men, is judged to be in error (e.g., *fautores*); those who confess their heresy to the inquisitor will have to perform penances or submit to public defamation.

Finally, this section gives the formulas for life imprisonment, sincere penitents and relapsed penitents.

4. *De forma abjurationis* (The forms of abjuration).

This section gives the wording to be used by heretics who wish to abjure. The opening words will give some idea: 'I, so-and-so, recognize the true, Catholic and Apostolic faith and detest all heresy, sects of the Valdenses, Cathars . . .'. The abjurer goes on to swear obedience to the Pope and the Church, and his belief in the literal presence of the body and blood of Christ in the sacraments.* He then had to promise to have no contact of any kind with known heretics, and to disclose the presence of heretics to his bishop – on the pain of eternal damnation.

5. *De forma purgacionis* (Formula for penances).

This section provides a simple formula for suspected heretics who are to perform public penances: 'I swear in the name of the omnipotent God and on the Holy Bible to keep to the Catholic faith . . .', etc.

6. *Qualiter compurgatores jurare debeant* (The method of oath-taking for *compurgatores*, or witnesses).

This is again a simple formula, in which the witness swears that he firmly believes that so-and-so was neither a Cathar nor any other kind of heretic, and that he – the witness – firmly believes that the suspected heretic himself swears truly.

7. *De Hereticis Insabbatatis in cimiterio sepultis quid sit agendum* (Of Cathar heretics buried in cemeteries . . .).

This is one of the most terrible provisions of inquisitorial procedure, and it is interesting to find it so prominently and clearly stated as early as 1242. The following is a full translation of the first paragraph, which will give a good idea of its flavour: 'If during the inquisition it is revealed that heretics or Cathars or believers are buried in the cemetery, their bones are to be exhumed, and burned if they are recognizable.' It goes on to say that *fautores* who died during the process of inquisition should also be exhumed, again with the terrible qualifying clause 'if

---

*The doctrine of transubstantiation, or the literal transformation of the sacraments into the body and blood of Christ, had been propounded by Innocent III. It was often a critical point for those who denied the Church, and was therefore prominent in trials for heresy. Gibbon, in *Decline and Fall of the Roman Empire*, ch. 59, wrote: 'Innocent may boast of the two most signal triumphs over sense and humanity, the establishment of transubstantiation, and the origin of the inquisition.'

their bones can be recognized'. This posthumous procedure had been sanctioned by the Council of Arles in 1234, and meant that even death could not provide refuge from the Inquisition.

8. *Qualiter sacerdos debet inquirere de confessione de facto heresis* (In which manner priests must enquire into a confession of a fact of heresy).

Priests are to search for heretics through confession, and if they find a heretic are to write out the confession and consign it to the local bishop. If the heretic does not confirm what he once confessed, it will then be necessary to proceed against him. The section stresses that it is necessary to be careful, since Cathars sometimes preach good words – saying that people must not lie or fornicate, and that they should go to church – and as the result of these words the people think that such a preacher is a good man, and that his sect is good.

9. *Purgacio et abjuracio fautorie* (Penances and abjuration of the *fautores*).

All *fautores* are suspected of heresy more or less as stated above, and must make a public abjuration of their heresy; those who have abjured are then immune to punishment. The formula for penance and abjuration is similar to that for heretics, given above.

10. *Forme penitentiarum* (Forms of punishment).

Heretics who persist in their errors are to be given over to the secular arm. In this section, the longest of the *Directory*, the forms of punishment are specified. A detailed list of penances is given, specifying that penitents should wear two-crosses (perpetually) of a colour distinct from that of their clothing, so that they will appear solemnly penitent; such penitents are obliged to observe Lent for ten years. Penances are divided according to the categories of convicted heretics, *fautores*, and strongly suspected persons. All these persons should always be present in their city and parish on feast days and church holidays, and must provide evidence by means of witnesses so that the bishop has proof that they have performed their penances on the days specified.

In this final section the local character of the *Directory* is emphasized by mention of the Bishop of Barcelona and references to the particular requirements of penances within the diocese of Barcelona, thus reminding us of the circumstances of the writing of this manual. It is fascinating to see the mind of a great jurist explaining to his local colleagues how the Inquisition should function. The penances and punishments will be analysed in the following chapter; for the moment, it is enough to see the inquisitorial mind at work – as if feeling in the dark for a new vocabulary, and a practical guide to procedure.

Processus inquisitionis[3]

The *Processus inquisitionis* was prepared in 1244 by the French inquisitors Bernard of Caux and John of St Pierre on the orders of Innocent IV and the Archbishop of Narbonne.[4] It was intended for friars who were to act as inquisitors in the ecclesiastical province of Narbonne, including the dioceses of Albi, Rodez, Mende and Le Puy. The manuscript was discovered in the nineteenth century by a Dominican friar in the library of the University of Madrid.[5]

It consists of nine sections, different from those of Raymond de Peñafort in many details. In particular, it differs from the Spanish manual in being much more a practical repository of phrases and formulas for inquisitors to use in their courts. It is assumed in this case that the inquisitors of Narbonne know who they are searching for, unlike their less informed colleagues in Barcelona, and require legal formulas more than anything else. Once again, in addressing themselves to the inquisitors of Narbonne, the authors unwittingly stress the local character of the Inquisition in the first twenty years of its existence. This manual goes straight to the point with the opening words, 'This is the procedure . . .', after which it explains how the inquisitors should first deliver a general sermon and then issue a summons to heretics to appear before them. After this echo of Gregory IX's letter to Conrad of Marburg, the other eight sections proceed as follows:

1. *Modus citandi* (Method of citation).

Throughout this manual, formulas are given with blank spaces left for the names and places of particular trials to be filled in.

Thus, the *Modus citandi* begins: 'The inquisitors of heretical depravity greet such and such a priest in the name of the Lord . . .'. There are new features not in the *Directory:* first, that the ages of fourteen for men and twelve for women are given as minimum for those who are to present themselves before the tribunal; second, that a period of grace is established. If no inquisition has previously been held in a locality, then all heretics coming forward voluntarily within a certain period will be granted an indulgence from imprisonment. This feature, with minor alterations, was to remain a constant through the Inquisition's history.

2. *Modus abjurandi et forma jurandi* (Method and form of abjuration).

This is a briefer version of Section 4 of Peñafort's *Directory*, with no significant divergence.

3. *Formula interrogatorii* (Formula for the interrogation).

This section provides a series of questions to use during the interrogation. It is noteworthy that the inquisitors who wrote this manual are conversant with the doctrines and rites of the Cathars – unlike the Spanish inquisitors. In the indications given, they mention that suspects should be asked if they have eaten bread blessed by the heretics, or have received the Peace (the *osculum Insabbatato* mentioned in the *Directory*). But they go on with greater precision to ask whether suspects have been present at the rites of *consolamentum* or *apparellamentum.*

Another interesting feature of this section is the evidence of bureaucratization, which becomes an outstanding feature of the Inquisition as it develops. Details of confessions are to be recorded in the presence of at least one of the two inquisitors, and then authenticated by a notary or scribe. Thus the records of confessions and abjurations were to be filed, and later became an important weapon in the armoury of the Inquisition.

4. *Modus singulos citandi* (Method of citing individuals).

In this section a formula for summoning individual suspects for inquisition is given. Interestingly, in view of later developments, two facts are stressed: first, that a legitimate defence is to be allowed to defendants; second, that normal legal procedure is used by officers of the Inquisition.

5. *Modus et forma reconciliandi et puniendi redeuntes ad ecclesiasticam unitatem* (Method and form of reconciling and punishing those who return to ecclesiastical unity).

This section includes a curious procedure which has often served apologists for the Inquisition: when the penitent heretic has sworn his oath of abjuration, and thereby reconciled himself to the Church, he is *to take himself* to the prison prepared for him, and make it his permanent home (*perpetuam mansionem*). Thus it may correctly be stated that the Inquisition never imprisoned anybody;* yet if the repentant heretic does not consign himself voluntarily to the prison he will be given over to the secular arm.

6. *Littere de penitentiis faciendis* (Letters on the carrying out of penances).

This section differs from Section 10 of the *Directory* in not giving the list of feast days on which penances should be performed. Otherwise, the substance is the same.

7. *Forma sententie reliquendi brachio seculari* (Formula of the sentence for release to the secular arm).

This section provides the detailed sentence to be used in the tribunal.

8. *Forma sententie contra eos qui heretici decesserint* (Form of the sentence for those who died as heretics).

Once again, the thoroughness of the Inquisition is manifest by this obsession with suspected heretics who may have escaped trial by dying before they could be brought before the tribunal. The sentence is similar to that given in Section 7 of the *Directory*. The *Processus inquisitionis* concludes with the remarkable declaration that if justice is fully carried out against

---

*For example, Maycock, *The Inquisition*, p. 122, states that 'Actually the Inquisition inflicted no punishments at all . . .'.

heretics, 'the Lord will appear glorious and marvellous in the fruits of the Inquisition'.*

These early and relatively elementary manuals give a clear idea of the work of the Inquisition, and the mental climate which conditioned it – although they were superseded by the sophistication and completeness of the manuals of Bernard Gui and Nicholas Eymerich.§ Their brevity is, however, a virtue in that it is possible to give an overall view of their contents in a short chapter. Now, with the legislation and the germ of a practical procedure, it will be useful to consider for a moment the roles and personalities of the men who were called upon to perform this new and exacting function.

The Inquisitor

We have seen that Coulton dismissed the inquisitors as 'fairly ordinary men', while on the contrary they often seem to have been exceptional men. Gui Foulques, an early inquisitor in France and author of another manual entitled *Quaestiones*, written about 1262, later became Pope Clement IV (1265-1268).† A prominent fifteenth-century Italian Inquisitor-General in Italy was St John of Capestrano, a Franciscan and national hero in Hungary for his crusade against the Turks. Later, in the sixteenth century, appointment to the Inquisition at Malta was considered a promotion and sure stepping-stone to future success.[7] But even in the thirteenth century Mariano da Alatri has shown how in the inquisitorial province of Venice a small group of men shared the posts of inquisitor and other important ecclesiastical posts on a rota basis: for instance, Timidio of Verona appears as the inquisitor at Venice from 1269 to 1273, and is then the Bishop of Verona when his successor causes two hundred Cathars to be burnt in the arena of that city in 1278.[8]

According to Innocent IV's Bull *Licet ex omnibus* of 1254, the

*'. . . *in fructu inquisitionis gloriosus Dominus et mirabilis appareret'*.

§For example, Part III of Gui's manual gives 47 formulas for sentences; Part V provides 38 formulas for citation and capture of heretics. Douais, *L'Inquisition*, p. 157, shows how Eymerich's *Directorium* was derived from Peñafort's *Directory*.

†Other inquisitors became Pope: Benedict XII (1334-1342) had been inquisitor in Palmiers; Fabio Chigi, inquisitor in Malta, became Alexander VII (1655-1667). The great sixteenth-century Popes, Paul IV, Pius V and Sixtus V were all ex-inquisitors.

inquisitors should be 'forceful in their preaching, and full of zeal for the faith'; after the Council of Vienne of 1311, a minimum age of forty was required, and inquisitors were supposed to be wise and mature men capable of asserting their authority. From 1300 they were usually *doctores legum*, or university trained doctors of law. Bernard Gui presents the essential requirements in these terms: 'The inquisitor should be constant, and should persist amidst dangers and adversities even to the point of death; he should be prepared to suffer in the course of justice, neither inviting danger nor avoiding his duty out of fear.'[9] He should also be diligent, zealous, honest, maintain self-control at all times, and never succumb to laziness. Furthermore, he should always take great care to proceed slowly in his legal cases, and seek to arrive at the best possible judgement. Such men must have been hard to find in sufficient numbers, and the assassination of the first inquisitors had served as a warning. As late as 1426, St John of Capestrano had to 'confront hardships, slanders and even attempts on his life'.[10]

Full indulgences were granted to inquisitors, and they possessed notable juridical authority* – having been given extensive powers by a series of Bulls promulgated by Alexander IV from 1254 to 1261.[11] Moreover, they held the important privileges of being able to sell goods confiscated from heretics, to proceed against people of any social standing, and to absolve excommunications.[12] The possibliities for corruption are evident. After the Bull *Catholicae Fidei* of 1260, Dominicans and Franciscans alike were directly responsible to the Holy See and were not required to obey the orders of their own Provincials.

Lea stated that under 'the canon law, any one, from the meanest to the highest, who opposed or impeded in any way the functions of an inquisitor, or gave aid or counsel to those who did so, became at once *ipso facto* ex communicate'.[13] As we have seen, after a year this 'suspect' would become legally a heretic and could then be handed over to the secular arm for burning. More recently, Lambert has suggested that the most important danger lay in 'misunderstanding and unconscious distortion, either through over-sophisticated questioning or over-rigid

---

*Civil authorities were required to submit to the Church: a civil judge was to suspend a trial already in progress and hand the accused over immediately if *suspected* of heresy (cf. de Cauzons, *L'Inquisition en France*, vol. II, p. 81).

adherence to some preconceived pattern of heresy derived from
treatise or handbook, then imposed by forceful interrogation on
a cowed suspect'.[14] The fact that the inquisitor was both
prosecutor and judge, acting in secret without even the
elementary requirement of informing the heretic or suspected
heretic of the charges against him, was clearly too great a
temptation for the unscrupulous. The room for abuse was
enormous, but we shall also see examples of extremely
scrupulous inquisitors. A recent historian of the Inquisition in
southern France has commented that 'implacable as they seem
to modern eyes, the inquisitors did act in a scrupulously legal
manner, as they saw legality in those early years, did use
discretion in fitting penance to the offence, and were not
without conscience'.[15]

As the Inquisition developed, its efficient organization quite
probably gave rise to more misunderstanding than the whims of
individual inquisitors. The accumulation of vast archives
throughout Europe made it virtually impossible to escape once a
person had entered its records. The power and secrecy of the
Inquisition impressed itself upon people. Lea shows how in
1316 a woman in Toulouse was taken before the tribunal, and
the inquisitors discovered from their records that she had
already confessed to heresy and abjured in 1268. As a result of
this previous record, the old woman was sentenced to perpetual
imprisonment in chains – perhaps even having forgotten the
incident of nearly a half century before.[16] It is easy to imagine
how such efficiency engendered terror.

Inquisitors did not work alone. Such organization and
bureaucratization necessitated assistants, who fell into four
categories: each pair of inquisitors had a companion known as
the *socius*; there were substitutes, called *comissari*, who could
take the place of inquisitors in trials; there were also *servientes*,
who were allowed to bear arms and performed the duties of
messenger and general help; finally, there were the notaries and
scribes who transcribed the proceedings of trials, and kept
records.[17] When this organization was fully established during
the last quarter of the thirteenth century, it effectively
represented the first international law-keeping force. The
detailed transcripts of trials have served such historians as Le
Roy Ladurie and Carlo Ginzburg in the reconstruction of entire
communities of medieval Europe.

The inquisitor's job was often dangerous, always difficult, and unlikely to bring popularity. On the whole, the fanatical zeal of men like Conrad of Marburg is off-set by the meticulous labours of equally famous inquisitors like Bernard Gui. The office was difficult, and the men often exceptional; but what has survived in folk memory and literature of the medieval Inquisition is not so much the zeal of individual inquisitors as the generalized and widespread terror of the Holy Office itself – generated as much by bureaucratic efficiency and omniscience. Trial transcripts reveal honest men working painstakingly for their faith. It is hardly surprising that so many fell short of the ideals advocated by Bernard Gui, and over-stepped the limits of the concept originated by two great canonists such as Innocent III and Gregory IX.

4. Trial and Sentence

With complete legislation, and manuals to aid the inquisitors, a standard procedure was soon developed in those countries where the Inquisition was established. No longer did Inquisitors ride through their provinces in search of heretics like twelfth-century bishops. When Bernard Gui summoned suspected heretics to appear before him they were required to travel to the 'Hôtel de l'Inquisition'. In his case this meant the Dominican convent at Toulouse;[1] elsewhere, it might be the episcopal palace, a large church or a monastery. From that moment the interrogation and trial followed their inevitable course, as the following outline – based upon Gui's procedure – will demonstrate.

Citation

There were two methods of citation commonly used: the *inquisitio specialis*, or individual inquisition, and the *inquisitio generalis* or general inquisition.[2]

In the case of an *inquisitio specialis*, the citation was usually addressed to the parish priest of a suspected heretic. The priest would inform the suspect at his home and then repeat the charges publicly at mass the following Sunday, usually for three successive Sundays or feast days. Then the suspect would be required to present himself at the inquisitor's office, or temporary lodgings, and would be imprisoned pending trial. Refusal to appear would result in temporary excommunication, which, as we have seen in the *Directory*, would become permanent after a year. The suspect was then effectively ostracized within the community, and hunted as a heretic.

Yet the Inquisition also displayed a degree of leniency amidst this remorselessness, since its main avowed task was to conduct heretics back to the Catholic faith. Penitent heretics were especially encouraged and rewarded, because they would be able to provide information about other heretics in the area: even a Cathar *perfectus* could be accepted as a penitent, and then made to join one of the Mendicant Orders;[3] the famous Italian inquisitor Raynier Sacconi had been a *perfectus* before his conversion to the Christian faith. Moreover, people who revealed to the inquisitors the presence of heretics in their area could be rewarded with up to three years of indulgences for their information.[4]

The *inquisitio generalis* was usually carried out in towns or districts where the presence of large numbers of heretics had been indicated. The entire population over fourteen years of age for men and over twelve for women was required to appear at a pre-arranged point if they considered themselves guilty of even the most minor infraction. In a village or town where such gatherings were rare, it is easy to imagine crowds joining such a proceeding out of pure curiosity; thus these gatherings tended to be large and spectacular – with the innocent maintaining a safe distance.[5]

When the people were gathered, the inquisitor would deliver a sermon to them, known first as the *sermo generalis* and later as an *auto de fe*. Sometimes advance notice of a *sermo generalis* was given, and indulgences promised to those who attended. Thus an impression of power and solemnity was created, and the *sermo generalis* itself increased respect for the Inquisition:[6] as time went on, these ceremonies became larger and better organized, achieving enormous dimensions in the great *autos de fe* of the Spanish Inquisition in the seventeenth century – which were more of a parade after lengthy trial proceedings.* But already in the thirteenth century inquisitors forced entire communities to appear before them and give evidence in areas where resistance to the Inquisition encouraged heretics to ignore the summons. In 1245-6, Bernard Caux and John of St

---

*John Coustos, who had experienced the *auto de fe*, renders it more pragmatically as a 'gaol delivery' (cf. *The Sufferings of John Coustos*, p. 173).

Pierre – authors of the *Processus inquisitionis* – took depositions from nearly 10,000 people in the area of Toulouse.[7]

After the *sermo,* heretics were able to confess and abjure their errors and were then absolved from excommunication. By benefitting from the 'period of grace' and making a voluntary confession, it was possible to avoid the more serious forms of punishment. Since the *sermo generalis* took place on a Sunday or holy day, sentences could not be carried out immediately; but they were pronounced as soon as the examination was completed. The example of an *auto de fe* carried out by Bernard Gui in April 1310 will give some idea of the process. From Sunday 5 April to Thursday 9 April he tried and sentenced 103 people as follows: 20 to wear the cross of infamy and go on pilgrimages, 65 to perpetual imprisonment, and 18 to be consigned to the secular arm for burning at the stake.[8] Thus it is obvious that the announcement of an *auto de fe* also promised dramatic entertainment – rather as public executions did in England until the nineteenth century.

Interrogation

The chief objective of the interrogation was to obtain a free confession, and lead the suspected heretic back into the fold of the Church. It was carried out in the presence of two religious, and recorded by a notary or scribe; the public were never admitted. As we have seen, defence lawyers were not allowed in practice, although both the 1215 Lateran Council and the 1246 Council of Béziers had ruled that the accused should be able to present their defence. The most disturbing element of the interrogation was the total secrecy that enshrouded it: the accused never knew the names of his accusers or prosecution witnesses, and often faced an elaborate battery of questions from sharp and sophisticated inquisitors without knowing the precise nature of charges against him. Only if the accused managed to guess the identity of witnesses against him, and demonstrate that evidence had been presented in personal enmity, was there a chance of defending himself. Thus defence was a matter of chance, as the suspect blindly answered the questions formulated by his inquisitor.

But a further obstacle lay beyond the confession, and provides an interesting insight into inquisitorial procedure: the concept of delation. It was not enough to confess, for the suspect was also required to inform against his former colleagues in heretical practices; the trial snowballed as delations incriminated new suspects, who in turn brought in others by their confessions. The refusal to betray friends was regarded as proof that conversion had not been complete, and rewards were often used to obtain further names in addition to threats and continued torture. An example of the success of this system is provided by Lea: in Toulouse in 1254, a woman called Saurine Rigaud incriminated 169 people, providing their names and addresses.[9] This essentially pragmatic aspect of inquisitorial procedure is stressed by Bernard Hamilton, who asserts that the 'inquisitors were less interested in formal breaches of canon law than in the willingness of offenders to co-operate with the Church authorities in extirpating heresy'.[10] It is yet another of those aspects of the Inquisition that helped to disseminate fear and hatred in tight-knit feudal societies.

Suspects who confessed and were willing to inform on others often received light penances, while a suspect who confessed his own heresy and at the same time refused to incriminate others made his own trial much longer and more complex.

Another notable feature of the Inquisition as an institution was its immense patience. Bernard of Caux and John of St Pierre interrogated thousands of people in a single area, and transcripts of inquisitorial trials reveal lengthy and complex sessions of questioning. But once a suspect was taken into prison, there was no time limit imposed upon the Inquisition's careful preparation and analysis of the case. Lea cites two interesting cases: the first, of Bernalde, the wife of Guillem of Montaigu, is a fairly straightforward matter of a woman imprisoned by the Inquisition at Toulouse in 1297, and sentenced in 1310; the second, the case of Guillem Salavert, is much more extraordinary. In 1299 he made a confession which was deemed by the inquisitor to be unsatisfactory, and then – still in prison – he made a fresh confession in 1316; he was finally sentenced in 1319, twenty years after his initial arrest.[11]

The inquisitor thus sought to obtain a confession, using all his dialectical skills of interrogation and powers of persuasion. Yet, in such a position of untrammelled authority, the exceptional zeal of these men often led them to adopt less orthodox means of persuasion. The inquisitor David of Augsburg, author of another manual for inquisitors, suggested four factors which would help in obtaining a confession: the fear of death, a dungeon, a visit from two 'sure, zealous and cautious' men, and torture – or *judicium seculare,* as he ambiguously refers to it.[12] Beyond questioning and waiting – themselves forms of torture when protracted for years – the explicit use of torture became more and more common towards the end of the thirteenth century, but remained one of several expedients. After an official investigation into the working methods of the Inquisition at Carcassonne in 1306, Clement V declared that 'prisoners were habitually constrained to confession by the harshness of the prison, the lack of beds, and the deficiency of food, as well as by torture'.[13]

Posthumous Trials

As the *Directory* and *Processus inquisitionis* indicated, one of the most atrocious practices of the medieval Inquisition – perhaps even worse than torture, which was commonly practised by secular courts – was the persecution of heretics beyond the grave. Death was no escape, as this vivid contemporary testimony of the Dominican inquisitor William Pelhisson illustrates:

> They dug up that Galvan and took him from the cemetery of Villeneuve where he had been buried, then in a great procession dragged his body through the town and burned it in the common field outside the town. This was done in praise of our Lord Jesus Christ and the Blessed Dominic and to the honour of the Roman and Catholic church, our mother, in the year of the Lord 1231.[14]

The case of Alderigo of Verona underlines two elements absent in Pelhisson's *Chronicle* – the patience, noted above, with which the Inquisition awaited its vengeance, and the extreme duration of posthumous trials. In 1287, the body of Alderigo was exhumed and burned, and the wealth he had left confiscated from his heirs; then sentence was pronounced against him. Mariano da Alatri has formulated the chilling hypothesis that this exhumation was due to simple revenge: Alderigo had helped a patarin to escape from the Venetian Inquisition over twenty years earlier, in 1262 or 1263, and the inquisitors had waited such a long time to lay their hands on him because their power of action was then limited by the large number of heretics in the area.[15]

The story of Castel Faure, 'bourgeois de Carcassonne', is even more remarkable.[16] Faure was a wealthy benefactor of the Franciscans who died in 1278 and was buried in the cemetery of their monastery at Carcassonne. As the result of a secret inquiry in 1300, the inquisitor Nicolas d'Abbeville became convinced that Castel Faure had been received into the Cathar Church on his deathbed. He invited friends and relatives of the dead man to defend his memory, proclaiming the fact in all the churches of the city. The Franciscans charged Brother Bernard Délicieux to defend what they perceived to be their rights in this affair, which represented an affront to them on the part of the Dominican inquisitors, but d'Abbeville refused to hear his petition.[17] Neither did Délicieux succeed at a further attempt, and the notaries refused to prepare an appeal to the Pope in their fear of the inquisitor's reaction. Eventually a foreign notary was found to write the appeal, and Nicolas d'Abbeville was informed by the unusual – but safe – means of a notice nailed to the door of his office.[18]

The trial was suspended as a result of the appeal, and in 1302 d'Abbeville was removed from his post. With the accession to the Holy See of Clement V three years later the affair of Castel Faure was forgotten for a further nine years – the length of Clement's pontificate.

Pope John XXII, elected in 1316, inaugurated a new era of suppression of heresy, and the case of Castel Faure was reopened by the then inquisitor Jean de Beaune. A papal Bull issued from Avignon on 15 March 1319, and published by Vidal, provides evidence of the eventual sentence against Faure – forty-one years after his death. After such a long time the order to exhume and burn his bones was clearly difficult to execute, especially amidst rumours that the Franciscans had deliberately mixed up the bones in their cemetery to render such an operation impossible. In this case the phrase from the manuals, 'if they can be recognized', which also occurs in John XXII's Bull, was amply justified. The body of Castel Faure was never exhumed, but his wealth was nonetheless confiscated by Jean de Beaune – and his townhouse was still the object of legal controversy as late as 1338.[19] Ten years later, Rixende Faure – Castel's wife – *was* exhumed and burned; then the family was at last left in peace by the Inquisition. But another consequence of this long process was that in 1319 Bernard Délicieux himself was imprisoned and tortured on charges of plotting against the Inquisition.

The climax of activity in posthumous trials was reached shortly afterwards with the inquisitor Henri Chamayou, 'who seems to have exercised his zeal particularly against the dead'.[20] In 1330 he began the trial of eighteen people from Narbonne and Carcassonne who were all long since deceased. Depositions went back as far as the period from 1284 to 1290, and the earliest of the 'errors' cited dated from sixty-two years earlier. As a result of complaints by the heirs of these eighteen victims of the Inquisition, Pope John XXII ordered the suspension of trials against the dead in the case that no conviction had been brought against them in their lifetime.[21]

Torture

Innocent IV's Bull *Ad extirpanda* had approved the use of torture only in Italy, but by the end of the century it was employed by the Inquisition throughout Europe. In 1291 Philip the Fair of France alluded to the new methods of torture of the Inquisition.[22] At first, inquisitors themselves were not allowed to torture, but in 1256 Pope Alexander IV gave them the right to mutually absolve one another and grant dispensations to their colleagues. With this legal and moral issue circumvented, one inquisitor could torture and his companion then absolve him. The Bull ordered Provincials of the Mendicant Orders to assign two or more companions to the inquisitors specifically for the task of absolving them from any 'irregularities' they might meet in the course of their work; this assumes that inquisitors were present during the process of torture.[23]

Although the mere sight of the instruments of torture was often enough to extract confessions of heresy,* and references to torture are not common in contemporary documents, it seems that the use of torture was quite as widespread in late thirteenth-century Italy and France as in later centuries in Spain. The later sophistication of methods, and proliferation of printed accounts of prisoners who had been tortured, belong to a different world and cannot be used to argue *a posteriori* that the absence of such documents in the thirteenth century means that

*Michel Foucault has observed that 'The first degree of torture was the sight of the instruments' (*Discipline and Punish: the Birth of the Prison*, London: Allen Lane, 1977, p. 40).

inquisitors then were more lenient. The verbal ingenuity used to bypass the rule that torture could not be repeated shows that it must have been common practice: Nicholas Eymerich argued that since torture may not be repeated on a suspect without fresh evidence, 'then a second or third day may be fixed to terrify him, or even in truth, as a continuation of his torture ...'.[24] Thus torture may be *continued*, but not repeated. Bernard Gui opposed a 1317 decree of John XXII limiting the use of torture on the grounds that it would cripple the efficiency of the Inquisition: he suggested the insertion of the 'meaningless phrase that torture should only be used with mature and careful deliberation'.[25] To be fair to Eymerich, he did argue elsewhere that torture was counterproductive, as some subjects preferred to die, others became insensible, and the weak confessed to everything without making useful distinctions.[26] The problem involved in judging from contemporary records is that a confession may be reported as 'free and spontaneous' *that time*, while the accused had been tortured in an earlier session.

In this early period, the Inquisition employed six main methods of torture: the ordeal of water, the ordeal of fire, the strappado, the wheel, the rack and the stivaletto.[27]

The *ordeal of water* consisted in the prisoner being forced to swallow a quantity of water, either by means of a funnel or by soaking a piece of silk or linen jammed into the throat. There were many possible variations of this ordeal, which, as we shall see later, was often applied in conjunction with other tortures. When the prisoner's nose was blocked and water was dripped continuously into his mouth, it could result in blood vessels bursting.[28] Clearly the quantity of water was the key factor: in Italy, five litres was considered 'ordinary', and ten litres 'extraordinary'.[29]

The *ordeal of fire* is immediately more terrifying, since there exists an everyday parallel in cooking over the fire. A prisoner was tied or manacled so that he could not move and placed before a good fire. Then fat or grease was applied to his feet, either all over them or simply on the soles, and they would be burned – literally fried – in front of the fire until a confession was obtained. A wooden or metal firescreen was used to interrupt this torture for fresh questioning, and to provide respite in the case of fainting.[30] John XXII explicitly mentions this form of torture in a letter of 28 August 1319, written at

Avignon, when he absolves an inquisitor who had used it against a woman accused of sorcery and heresy in Toulouse: the inquisitor 'made the woman place her feet against the burning coals'.*[31]

The *strappado,* or pulley torture, was universally recognized as the first torture of the Inquisition and is often seen in illustrations of its prisons.[32] For this torture, the prisoner, male or female, was stripped to his underwear and then had his ankles shackled and his hands tied firmly behind his back. His wrists were then tied to a further rope that ran over a pulley on the ceiling above him. The prisoner was hoisted about six feet above the floor, sometimes with iron weights attached to his feet, and left hanging there from his wrists tied behind his back. In this uncomfortable position the prisoner was often interrogated further, and perhaps lashed with a whip. If he still failed to answer the inquisitor's questions, he was subjected to the full strappado: the body was hoisted higher still, as far as the ceiling until the torturer suddenly allowed it to drop towards the floor – allowing enough slack to create a good drop without letting the prisoner's body reach the floor. The strain usually caused dislocations, and must have been terrible to bear repeatedly. Only a confession or unconsciousness would halt the process.

The *wheel* existed in many variations, and has been used since ancient times; it was still used in the West Indies as late as 1761.[33] It involved the prisoner being tied to a large cartwheel, where his body was beaten and broken by battering it with hammers, bars or clubs. It would appear that this torture was used much less often by the Inquisition than the previous methods.

The *rack* is one of the most notorious forms of torture in all countries and periods. Later, we shall see a detailed description of its application by the Inquisition in Spain; but the form used by the medieval Inquisition was a fairly simple affair consisting of a wooden frame raised from the ground, with planks placed across it like the rungs of a ladder. At each end of the rack were rollers to which the victim's ankles and wrist were attached. The inquisitor would continue to put questions to the victim while he was being positioned on the rack; once ready, the process of

---

'fecisti plantas pedum eiusdem mulieris iuxta carbones accensos apponi . . .'

tightening the rack by turning the rollers would start. The victim's body was thus stretched until breaking point – or until a full confession was obtained to satisfy the inquisitor.[34]

The last form of torture used by the medieval Inquisition was the *stivaletto,* sometimes known as brodequins. It was a vicious form of the boot-type of torture: four thick boards were attached two to each leg with strong rope, as tightly as possible. Then wooden or metal wedges, four for the 'ordinary' torture and eight for the 'extraordinary', were driven between the two boards and the leg until the pressure became intolerable and the ropes began to cut into the victim's flesh. If continued, this torture could easily result in the splintering or crushing of bones, and therefore cause permanent disablement.

Torture is the aspect of inquisitorial procedure that has caused apologists the most difficulty, and there is ample evidence that the use of torture was as widespread and frequent in the medieval Inquisition as in the more notorious Spanish Inquisition of the sixteenth and seventeenth centuries. As the result of constant complaints, Clement V ordered an inquiry into the use of torture in 1306; this concern eventually led to new legislation *limiting* the use of torture – promulgated by John XXII in 1317. From that date agreement between the bishop and inquisitor was required before a prisoner could be tortured. Yet abuses continued, and the same Pope – as his letter cited above attests – was willing to absolve an inquisitor accused of applying the fire torture in 1319. It is in the last resort hard to disagree with Lea's observation that the 'whole system of the Inquisition was such as to render the resort to torture inevitable'.[36]

The Sentence

It was theoretically possible for an accused person to make an appeal to the Pope, although such appeals were difficult, expensive and therefore fairly rare. But there were instances where such appeals were successful, especially because an accused person's readiness to subject his fate to a papal decision was often taken as evidence of innocence.[37] Once sentence was pronounced, there could be no appeal,* but inquisitorial sentences were susceptible to commutation and even to later revisions.[38]

Final judgement was passed before a mixed court of religious, secular clerks and lawyers – so that a single inquisitor was unable to exercise arbitrary powers over court proceedings. In fact, from a technical point of view, the inquisitor was not empowered to pass sentence at all;[39] inquisitors only pronounced sentence in the case of suspects who had confessed and abjured their errors. Such sentences usually consisted of penances that ranged in severity from light and easy to long-term and difficult. In the case of a conviction for heresy, with customary verbal dexterity and ambiguity, the Inquisition merely declared the existence of a crime and then handed the victim over to the secular arm. Thus the fiction that inquisitors had no power to inflict punishment was maintained, and in the formula for requisition of an escaped prisoner perhaps reached the height of absurdity: the escapee was described as '. . . one insanely led to reject the salutary medicine offered for his care'.[40]

After the secrecy surrounding the process of interrogation and the scenes of torture, the work of the Inquisition again became public at the moment of sentence. At a *sermo generalis* the inquisitor preached a short sermon to townspeople congregated before him, and then announced the sentences in ascending order of severity. First were the simple canonical penances, and then the more humiliating penances (or *penitentie confusibiles*); the ceremony would conclude with sentences of imprisonment and other consignments of prisoners to the secular arm.§

*As always, there were exceptions to this rule. J. M. Vidal points out that after the reforms of the Council of Vienne in 1311, appeals to the Pope became more frequent. He cites three cases of condemned men successfully appealing (*Bullaire*, pp. lxxii-lxxx). In a letter of 1 August 1377, for instance, Gregory XI exculpated Jean de l'Isle, clerk of Cahors, who had been excommunicated for admitting visions that the Inquisition had judged to be inspired by the Devil. The Pope ordered a penance to be inflicted on the inquisitor responsible if it were shown that an injustice had been committed (*Bullaire*, pp. 437-40).

§The often quoted figures of Bernard Gui are interesting for the proportions they provide: of 930 prisoners sentenced by Gui from 1308 to 1323, no less than 423 were for various forms of penance, and 307 for imprisonment. Other sentences were for minor forms to be reviewed later in this chapter (cf. 'Liste des Condamnations de Bernard Gui', in Vacandard, *L'Inquisition*, p. 522).

Simple Penances

The simple penances included recitation of prayers, pilgrimages, regular church attendance, the discipline, fasting and fines. But although they were often extremely light they were nonetheless serious – since a person who did not complete them was considered a relapsed heretic, and whoever refused to make these penances was immediately handed over to the secular arm.[41]

Until the thirteenth century penances had been voluntary, an act of contrition to God for some error committed; for example, men went to the Crusades as an act of penance. But the Inquisition institutionalized the system of penance by making the penances they issued into obligatory punishments – and therefore, as in other cases of institutionalization, it destroyed the system by bringing it into disrepute. Thus, although again it is easy for apologists to claim that penances were not a real punishment, legal enforcement made them so.

All the simple penances were variable, and depended upon the decisions of local tribunals. Bernard Gui divided the pilgrimages into major and minor penances: for his tribunal, the major pilgrimages were to Compostella, Cologne, Canterbury and Rome, in the last of which cities the pilgrim was to remain a fortnight in order to visit all the saints' tombs and the churches with special indulgences; the minor pilgrimages were to churches near Toulouse, which numbered twenty-one, and annual pilgrimages for life to specified churches in Toulouse, Carcassonne, Albi and Palmiers on major feast days.[42] In this way the whole of a repentant heretic's future life was punctuated by a series of essential pilgrimages, which had more than a passing influence on family life. And these pilgrimages were controlled: the penitent carried with him a special letter from the inquisitor which was to be signed or stamped at each of the churches named, and then presented to the inquisitor on returning to Toulouse. Fasting and the discipline – a whip or scourge used for self-inflicted mortification of the flesh – were commonly added to these pilgrimages as a form of subsidiary penance.

Yet the local nature of penances also allowed for a certain amount of discretion and mitigation by inquisitors. The Italian Inquisition of the fifteenth century furnishes an interesting example under St John of Capestrano. In 1430 two sisters called

Mariola and Perna di Pietro di Angeletto, from Rieti in Central Italy, were sentenced to make penance by going on an annual pilgrimage to the churches of St Peter and St Paul at Rome. But they were old women and found even this relatively light penance to be difficult. Their brother requested an audience with the Inquisitor-General, John of Capestrano, and pleaded with him on behalf of his sisters; the result was a sentence of mitigation entitled *Mitigatio pene sororum Angeli Rubei Stacchoni.*[43] This *Mitigatio* gives the two sisters permission to make their annual pilgrimages to churches in and near Rieti, 'inasmuch as they cannot make the said visits'.

Signs of Infamy

This penance, the *penitentie confusibiles*, was designed to degrade and humiliate the penitent, and was thus considered a degree more severe than the penance of pilgrimages. As we have seen in the *Directory* and *Processus inquisitionis*, it consisted of wearing two yellow crosses, one on the chest and one on the shoulders, for the entire life of the penitent and never over yellow clothing.[44] Although it required no special effort like distant pilgrimages, and caused no physical discomfort, it was perhaps the most severe of the penances. Penitents sentenced to wear the crosses complained 'that they found difficulty in obtaining work, that their neighbours ostracized them, and that their children's marriage prospects were diminished, because people were afraid of associating with those whom the Inquisition had defamed as former heretics'.[45] In a feudal society this ostracism was indeed a terrible punishment.

Confiscation

Equally feared, and equally severe, was the policy of confiscation, which the Inquisition adopted from the beginning of its existence. The policy differed in its application between countries such as France and Italy, but in principle was universal. Mariano da Alatri has argued that among all the punishments used by the Inquisition that of confiscation had the greatest social repercussions,[46] and we shall see how the obviously attractive elements of such a policy were soon to be perverted for political motives. One of the most disastrous aspects, especially for wealthy suspects, was the widespread practice of confiscating property even before a trial had taken place. Arrest entailed conviction.[47]

In Italy, proceeds were divided into three parts: one for the town, one for the officials of the Inquisition, and one to be deposited and used for the extermination of heresy.[48] Again, the scope for possible abuse was considerable. Some secular rulers like Charles of Anjou – who was invited to accept the crown of Naples and Sicily when Frederick II's dynasty came to an end – were notoriously rapacious. The policy had an unexpected but interesting influence in Florence, where the sellers of land or houses were at one point required to provide security against possible future confiscation sentences by the Inquisition.[49] A purchaser might find himself losing both his money and the property if a charge of heresy was subsequently brought against its former owner.

In France, the proceeds of the confiscation policy were given to the king, who in turn made regular payments to French inquisitors and to the chief guards of the Inquisition's prisons. He also provided further sums as expenses for the maintenance of prisoners.[50] Here, too, action was taken before sentences had been passed against suspected heretics – perhaps to avoid the possibility of potential heirs transferring the wealth they were about to inherit. Royal tax officials mortgaged the properties of suspects who had been arrested, and then passed them to the legal heirs as temporary usufructuaries. In the case of deceased heretics, heirs were allowed to contest the inquisitor's action; but if they omitted for any reason to respond to the citation, an automatic sentence of confiscation was pronounced.

The physical destruction of the dwellings of convicted heretics was another pernicious sentence, as economically disastrous as the policy of confiscation. It was usually applied in Toulouse to houses in which dying heretics had received the Cathar *consolamentum*, or to the homes of *perfecti*.[51] The houses could never be rebuilt, although materials retrieved from the demolished building could be reused in the construction of such pious buildings as hospitals and monasteries. Elsewhere, this provision does not appear to have been so strict. In 1298, for example, Boniface VIII gave permission to the descendants of a heretic condemned by the inquisitor Andrea da Todi in 1260 to rebuild the house that had been destroyed at the time of sentence.[52]

It is easy to imagine the terror that such a provision provoked in the families of potential suspects, and the extent to which an economic sanction of this kind must have influenced areas like Toulouse, Carcassonne and Albi, where confiscations and the destruction of houses were relatively common at the end of the thirteenth century and the beginning of the fourteenth century.

Prison

After penances, the next most common form of punishment by the medieval Inquisition was imprisonment. As we have seen, of the sentences passed by Bernard Gui from 1308 to 1323 almost exactly a third were sentences of imprisonment.[53] In Gregory IX's Bull *Excommunicamus* of 1231, life imprisonment had been specified as the sentence for repentant heretics and was considered as an extreme form of penance.[54] Thereafter, it became the standard practice, although life sentences were often in practice commuted.

Prison conditions were often harsh, as the complaint of Clement V that the prisoners at Carcassonne were induced to confess by their sufferings attests. But, as in the case of torture, they were no worse than other ecclesiastical or secular prisons at that time. Normal diet was, in Bernard Gui's words, 'the bread of suffering and the water of tribulation'.[55] But both diet and general conditions varied according to the category of imprisonment. There were two main types of prison: the *murus largus*, wide walls or ordinary prison, and the *murus strictus*, or narrow walls – comparable to dungeons.

The *murus largus* appears to have been based upon the monastic ideal of separate but interconnecting cells. It was the most common form of imprisonment, used both for suspects awaiting trial and for the greater part of condemned penitents – who, it will be remembered, had betaken themselves there voluntarily to do penance. Prisoners met, could talk together and take exercise, although the basic diet was the same as in the *murus strictus*. The most important difference was that in the *murus largus* the Inquisition sanctioned the giving of presents – such as food, drink, clothing, and cash for bribing the guards – and a certain amount of liberty and trade with the outside world were therefore maintained.[56] Wives and husbands were allowed to make visits to prisoners, and occasionally other people could be introduced to the prisons: there are cases of Cathar *perfecti* who risked their lives by going into prisons in disguise to console believers at the moment of death.[57] In such cases, it was clearly the complicity and corruptibility of the Inquisition's lax staff that were responsible.

Yet there are many examples of surprising leniency on the part of bishops and inquisitors, suggesting that the reality was often different from the horrors that might be imagined. Guiraud cites the case of Alzais Sicre, who on 13 August 1250 was given a holiday from prison until All Saints' Day by the Bishop of Carcassonne – with permission to travel wherever she wished as long as she returned to the prison.[58] Similarly, Raymond Volguier of Villar-en-Val had a holiday which was due to expire on 20 May 1251 extended to the 27th of the same month.[59] Guiraud gives thirteen other similar examples of leave from prison and permits being extended. In such cases, the renowned efficiency of the Inquisition's network throughout Europe could stand as sufficient guarantee of the prisoners' return. But there are also cases of prison sentences commuted into fines when such pressing needs as the Crusades made the quick recruitment of extra men necessary.

No such freedom existed in the dungeons of the *murus strictus*. Here, cells were smaller and darker. Prisoners were chained by their feet, and often to the walls of their cell. It was reserved for prisoners whose offences were particularly serious, for those who had perjured themselves by making incomplete confessions, and for those who had committed additional offences once confined to the *murus largus* – for instance, attempting to escape. A further form of imprisonment, known as the *murus strictissimus*, a kind of super dungeon, existed in some prisons. In this case, prisoners were permanently chained by their hands and feet: it could be compared to the monastic *in pace* – ironically, in peace – where nobody could see the prisoner and food was passed to him through a slit in the wall of his cell. This latter form of imprisonment was very rare.

As with most aspects of the Inquisition, prison conditions and treatment by inquisitors and guards varied widely from region to region. The personality and whims of individual inquisitors could transform a prison into a kind of hell, or equally into a relatively easy regime with all the above privileges freely available. It is important to remember, however, that the Inquisition conceived imprisonment as a form of penance. Even allowing for its excesses, and the constraints involved in life imprisonment, the conditions of prisoners can be compared with those of voluntary anchorites or monks who chose to spend their lives as a form of suffering for God, which is the spirit with which the penance of life imprisonment was originally adopted.[60]

The Stake

The stake was rarely used in this early period of the Inquisition; it was originally intended to impress and terrorize rather than to eliminate heresy, and was used as the last resort for unrepentant or relapsed heretics. Relapse into heretical doctrines was the principle cause of capital punishment.[61] Once more, Bernard Gui serves as an approximate guide: in fifteen years of activity he consigned not more than forty people to the secular arm for burning at the stake. It was an act of desperation. In Lea's words, once a prisoner had admitted heresy, defended it, and refused to recant, 'the Church could do nothing with him, and as soon as the secular lawgivers had provided for his guilt the awful punishment of the stake, there was no hesitation in handing him over to the temporal jurisdiction to endure it. All authorities unite in this, and the annals of the Inquisition can vainly be searched for an exception.'[62]

Burning at the stake was carried out in public, and usually took place after a *sermo generalis*. The combined spectacle of burning live heretics and burning the bones of deceased heretics must have acted as an impressive admonition to the crowds who gathered, although Cathar *perfecti* were probably undeterred. But this almost theatrical aspect also encouraged those eager for martyrdom, who were further incited by the fact that the *sermo generalis* always took place on a holiday – when a large public could be guaranteed. This choice of Sundays and feast days was deliberate: 'The Inquisition intended these macabre *autos-de-fe* to be outrageous, since it wished to demonstrate that unrepentant heretics had no place in Christian society, and that even after their death they polluted graveyards by their presence.'[63] This function was best performed in the presence of the largest possible audience, which would then report the ceremony to friends and relatives in neighbouring villages and towns. As a result of this, the stake is often given a disproportionate role in the literature of the Inquisition.

When the sentence was pronounced, the victim was tied to a post high enough for the entire audience to see, while friars tried to the last moment to obtain the confession they had been seeking. A detailed account of the burning of the Bohemian reformer John Hus, at Constance in 1415, will illustrate the ceremony of burning at the stake in all its macabre aspects.

Hus was first bound to the stake by ropes around the ankles, above and below the knee, groin, waist and arms; then a chain was placed around his neck. Faggots were piled up to his chin. But at the moment of setting light to these faggots it was noticed that he was facing towards the east; thus his body was turned until it faced west. Then the fire was started. When he had been burned to death, and the flames had diminished, his body was torn to pieces and his bones broken one by one. Remaining fragments and the viscera were then thrown onto a fresh pile of logs, and the burning repeated. When the whole process was at last finished, Hus's ashes were thrown into a stream for final dispersion.[64]

The political implications of the trial of John Hus were at least partly responsible for this thoroughness.* As so often in the case of the Inquisition, a relentless logic determined the almost military nature of the destruction of a human body in this ceremony. The shifting of the body from east to west is comprehensible even today, but the breaking of Hus's body and distribution of the ashes were equally important. In an age when the cult of relics was at its peak, and churches and cemeteries all over the Christian world were ransacked for the bones, or a bone, of saints and martyrs, it was essential that the execution of a politically dangerous heretic like John Hus was not converted to a martyrdom and the victim become an object of a cult by the preservation of his relics. Other important heretics burned at the stake – Arnold of Brescia, Savonarola and the Spiritual Franciscans – suffered a similar fate for much the same reason.

At this early stage, the public burning of books was less frequent than later in the history of the Inquisition – since fear of their potential influence was clearly minimal in an age of

---

*Bishop Jewel of Salisbury, about 1560, commented: 'As for John Wycliffe, John Huss, Valdo and the rest for ought I know, and I believe setting malice aside, for ought you know, they were godly men. Their greatest heresy was this ... That they desired the reformation of the church.' Quoted by the Revd Jack Putterill in the pamphlet *550th Anniversary Service of the Martyrdom of Blessed John Hus of Bohemia*, available at Thaxted Parish Church, Essex.

widespread illiteracy amongst the laity, and before the introduction of printing. But it is worth noticing that this process did already exist. In 1239, Gregory IX ordered all Jewish books to be seized the following Lent, and delivered to the mendicant friars for burning; twenty wagon-loads of books were said to have been burned in Paris in 1248; Bernard Gui records the burning of a copy of the Talmud in 1319. George Haven Putnam lists thirty-six single and multiple instances of books being burned before the Index was introduced in the sixteenth century.[65]

It would be wrong to underplay the role of the stake in the medieval Inquisition, and Bernard Gui is perhaps in this case atypical. We have seen evidence of the holocausts of Robert le Bougre, and the mass burnings of Cathars by the Venetian Inquisition in the arena at Verona; at the beginning of the fourteenth century, while Gui was at work in Toulouse, there were further mass burnings of the Knights Templars in Paris. In the same period, there are numerous examples of witches and sorcerers being burned at the stake throughout Western Europe.[66] The fact that many of these executions were by secular courts only serves to illustrate how common the procedure was at that time.

Nevertheless, it is obviously true that the stake was inflicted upon a relatively small proportion of the Inquisition's prisoners, and thus had a limited social impact. There were many towns and villages where it was completely unknown, while other penances and punishments seem to have filtered through the greater part of society – in southern France and northern Italy in particular. The Inquisition was less efficacious in other parts of Europe in the Middle Ages, since its main effort was concentrated on the Cathars who were to be found in those two areas. It was not until the Cathars were effectively exterminated around 1325 that the Inquisition managed to turn its full attention to other matters, and to other areas.

5. The Medieval Inquisition in Italy

Legend, popular history and the influence of propaganda against the predominantly Dominican Spanish Inquisition have accentuated the links between the Inquisition and St Dominic, while as the result of a strong hagiographic tradition deriving from St Francis's own writings and the frescoes of his life by Giotto, the Franciscans have usually been perceived as gentle, smiling monks, always laughing. A popular biographer of St Francis like G. K. Chesterton mentions the Inquisition in his Life of the saint in passing, '. . . not because it is especially connected with St Francis, in whatever sense it may have been connected with St Dominic'.[1] Similarly Moorman, historian of the Franciscan Order, deals with the Inquisition in a single page. He asserts, rightly one would imagine, that the Inquisition was a thankless job, that the inquisitors were unpopular, and that 'several inquisitors had to be removed from office' as the result of temptations to graft and dishonesty.[2] Yet there is no sense in either of these authors of the important role played by the Franciscans in the history of the Inquisition, nor of the development of the Inquisition itself in early Franciscan history.

It is true that a relatively small proportion of Franciscan friars were inquisitors or otherwise worked with the Inquisition. But it is equally true that from 1260 the Provincials were personally responsible for selecting Franciscan inquisitors and that they played a significant role for at least two centuries, from 1229 – when Gregory IX invited some Franciscans to assist at an episcopal inquisition in Milan – to 1430, when St John of Capestrano was the Inquisitor-General in Italy. We have also seen that the Franciscans were directly responsible for the burning of the Cathars in the arena at Verona – carried out by a Franciscan inquisitor with the approval of the Franciscan bishop. Furthermore, it is clear that the Franciscan Order was allowed to come into being in order to combat heresy, although St Francis himself was never actively engaged in this function.

St Dominic's role is better known. Within a century of his death he was characterized by Dante as: '. . . the holy athlete,|kind to his own and cruel to his enemies'.* The poet would appear to be closer to the mark than a recent historian of the Dominican Order who admits condescendingly that 'there are official statements that link the Friars Preachers to the suppression of heresy',[3] as if the tens of thousands of pages of existing trial reports and papal letters, and research by Dominican scholars into their part in the history of the Inquisition, did not exist. The same author records Bernard Gui merely in his guise as the first historian of the Order.[4] While it is true that the Dominican friars also put great emphasis on preaching as a means of combating heresy, we must remember Maisonneuve's observation – cited earlier – that preaching leads naturally to inquisition.

Earlier Dominican writers such as Louis de Paramo, Spanish inquisitor in Sicily and author of the *De origine et progressu officii sanctae Inquisitionis*, published in Madrid in 1598, referred to the founder of their Order as *Primus inquisitor*. La Mantia suggested that the attempt to disassociate St Dominic from the Inquisition began after Voltaire's assignment of the saint to Hell in his play *Pucelle d'Orléans*.[5] The desire to create a new image of their founder appears to coincide therefore with the decline and final closing of the Spanish Inquisition; their medieval counterparts had no such qualms.

William Pelhisson recounts an extraordinary event that occurred at Toulouse in 1234. The Bishop of Toulouse was at that time Raymond of Falga, also known as Raymond of Miramont, who had been a follower of St Dominic himself and also Provincial Prior of the Dominicans in the Toulouse area. He had gained notoriety for his enthusiastic support of the

---

*'. . . il santo atleta,|benigno a' suoi e a' nemici crudo' (*Paradiso*, XII, 56-7).

inquisitors working there. When this bishop received news of the canonization of St Dominic, on 4 August 1234, he celebrated his immense joy publicly by burning a woman and some male heretics. The woman was sick, and had to be carried on her bed to the place of execution in a meadow belonging to the Count of Toulouse. William concludes his account of this event as follows: 'And after the bishop and the friars and their companions had seen the business completed, they returned to the refectory and, giving thanks to God and the Blessed Dominic, ate with rejoicing what had been prepared for them. God performed these works on the first feast day of the Blessed Dominic . . .'[6] His terrifying words provide an accurate and authentic view of the role of the early Dominicans in the Inquisition. Such testimony, the references of Dante, and the work of Bernard Gui, cannot be manipulated to provide an alternative view.

But the Dominicans were not totally responsible. At various stages of the Inquisition's lengthy history, most of the monastic orders have performed minor functions when necessary, and it is clear from Pope Alexander IV's decision to employ the Franciscans in Italy as full-time inquisitors that there was little difference between the two orders. Again, contemporary documents are eloquent, and in order to correct a common bias towards the Dominican Inquisition we shall now examine in more detail the role of the Franciscans in central and north-eastern Italy in the thirteenth and fourteenth centuries.

Central Italy

It was in Central Italy that the intimate connection, almost an interdependence, between inquisitorial power and political exigencies was made clear even at this early stage of the Inquisition's history.

Encouraged by the death of Frederick II of Swabia, the protector of heretics, in 1250, and the martyrdom of Peter of Verona in 1252, Innocent IV had divided the territory of Italy into two inquisitorial provinces for the Dominicans and Franciscans with his Bull of 1254. The efficiency of the Inquisition was further enhanced by the financial support of the *Crocesegnati*, and by guards that they provided. But Cathars and other heretics still flourished, and Lombardy in particular was still regarded as a secure haven for Cathars fleeing from

Languedoc. Innocent's reaction was to preach a crusade against
the heretics, to be led by Dominicans from the Roman province
and offering the same indulgences as for a crusade to the Holy
Land (as his predecessor Innocent III had done for the
Albigensian Crusade). This strange crusade eventually set out
from Venice in June 1256, after Innocent's death. It was led by
the Archbishop-elect of Ravenna and his personal astrologer,
but after having successfully sacked Padua they were halted by
fierce resistance at Brescia. The unfortunate effect was further
to increase the independence and power of the heretics in
Lombardy. By 1260, in Lea's words, 'Inquisitors were no longer
able to move around in safety, even in the Roman province, and
prelates and cities were ordered to provide them with a
sufficient guard in all their journeys.'[7]

The period marks a paradoxical pause in inquisitorial activity.
The definitive juridical structure of the Inquisition was at last
realized in the same years, during the pontificate of Urban IV
(1261-1264), at the same time as the political instability and
uncertainty in Italy rendered the work of the Inquisition
difficult, if not impossible.[8] The change was wrought by Charles
of Anjou, who 'came as a crusader and champion of the
Church'.[9] His arrival in 1266 – invited by the Pope after Henry
III of England had refused to step into the power vacuum left by
Frederick's death – and the foundation of the House of Anjou
that was to rule the kingdom of Naples for two centuries,
dramatically changed both the history of Italy and the history of
the medieval Inquisition. In the longer term, it also marked a
shift towards France that eventually led to the transfer of the
papacy to Avignon.

There was now no refuge for heretics: soon afterwards
twenty-eight wagon-loads of heretics were burned at Piacenza,
and 174 *perfecti* were taken at Sirmione. Inquisitors worked
through the two main Cathar dioceses in Central Italy, that of
Florence and of the Valle Spoletana. The latter diocese had
origins as early as 1190, and included such towns as Spoleto, St
Francis's city of Assisi, Gubbio, Perugia, Todi, and Terni.[10]
The province had been assigned to the Franciscans by Clement
IV in 1265, with two inquisitors – one based at Spoleto and one
in Perugia. From about 1250 this area had been a Cathar
stronghold: fleeing Cathars from France and Lombardy had
moved south, while the town of Rieti served as 'a bivouac for the

perfecti who travelled from Umbria and Lazio into the Marches
and into the Kingdom of Naples, where, in these years, one
meets an unexpected number.'[11] It was to halt this dangerous
spread of Catharism in Central Italy that Charles I, who had had
experience of this heresy in his native country, provided such
support for the Inquisition as soon as he took power. The
Inquisition in those years was closely modelled on that promoted
in Toulouse by his brother Alfonso, Count of Poitiers and
Toulouse.

Once established, Charles set about organizing the Inquisition throughout the peninsula. In 1269 he sent a letter to the
counts, marquises and consuls of his new realm, ordering them
to assist the inquisitors in their work; in the same year Brother
Matteo of Castellamare was nominated Inquisitor to Calabria
and Sicily. In cities such as Orvieto, long a seat of Catharism,
the Guelph faction finally managed to take over from the
pro-Frederick Ghibellines and actively supported the
Inquisition.[12] And as always the efficiency of the Inquisition's
battle against heresy was determined by this collaboration from
the secular arm. This new period marks the beginning of the
greatest power of the medieval Inquisition in Italy, which lasted
for approximately thirty years – until the end of the century, and
the transfer of the papacy to Avignon.

Venice

Venice, as in the later history of the Inquisition, was a particular
case, with rulers whose first loyalty was always to the Republic
and who often worked against the interests of the Holy See at
Rome. When Doge Marino Morosini swore in 1249 to appoint
men to search for heretics within the Republic, creating what
Lea describes as a 'kind of secular Inquisition', it was specified
that the Venetian Council retained the power to revise
judgements made by inquisitorial courts, and that non-Venetian
heretics would be banished rather than sentenced.[13] Thus the
Republic of Venice contrived to conform with the desires of the
Pope while maintaining its independence. Even when Franciscan inquisitors later began to operate in Venice, this secular
inquisition composed of three Venetians continued to function
as a parallel force.

Cathars had fled to Venice during the persecutions in
Lombardy, so that when Innocent IV inaugurated the

Inquisition in Treviso in 1254 he sent a copy of the Bull to the Franciscans in that city as well. But here too a fresh impulse was provided in the 1260s after the coming to power of Charles I – although he played no direct part in the history of the Venetian Republic. From about 1262 to 1302 a small group of six or seven Franciscan friars, 'powerful and at times even tyrannical',[14] controlled both the Inquisition and the Church in Venice. These friars frequently interchanged roles from inquisitor to bishop or prior, and maintained an effective stranglehold on ecclesiastical affairs in that province. Their abuses of power were eventually punished by Pope Boniface VIII, who ordered an inquiry into their activities.

The first of these remarkable Franciscan inquisitors was a certain Brother Florasio of Vicenza, who from the moment of his appointment in 1262 fought for the inclusion of anti-heresy legislation in the laws of Venice. His success was rewarded with promotion to the Curia in Rome, whence he used his increased influence to the benefit of his successors in the Inquisition at Venice. He was followed by Brother Mascara of Padua, who according to Brother Mariano da Alatri was still renowned twenty years later for the vast sums he had managed to confiscate whilst in office.[15] His enormous power in the province lasted for over forty years, often financed by money he extorted for his own use by the blatant use of his relatives as 'fronts'.

The famous burning of Cathars in the arena at Verona was the work of two of these inquisitors. Even before that holocaust, Brother Timidio of Verona – inquisitor at Venice from 1269 to 1276 – had directed his efforts against the powerful Cathar communities of Lazise and Sirmione, near Verona. But his moment of greatest notoriety came after his appointment in 1276 to the bishopric of Verona, when his friend and successor as inquisitor, Brother Filippo Bonnacolsi of Mantova, led a military expedition against the Cathars of Sirmione. This mini-crusade, led in person by the bishop and the inquisitor, was a great success: nearly two hundred Cathars were captured and taken to the Inquisition's prison in Verona. Bishop Timidio presided over the public execution of these Cathars in the Roman amphitheatre on 13 February 1278. Perhaps it was as a reward for his zeal in this case that Filippo Bonnacolsi was appointed Bishop of Trent.[16]

But the scandals that were eventually to end the Franciscan domination of the Inquisition in the Venice province derived from corruption rather than zealous treatment of suspected heretics. It was a wealthy province, and the potential pickings were correspondingly rich; there is ample evidence that the friars enriched both themselves and their families, with little concern for the Order to which they belonged. Brother Antonio de Luca of Padua, for example, sold during a single auction the property of twenty-two convicted heretics – entirely for his own benefit. An illustration of the friars's awareness of their good fortune is the long and ferocious battle fought by the inquisitor Buonagiunta of Mantova to retain the privileges of the Franciscan inquisitors against the Dominicans. The Dominican inquisitors of Lombardy, Brother Pagano and Brother Viviano, were keen to gain jurisdiction over the rich city and province of Verona – which fell within the inquisitorial province of Venice.

The climax of this arrogance and corruption was reached with Brother Pietrobuono of Padua, inquisitor at least from 1296 to 1298 and perhaps considerably longer. This totally unscrupulous friar committed a long series of frauds against the Church and the Inquisition itself, and amassed a considerable personal fortune. He sold clandestine absolutions to notorious heretics, bought for himself at minimal cost the property of heretics put up at auction, sold the belongings and property of the Holy See at a loss to his friends and relatives, and bought buildings in Padua for the offices of the Inquisition – later selling them for his own profit. When the time came for this inquisitor to hand over his office to a successor, he refused to consign the registers that recorded financial transactions. It was his excesses, and this refusal, which brought the scandalous state of affairs in the Venetian Inquisition to the attention of Boniface VIII. The Pope ordered an immediate inquiry. He suspended the activities of the Inquisition at Venice on 1 May 1302, once the details of corruption, injustices and decadence had been made clear by a report. Six months later, he transferred the duties of inquisitor for Venice to the Dominicans of the dioceses of Padua and Piacenza.

Thus the Venetian Inquisition in the thirteenth century appears to have provided a provincial political and ecclesiastical power base – with numerous financial incentives. Fines and confiscations were the most common type of sentence, especially of deceased heretics. There were endless cases in which confiscated property or money was 'misused': properties of heretics put up for sale were often purchased by relatives of the previous owner, and even in some cases by the heretics themselves; inquisitors traded in these properties and confiscated goods, made loans at interest and performed other commercial transactions. All these activities were in open contrast to the explicit ban against the use of money which had been promulgated by St Francis in his Rule less than a century before.

The activities of the Inquisition in Venice accurately reflected the prosperity and trading mentality of a great mercantile centre, of which the chronicler Martino da Canale wrote in the same period that 'merchandise passes through this noble city as water flows through fountains'.[17] In fact, as Mariano da Alatri concludes, many other aspects of the Inquisition were conspicuously absent in Venice. Consignment of convicted heretics to the secular arm was extremely rare, and prison is only mentioned once in the surviving documents.[18] The example of Venice illustrates how the Inquisition assumed the characteristics of the area in which it was established as soon as there was no direct papal interest or control.

A Trial by Lake Garda

An interesting insight into the activities of the monks and inquisitors is provided by the trial documents of an *inquisitio generalis* carried out at Riva sul Garda between December 1332 and March 1333. This small town had already been the scene of inquisitorial activity when Brother Aiulfo of Vicenza, 'a man without scruples, and a judge without mercy',[19] had burned two women and a local blacksmith on the public square in 1304. But in 1332 it became the seat of a long and complicated trial in which between thirty and forty Franciscan friars were present or participated over the three months that it lasted. Their names and details of the trial are recorded in notarial archives preserved in Padua.

The trial was attended by fascinating and surprising personalities who spring to life from the detailed accounts kept by the Inquisition, and incidentally substantiate earlier comments about the corruption of the clergy in the Middle Ages. There appears a certain Brother Stefano of Brescia, for instance, referred to by his picturesque nickname of 'block-head', who openly confessed to practising all the sacerdotal virtues and the Rule of the Franciscans *in reverse*.[20] But one of the most frequent matters discussed is the problem of concubinage. Three priests who lived with concubines attempted to justify their practice by making an appeal to the authority of St Paul – although the inquisitors did not accept their argument. Another priest, Gentile of Verona, had provided a more convincing defence. A witness called Ottonello di Giovannino Dentelli swore that he had heard Gentile 'say that he would well have and keep women, because he's a man like others although a priest; and it was better to have one than go out and search for many. And at the moment of death, since he had got somebody with a child that he called his nephew, he replied: "Because I cannot have women like you, it's better that I have one of them rather than cause trouble with other men's wives'.*[21] This enlightened defence speaks eloquently for the importance of celibacy in the minds of the thirteenth- and fourteenth-century clergy.

Even more remarkable is the case of the widow Ida, whose hobby appears to have consisted in persuading priests and monks to break their vows of celibacy. One day she met two Dominicans who claimed to be out searching for grain. Ida boldly declared: '"I know what grain you want, because you want to screw!" At this the friars said: "You are a wicked woman. What words are these? Perhaps you don't know that this is a sin against God?" She replied: "Why is it a sin? It's not a sin, because God ordered it, because friars and priests are men like the others, and they screw well and serve women. And if this were a sin and God were displeased, he would not allow it to happen."'§[22] The similarity of Ida's argument to that of Gentile

---

* '*Dicere quod bene potest tenere et habere feminas, quia est homo sicut alii, licet sit sacerdos; et melius est quod habeat unam, quam ire per multas. Et cum increparetur, quod gravidaret quandam, quam dicebat nepotem suam, respondebat: "Quare non possum ita bene habere mulieres sicut vos, melius est quod habeam unam, quam ire ad uxores vestras".*'

§ Again, the Latin text will give the full flavour of Ida's conversation: '"*Bene scio quale bladum queratis, quia vultis coire*". *Et cum dictus frater diceret:* "*Mala mulier es! Que verba sunt ista? Nescitis ... quia peccatum est et contra Deum?*" *Que respondit:* "*Quo modo est peccatum? Non est peccatum, quia hoc Deus ordinavit, quia fratres et sacerdotes sunt ita homines sicut alii, et ita bene coerunt et serviunt mulieribus. Et si esset peccatum et displiceret Deo, ipse non permitteret facere talia!*"' The pun on *bladum* is lost in English.

suggests that it was common enough to justify the breaking of celibacy in such a way. Ida's only mistake was to choose two Dominicans belonging to the Inquisition.

One further incident in this trial which is of interest in a history of the Inquisition also concerns Gentile of Verona. The same friar who had justified his keeping of a concubine, and had a son by one of his mistresses, was capable of exhibiting extraordinary outbursts of zeal. During a sermon preached by a Franciscan from Venice, Gentile interrupted to deny vehemently that 'the cord of contrition' was necessary to prepare a good confession. He emphasized his dramatic intervention by grabbing the poor preacher by his tunic, shaking him violently, and shouting: 'He's a Cathar!'* The preacher was forced to conclude his sermon immediately, but the story is important for its indication of the readiness with which the term 'Cathar' could be used – even within the delicate circumstances of a trial for heresy. It also illustrates the extent to which fear of heretical doctrines lay close to the surface of the minds of the clergy at that time, and how explosively it could erupt.

The Fraticelli or Spiritual Franciscans

The Franciscan brotherhood had already split into opposing factions before the death of its founder. This division was based on how closely the Rule of St Francis should or could be observed: the *conventuali* held that 'the original Franciscan ideal was beyond the reach of most people', while the *spirituali* represented the rigorist wing and maintained that St Francis had 'revealed a new spiritual epoch and that his Rule therefore had the authority of Gospel'.[23] That such a doctrine, which during the course of the thirteenth century produced several mystics and such a poet as Jacopone da Todi, should be considered heretical is one of the great ironies of that century. The injustice of their persecution did in fact derive from a mistaken identification of the *fraticelli* with a so-called third order of Franciscans who broke completely with the Roman Church and set up an alternative Church with priests and bishops of their own.

Perhaps the root cause of the heresy of the *fraticelli* was their association in the minds of successive Popes with the

*'. . . *quia catharus est!*' (Alatri, *Rileggendo*, p. 186).

arch-heretic Frederick II, and their adoption of the prophetic doctrines of Joachim da Fiore – whose eschatology, described by Norman Cohn as 'the most influential one known to Europe until the appearance of Marxism',[24] was based upon a mystical interpretation of the Scriptures and claimed predictive powers. Joachim's vision was developed from a concept of history divided into three successive phases: the age of the Father, the age of the Son, and the age of the Holy Ghost, corresponding respectively with an age of fear, an age of faith, and a final age of love and freedom when 'the knowledge of God would be revealed directly in the hearts of men'.[25] In this final, ecstatic age the world would be like a vast monastery which would last until the moment of the Last Judgement.

It was Joachim's placing of the culmination of human history between 1200 and 1260 that focused attention on Frederick II, who was burdened throughout his life by this role as Emperor of the Last Days. For this reason, his death in 1250 had a traumatic and decisive influence on the history of both Italy and Church. At the end of the century Dante was still inspired by the Joachite vision, and lived his creative life in a kind of mystical fervour for the eschatological myth of Empire. The *Divine Comedy* climaxes with an ecstatic invocation to the 'eternal light of God which loves and rejoices' in the Holy Spirit.* Equally, Dante's conception of world government was derived from and closely linked to Joachite dreams; so much so that, as we shall see, his *De Monarchia* was placed on the Index of prohibited books by the Inquisition 250 years later. Thus these visions, transmitted by the *fraticelli*, permeated thirteenth-century religious thought.

When the Franciscans expanded rapidly into one of the greatest of religious orders, and their friars began necessarily to deal with money, teach in the new universities and face other problems of worldly life, some of them refused to accept this revised form of a brotherhood founded on total poverty and with obedience to a strict Rule:

These men – the Franciscan Spirituals – formed a minority party, at first within the Order, later outside it. By the middle of the century they had disinterred Joachim's prophecies (which had hitherto

*Cf. *Paradiso*, XXXIII, 124-126.

attracted little attention) and were editing them and producing commentaries upon them. They were also forging prophecies which they successfully fathered upon Joachim and which became far better known and more influential than Joachim's own writings. In these works the Spirituals adapted the Joachite eschatology in such a way that they themselves could be seen as the new order which, replacing the Church of Rome, was to lead mankind into the glories of the Age of the Spirit.[27]

In this way the *fraticelli* entered into direct competition with Rome, and it became the business of the Inquisition to eliminate them.

As with other heresies, however, precise definition of the *fraticelli* is complicated by the agglomeration of other fringe religious orders under the cover of their name, and the attribution of men and ideas which have little to do with them. Bernard Gui thought that they were an Italian version of the *beguines*, for example. But it is interesting to note that one of the areas in which the *fraticelli* 'heresy' persisted well into the fifteenth century was approximately equivalent to the old Cathar diocese of the Valle Spoletana, with related phenomena in the nearby Abruzzi – where many Cathar refugees are thought to have fled the persecutions of the Inquisition in Central Italy.

The obsession of Boniface VIII with the *bizochi*, as the *fraticelli* were known in the Abruzzi, is a case in point. It was from the same wild and remote area that the hermit who was later to become Celestine V had come. His austere lifestyle, and that of his own followers known as the *celestiniani*, conformed closely to that of the *fraticelli*, and there seems to have been little difference between them. The story of his journey to the 1274 Council of Lyons to gain recognition for his followers cannot have failed to obtain the consensus of the *fraticelli* and remind them of St Francis himself. The iconography of Celestine V is reminiscent of that of St Francis, with the Pope usually portrayed talking to animals and birds, or feeding himself with the spartan produce of his hermitage near the town of Sulmona. This mysterious and often ambiguous man named the first monastery he founded after the Holy Spirit.

The historical problems of the papacy of Celestine V, his surprise election to the Holy See in 1294 and equally surprising renunciation of the papal crown five months later – famous from Dante's characterization of him as 'he who from cowardice made the great refusal'* – might be explained in terms of the *fraticelli*. Boniface VIII, who persecuted the *bizochi* (often confused with the *celestiniani* and *fraticelli*, perhaps even in his own mind), was also the Pope who succeeded Celestine V; he captured Celestine after pursuing him through southern Italy, imprisoned him at Fumone south of Rome, and was almost certainly responsible for murdering him. This strange and dramatic conclusion to the life of an ex-Pope, together with the Inquisition's newly intensified operations in the area from which he came, suggest the intriguing hypothesis that Celestine V was himself a heretic. If this is the case, then his story stands as a monument to the complexity of religious life at the close of the thirteenth century. And Alatri's observation *vis-à-vis* the Venetian Inquisition that 'in the light of the corruption of these Franciscans, the drama of the spirituals becomes a little more comprehensible'[28] underlines the intense drama of men such as Celestine, who perceived their mission in terms of St Francis and the early Church Fathers.

Pope John XXII, in his Bull *Sancta romana atque universalis Ecclesia* of 30 December 1317, excommunicated and suppressed the *fraticelli*. But five years later he found it necessary to insist that his Bull was put into effect in a letter to bishops, archbishops and inquisitors of Sicily, Italy, Provence, Narbonne and Toulouse. In this letter he complains that the *fraticelli* claim that they were given the privilege to live as they do by Celestine V, and then goes on to describe them as deviants from the Catholic faith.[29] In 1323 the Franciscan concept of poverty was itself condemned, a fact that indicates fear within the Church of extremist movements.§

The Inquisition tried and condemned many *fraticelli* in two full centuries of persecution. The anonymous author of the Vatican manuscript *codice Urbinate 1638* states that over 15,000 were executed, but that is probably an exaggeration. Mariano da Alatri concludes that 'as far as Central Italy is concerned, notwithstanding the lack of documentation, we believe that few were consigned to the secular arm. In any case, those who were

---

*Cf. *Inferno*, III, 60. The most complete life of Celestine is that by Giuseppe Celidonio: S. Pietro del Morrone, Pescara: Artigianelli, 1954.

§Lester K. Little has shown how the voluntary poverty movements reflected a crisis provoked by the emergence of a profit economy. Such extreme reaction generated fear in an institution which had necessarily become part of this profit economy (cf *Religious Poverty*, pp. 99–160).

consigned can be counted on the fingers of one hand . . .'.[30]

The essential fact is that during the thirteenth century, inspired by the lawyer-popes and the need to combat Catharism, the Church had been gradually developing a dogma. The detailed presentation of Cathar doctrines by inquisitors, and subsequent confutation with scriptural texts in pages of biblical language, contributed to the formation of this body of dogma. Treatises such as the *Summa contra haereticos* of the Franciscan inquisitor Giacomo de' Capelli (c.1240), which used the Gospels for argument and illustration without reference to the Church Fathers,* worked towards the synthesis triumphantly achieved by Thomas of Aquinas in his *Summa Theologica* and *Summa contra Gentiles* towards the end of the century. Most important in this context are the continued references to the New Testament, which owe much to the insistence on the Gospels given by both the Cathars and the followers of Waldo.

With such rigid dogma the slightest variations can be defined as heretical, whereas earlier space for manoeuvre had been much greater; it seems to have been this dogmatic narrowing which produced the 'heresy' of the *fraticelli*, perhaps also that of Pope Celestine, and created enormous difficulties for other orders with even minor liturgical variants. But the case of Celestine, the persecution of the *fraticelli* – and even the suppression of the Knights Templar – marked a severe wrenching of the theoretical system which had sustained the structure of medieval society. They also marked the enhanced papal fear of extremism that was consolidated as the new orthodoxy was perfected.

With the *fraticelli* the frail and artificial dichotomy between saint and heretic – later evident in the case of Joan of Arc and other 'witches' – first became apparent. Some men and women were both mystics and heretics, a fact which demonstrates how the term 'heretic' had become a useful label to circumscribe the abnormal, the deviant or the uncategorizable. By this time the slightest indication of unorthodoxy, even as the result of ignorance, was considered equal to heresy and therefore brought with it the full weight of the Inquisition. St Thomas Aquinas codified this new attitude and then provided the basis for punishment in such sections of the *Summa Theologica* as that

*Cf. the summary of Capelli's *Summa* in Alatri, *Inquisizione francescana*, I, pp. 239-50.

where he declares that opposition or resistance of any kind to the authority of the Church could be taken as heretical (II-II, 11, 2 ad 3). The first Jubilee called by Boniface VIII in 1300 was a public recognition of this new certainty and superiority. Generously interpreted by both Popes and inquisitors, this authority expressly condoned the extermination of potential enemies of the Church – whether spiritual, financial or military.

The Forcing Underground of Heresy

In the final thirty years of the thirteenth century, the Inquisition almost succeeded in exterminating Catharism; yet it survived, and even filtered back into France with the missionary zeal of Cathars like Pierre Autier. An important consequence of this partial success of the Inquisition, neither anticipated nor fully understood, was to drive the surviving Cathars away from cities like Milan and Florence into mountainous regions or secure havens distant from centres of ecclesiastical power: 'Cathari driven from Languedoc, who perhaps found even Lombardy insecure, were tolerably sure of refuge in the wild and secluded valleys of Calabria and the Abruzzi, lying aside from the great routes of travel.'[31]

It is at this difficult moment, scarcely documented, that the first intimations of a link between heresy and sorcery become apparent. If there is any truth in the derivation of magical rites such as the sabbat from Cathar ritual, then it is in this obscure period of history that such a transition could have been made. Heresy did not disappear, but went underground; the areas where the last traces of Catharism in Italy were found have consistently represented the epicentres of other heretical movements throughout succeeding centuries. Even today, the last surviving centres of magical activities such as sorcery and sympathetic magic that may be derived from medieval sorcery are to be found in the remote areas of Piemonte, the Abruzzi and the area of Naples.

When Franciscan inquisitors demanded of Alexander IV in 1257 whether magic, sorcery and usury fell within their jurisdiction, he replied that such practices were outside the scope of their work unless heresy was directly involved.[32] Yet the new question, and the doubts that it formulated, bears its own interest since there is little record of a similar concern before this date. It seems that many people actually preferred to be tried by the Inquisition for sorcery, because at that time it was possible to escape with simple penances, while secular courts often burned suspects immediately. Alexander's Bull *Quod super nonnullis*, replying to the inquisitors, marks the beginning of a new attitude towards sorcery, and its existence would appear to reinforce Guiraud's statement that 'these practices multiplied, especially when the sects were attacked and became secret'.[33] There is ample evidence that soon after 1257 inquisitors throughout Europe began to interest themselves in matters concerning sorcery. Jeffrey Burton Russell shows how two French inquisitorial formularies of 1270 and 1280 included new questions designed to discover whether suspects had done anything involving the use of demons, or had called up demons in their rooms.[34] He gives examples from the *Anecdotes* of the French inquisitor Stephen of Bourbon, with details taken from the accounts of suspects arrested for *maleficium* – or sorcery – as early as the 1250s.[35] But these were still isolated cases, both in Italy and in France, and were virtually non-existent elsewhere at such an early date; the full attention of the Inquisition was not yet turned to sorcery and witchcraft.

Generally speaking, the Inquisition in Italy seems to have been fully occupied with the Cathars and the threat it perceived in them from its inception to around 1270. From 1270 to 1300, as heresy went underground beyond the Inquisition's direct control, there is a distinct decline in attacks against the Cathars; emphasis is placed on posthumous trials and confiscations, almost as if it were an acknowledgement of the lack of more legitimate activities. Then, around the turn of the century, there was another noticeable shift as the attention of Italian inquisitors turned towards the *fraticelli* and related movements. The apogee of the Italian Inquisition, and in particular that of the Franciscan Inquisition, had already passed. With the transfer of the papacy from Rome to Avignon the part the Inquisition played in Italian history diminished dramatically; it suffered a slow but irrevocable decline throughout the fourteenth and fifteenth centuries.

The Transfer of the Papacy

When Pope Clement V moved the seat of the papacy to Avignon in 1309, the Church effectively abandoned its claim to universal political supremacy. There was a widely diffused feeling that

Christian society had reached a 'conclusive moment of its development'.[36] The great Jubilee proclaimed by Boniface VIII in 1300 had represented the final assertion of the medieval Church as the lawyer-popes had conceived it. The very fact that a Pope could imagine the Church directed from a city other than Rome demonstrates the fundamental changes that were taking place; such a move would have been inconceivable to Innocent III, a mere century earlier.

R. W. Southern believes that the transfer of the papacy was a good thing: 'It removed the papacy from the fierce tensions of Italian politics and installed it in a low-pressure political area. Geographically the new seat of government was more convenient: for the inhabitants of four fifths of western Christendom it cut the time spent on a visit to the papal court by five weeks'. Furthermore, 'if the work of the papacy was to lie mainly in the daily routine of judicial business – and from this there was now no escape – then Avignon was a much better centre than Rome. It had the atmosphere of an up-to-date governmental headquarters.'[37]

The arrival of Charles of Anjou had turned the face of the Church inevitably towards France; Clement was the fourth French Pope since the 1260s, while the number of French cardinals had been constantly increasing. One of the first actions of Celestine V, elected to the Holy See with the support of Charles II of Anjou, was to create seven new French cardinals – against five Italians. France rather than the papacy stood at the centre of the Western world. The issues that had dominated the thirteenth century – Frederick II, the invasions of Mongols and Turks – were forgotten as the papacy became a tool of the French state. In this process of change the Inquisition was to play a fundamental role, demonstrated most dramatically by the Templar trials. The function of the Inquisition, and its power in Italy, were irrevocably changed by Clement's transfer to Avignon.

6. The Medieval Inquisition in France

At the beginning of the fourteenth century France was divided into six inquisitorial provinces, which increased temporarily to seven or eight in response to specific needs during the century. These provinces were in fact never static, but were frequently modified, amplified or closed; the inquisitors themselves often received different titles and jurisdictions from successive Popes, whose Bulls constantly adapted the situation to their personal view of heresy. In addition, the borders between the provinces fluctuated and were often the cause of disrepute between the two main Orders of inquisitors.

An example of this situation is the case of the Inquisition at Rouen. Until the fifteenth century the office of inquisitor in Rouen was considered to be a lieutenancy, delegated by the inquisitor at Paris. Thus at the beginning of the proceedings against Joan of Arc the inquisitor-delegate, Jean Le Maître – appointed in 1424 by Jean Graverant, Inquisitor-General at Paris – participated in the trial. When the ramifications of the trial, and therefore the importance of the post at Rouen, developed beyond initial expectations, it was thought necessary to appoint an inquisitor of greater rank. In 1431, a month and a half after the execution of Joan of Arc, Jean Graverant himself became the inquisitor at Rouen. From that date, the Inquisition in that city appears to have become autonomous.[1]

The eight provinces which existed during the course of the fourteenth and fifteenth centuries were as follows:[2]

Provence. This Franciscan province included Arles, Aix, Embrun and Vienne, although papal Bulls often include other towns. In this area of active heresy, temporary branches were quite often established.

Toulouse. Again a varied province, it usually included Auch, Gascoigne and Languedoc. It is perhaps the best known of the French Dominican inquisitorial provinces as a result of the detailed information provided by Bernard Gui.

Carcassonne. This province included Montpellier and sometimes Albi, with a total of seventeen dioceses. Again temporary branches were common.

Kingdom of Majorca. Controlled from its seat at Perpignan, this province included Roussillon and Cerdagne. It existed from 1262, when the Kingdom of Majorca was created, to 1348, when it was annexed by Aragon. But it was fully occupied with heretics who sought refuge in the islands under its jurisdiction, and Roussillon remained an independent Inquisition after the annexation of Majorca.

Corsica. Franciscan missions were sent to Corsica in 1340 and 1369 to search out Cathars and Waldensians who had escaped there, and from 1372 there was a permanent inquisitor based on the island. In 1377 Pope Gregory XI ordered the Franciscan General to appoint a further inquisitor in Sardinia and Corsica, since the islands were 'infested with heretics'.

Lyon, Burgundy, Franche-Comté and Lorraine. This province was run by the Dominicans, and after the establishment of an Inquisition at Besançon in 1290 it comprehended Geneva, Lausanne, Sion and Metz (from 1458 an Inquisition based at Lausanne presided over French-speaking Switzerland). An instance of the constant friction between Dominicans and Franciscans can be seen in the Franciscan attempts to annex Geneva to the province of Provence. Although detailed records are missing, it appears that this enormous province disintegrated after about 1450 and instead of a single inquisition 'each diocese ended up having its own'.[3]

Tours and Poitiers. This seems to have been short-lived as an independent province, since its existence can only be documented from 1317 to 1343 – with a total of three inquisitors. Otherwise, it seems to have fallen within the jurisdiction of the Inquisition of Paris. It included Brittany, and Anjou and Maine (except between 1290 and 1351, when these two dioceses were exempted from the Inquisition as belonging to the King of Naples).

Paris. The remainder of France came under this Inquisition, by far the largest; it included the large and important dioceses of Rouen (until 1431), Reims and Sens. The inquisitors at Paris were given the titles of *inquisiteurs in regno Franciae* or *inquisiteurs généraux de France,* which testify to the importance of the Parisian office.[4] Each subservient diocese had a vicar representing the Inquisitor-General, and again the staff was expanded or contracted according to temporary requirements.

This vast capillary organization was reinforced or weakened by the positive or negative personal interest of the Popes resident at Avignon. A long series of papal interventions demonstrate this fact: Clement V (1305-1314) substantially curtailed the abuse of the Inquisition by his investigations and the reforms he pushed through the Council of Vienne; John XXII (1316-1334) and Benedict XII (1334-1352) both used the Inquisition as an instrument in their personal battles against sorcery and heresy, although both also intervened personally in favour of suspected or condemned heretics.[5] John XXII once pardoned a *fraticello* who was his declared enemy, ordering in a letter dated 23 November 1330 from Avignon that the German Conrad could be released from perpetual imprisonment if he were to show some sign of repentance.[6]

But in the first half of the century the inquisitors were often encouraged by frequent letters of exhortation from John XXII and Benedict XII to exterminate sorcery and heresy. Benedict, whose name was Jacques Fournier, had been a Cistercian monk who later became Bishop of Palmiers and founded a branch of the Carcassonne Inquisition there. He continued his battles against heresy as Bishop of Mirepoix, and once promoted to Cardinal worked closely with the Inquisition. John XXII made him responsible for dealing with the appeals made to the Holy See by suspected heretics imprisoned by the Inquisition, and also for the work of inquisitor within the papal Curia. Throughout his long pontificate, Benedict maintained this close interest. As Vidal says of the 350 documents contained in his collection of papal Bulls concerning the Inquisition: 'Nearly all the documents of this collection witness the importance that the Popes attached to the action of the Inquisition.'[7]

This period was in fact to be the climax of the Inquisition in the Middle Ages. Once adapted to secular needs by such monarchs as Philip the Fair of France, the Inquisition fulfilled its role in the conception and successful implementation of one of the largest simultaneous international police operations before modern times.

The Trial of the Knights Templar

The trial of the Templars presents several anomalies with respect to normal inquisitorial procedure, being essentially based upon the use of heresy charges for secular and financial gain by a secular authority. The initial arrests were made by agents of the King of France, and not by inquisitors – although Philip the Fair cleverly asserted that they were being made in 'the name of the Inquisition'. Moreover, the action taken by the French king in destroying one of the greatest religious orders can be interpreted as being against the interests of the papacy, which was paradoxically the sole arbiter of the Inquisition. It was not therefore so much the Inquisition itself, but rather its methods that had attracted Philip. Lambert has expressed this paradox as follows: 'Novel forces were arrayed against the papacy when an advanced secular monarchy ... made uninhibited use of inquisitorial techniques in order to gain the Templar's wealth.'[8]

The close personal relationship between Philip the Fair and Guillaume de Paris, the Inquisitor-General at Paris and also the king's confessor, also represents an anomaly. At the moment of the arrest of the Templar brothers in France, on 13 October 1307, Philip claimed that the Inquisitor-General had informed him of the corruption of the Knights Templar. This information, never specified or mentioned again in the trials, was supposed to be his only motive in ordering the arrests. Thus he could claim that he was 'following the just request of Guillaume de Paris'.[9] Philip had devoted over a decade to bringing the Inquisition in France under his personal control, and this action was the fruit of his success. Inquisitors played a vital role in torturing Templar brothers and knights, and later carried out further arrests and trials throughout Europe on the orders of the Pope.

It is also important to remember that the Inquisition itself was to a certain extent under trial in the same period as the Templar trials. On 13 March 1306, one and a half years before the arrest of the Templars, Clement V had charged two Dominicans – Bernard Blanc and François Aymeric – to investigate into the complaints of the people of Carcassonne and Albi against what they described as the persecutions of the inquisitors in that area and the bishop, Bernard de Castenet.[10] This followed the earlier investigations made for Boniface VIII in Italy. Although the Inquisition continued to function, these long-term inquiries clearly had some effect and it was temporarily weakened during the period up to the Council of Vienne in 1311. At that Council, reforms were imposed on the Inquisition: thereafter, for example, the presence of the bishop was required at trials and new restrictions were made on torturing; Inquisition prisons lost their previous autonomy, with the rule that each cell and prison should have two keys – one each for the inquisitor's gaoler and the bishop's representative. This period of relative weakness and uncertainty, from 1306 to 1311, roughly coincides with the long-drawn-out business of the Templar trials – which lasted from the initial arrests of 1307 to the burning of the Grand Master in 1314.

Furthermore, whatever heresies might have emerged in the course of the Templar trials, it seems clear that financial rather than religious motives prompted Philip into action. The need for money had already been the cause of a violent argument with Boniface VIII, who had attempted to impose taxes on the French clergy in 1296, when Philip was raising cash for his war against England.[11] Although arrests were made 'in the name of the Inquisition', as soon as the Templar brothers were taken into custody their property was confiscated by representatives of the king. Barber has stated that in successive stages the counsellors of Philip were well suited to making the 'conversion of the Templar's unpopularity into "heretical depravity"'.[12] Thus the origin of the battle to exterminate the Knights Templar had little to do with the Inquisition's avowed and customary function, and Clement V was himself reluctant to be dragged into the fray. This continued reluctance itself shows that it was the royal will – and exigencies – which caused and directed the trial. Lambert's observation that it was more a matter of the ruthless political use of inquisitorial techniques is pertinent.

In fact, for nearly a year after the initial arrests hundreds of Templar knights and brothers languished in French prisons without much progress being made in their trial. King Philip was engaged in a struggle for power with the Pope, who was forced to concede passive assistance even though he was never convinced of the truth of accusations made against the Order. From the beginning he insisted that property and money confiscated from the Templars should go to the Church rather than to the French State.* But it was soon clear that Philip the Fair's ambitions went far beyond the mere acquisition of Templar wealth: he was attempting the definitive subordination of the papacy to the French crown.

The role of the Inquisition in the trial of the Templars was twofold. It was instrumental in obtaining the first confessions, which were to set the pattern for trials throughout Europe; and it carried out the minor trials of Templars in other countries once Clement V succumbed to Philip's persuasion.

As we have seen, the French Templars were arrested on 13 October. Within a week the Inquisitor-General of Paris and France, Guillaume de Paris, personally started the interrogation of the most important prisoners. From 19 to 26 October he questioned thirty-seven witnesses and obtained confessions from Jacques de Molay, the Grand Master, and Geoffroi de Charney, the Preceptor of Normandy. The confessions of the two most powerful Templars made the continuation of the prosecution possible, and 'set the pattern for the remaining hearings'.[13] Royal officials participated more in the questioning in the provinces, but it seems that key figures were questioned and tortured by the Inquisition. The Dominican inquisitor Nicolas D'Ennezat was responsible for the interrogation of Hugues de Pairaud, Visitor of France, Geoffroi de Gonneville, the Preceptor of Aquitaine, and Raimbaud de Caron, the Preceptor of Cyprus.

Then, when Clement V eventually made up his mind after lengthy negotiations, the fate of the Templars was sealed as the

---

*This wealth has often been exaggerated. Partner points out that any available cash would have been used up in re-equipping forces in Cyprus after the fall of Acre (*Murdered Magicians*, p. 66). Perkins asserts that 'The value of the Templar's movable property was much less than we might expect', and provides the figures. He concludes that the result was a 'wild orgy of plunder' that minimized possible advantages for Philip (*The Wealth of the Knights Templar*, p. 254 and p. 263).

full machinery of the Inquisition was brought to bear on the case. 'On 12 August 1308 no fewer than 483 separate papal letters were issued on a single day, in order to effect these arrangements. All over the Catholic world, governments, bishops and inquisitors were mobilised for the enquiries. The methods to be employed, which included interrogation under torture, were minutely specified.'[14] The inevitable consequence was the first public burning of Templars, when fifty-four of them were executed at Paris on 12 May 1310; Barber describes that mass burning as the 'decisive stroke' in breaking the Templars.[15] Torture by the inquisitors soon brought a sufficient number of confessions to prove Templar guilt of the charges of heresy and witchcraft – whether we consider them to be 'an extraordinary farrago of nonsense'[16] and 'certainly exaggerated, if not wholly fabricated',[17] as two reliable historians have recently described them, or accept them at face value. Fantasies produced in desperation under torture were then used by inquisitors to stimulate fresh confessions, until it was virtually impossible to disentangle fact and fiction.[18]

The enigma remains. Were the Templars destroyed because their power was feared and their wealth desired by Philip the Fair, or was there some basis in the accusations made against them by the Inquisition?[19] The answer is beyond the scope of a history of the Inquisition, but from that point of view there are two further features of interest.

First, the arrival of the two French inquisitors Dieudonné, Abbot of Lagny, and Sicard de Vaur, a canon of Narbonne, at London in September 1309. They were sent from France to search out and try English Templars, and this occasion marks the only attempt by the Inquisition throughout its long history to work in the British Isles.* Thwarted by the provisions of common law, which expressly forbade torture and which they did not manage to circumvent in repeated attempts, they soon returned to France without the elaborate and fantastic confessions that their fellow inquisitors had obtained in France.[20]

The second feature is the distant role played by the most

---

*Hamilton points out that although these clerics are usually called inquisitors, there is no evidence for this supposition (*Med. Inq.* p. 84). However, Barber describes them as inquisitors and provides a detailed account of their mission (*Trial of the Templars*, pp. 195-204).

famous inquisitor of the time, Bernard Gui. Cheney describes Gui as 'baffled by the contradictory evidence',[21] a state of mind which is difficult to imagine in an inquisitor of such experience and certainty. We are led to ask how any other man could understand what was going on if such an expert heretic hunter was baffled. As far as the accusations made against the Templars of sorcery or supposed similarity to Cathar doctrines are concerned, Henry Lea's conclusion remains valid: 'Perhaps the most detailed and authoritative account of the downfall of the Templars is that of Bernard Gui. It is impossible to doubt that had there been anything savouring of Catharism in the order he would have scented it out and alluded to it.'[22]

Thus the most celebrated of inquisitors stands aside from the trial, but there is no doubt that the Inquisition played a decisive, if minor, role. Until it was called into action, the success of the trial was in doubt; once it entered the fray there was no longer any doubt. This simple fact stands as awesome witness of the terrible efficiency of the Inquisition. Yet again, it seems that Lea does not exaggerate when he argues that the destruction of such a powerful order could not have been contemplated without the facilities that the Inquisition made available to an unscrupulous man like Philip the Fair. The trial of the Templars offers 'a perfect illustration of the helplessness of the victim, no matter how high-placed, when once the fatal charge of heresy was preferred against him, and was pressed through the agency of the Inquisition'.[23]

Pope John XXII

John XXII accurately reflects the ambivalence of the medieval Church in being both the fiercest persecutor of sorcery and at the same time superstitious to the point of inviting accusations of being a magician himself. There is reason to believe that Peter of Abano, a magician and necromancer tried by the Inquisition in 1306, wrote his work on poisons, *Tractatus de Veneris*, for this Pope. As Thorndike says of the *Ars Geomantie* of Bartholomew of Parma, written in 1288 for the bishop-elect of Reggio, 'the interest of the canon of Laon and bishop elect of Reggio in the art of geomancy is another of numerous indications that we have that such occult and superstitious arts were at least not consistently condemned by the Church and clergy'.[24]

In this respect it is fascinating to note a 1312 statute forbidding Franciscans from the possession of necromantic books, or from participating in alchemy, necromancy, divination, incantation or invoking demons.[25] That such a statute was considered necessary presumes the widespread distribution of such books and practices within the Franciscan Order at the beginning of the fourteenth century. And such beliefs were certainly prevalent among John XXII's own predecessors, rendering possible the attacks for political motives which multiplied and became almost endemic at the turn of the century. These attacks culminated in 1307 when, as Partner affirms, 'magical charges became one of the standard methods of aggression among the jealous and competitive servants of King Philip the Fair'.[26]

Yet, as in the case of the Knights Templar, these accusations may often have harboured some element of truth. Celestine V chose for his personal emblem a symbol curiously resembling an alchemical sign, and Boniface VIII was suspected of a deep interest in alchemy, together with his personal doctor Arnold of Vilanova. John XXII was subject to a necromantic plot on his and his cardinals' lives in Avignon, when sympathetic magic was worked using images of the Pope and the cardinals.[27] The use of magical talismans, deriving from Moslem practices, was fashionable in papal and court circles: Clement V, Benedict XI and Boniface VIII are all said to have used them.[28] Moreover, this papal ambivalence was only confirmed by their actions against so-called sorcerers: Thorndike has observed that the condemnation and burning at the stake of the astrologer Cecco d'Ascoli by the Inquisition seems 'to have advertised rather than repressed his writings'.[29] Similarly, the insistence of St Thomas Aquinas and the Church on the real existence of evil spirits and their presumed powers did little to abate general interest in such phenomena.

A curious example in connection with John XXII is his use of a curved horn, or *corno serpentino* – still used in Naples and southern Italy today against *la jettattura*.* The Pope borrowed a silver one, said to have been used previously by Clement V, from the Countess Margaret of Foix. Luigi Fumi has described the occasion in these words: 'The pope, after having received it

---

*The Neapolitan word for an evil spell, against which professional 'witches' or 'wizards' use the curved horns. According to Llorente, the great Spanish Inquisitor-General Torquemada himself used one in the early sixteenth century.

from the hands of two legal representatives of the Countess . . . promised in the written receipt which begins *Ecce filia cornu illud serpentinum* to restore it at any eventual request, binding himself in good form with all his fixed and movable property. He used it at table, driven into his bread and surrounded by salt.'[30] This indicates that it was not a straightforward loan, but one guaranteed in an extraordinary manner, testifying to his eagerness to possess this curved horn. John XXII is often described as having been superstitious,[31] but this seems to go beyond simple superstition. It was perhaps his real belief in the efficacy of such magical practices that nurtured his great fear of them, and led him to persecute sorcerers with such venom throughout his long pontificate.

John XXII, who was born Jacques d'Euse in Cahors, was elected at Avignon on 7 August 1316. He began his pontificate with great energy, devoting his attention first to the *fraticelli*; he launched an unprecedented campaign against them with four Bulls issued within the next eighteen months. The first, of 7 October 1317, demonstrates a degree of attention to detail which might appear strange to modern eyes; he specifies the correct interpretation of some obscure articles of the Franciscan Rule, banning, for instance, the short tunic adopted by the *fraticelli* and ordering them to wear the prescribed dress.[32] A month later he ordered the inquisitor of Provence to proceed against twenty-six *fraticelli* individually named in a further Bull.[33] On 30 December 1317 he excommunicated and suppressed the *fraticelli*, *bizochi* and Beguines, who – according to his judgement – had proliferated in Italy, Sicily, Provence, Narbonne and Toulouse.[34]

When he considered that the question of the *fraticelli* had been dealt with satisfactorily, John XXII turned to magic and demons. On 28 July 1319 he ordered the Bishop of Palmiers – the future Benedict XII – to proceed against two men and a woman suspected of making images for magical practices and consulting demons.*[35] Whereas Alexander IV had distinguished between diviners and sorcerers, who came under the jurisdiction of the diocese, and heretics, who came under that of the Inquisition, John XXII made no such distinction. Within a year of the issuing of this Bull he made the fundamental order to the

---

'. . . factionibus ymagiunum, incantationibus et consultationibus demonum'.

Dominican Bishop William Goudin of Toulouse and Carcassonne to proceed against sorcerers as if they were heretics.

This Bull marked the beginning of an accentuation of the
repression of the 'crime' of sorcery. The bishop, who bore the
title of Cardinal of St Cecilia from 1312, went beyond the
conventional language of accusations against heretics when he
expressly stated that they 'sacrificed to and worshipped demons,
and made homage to them by giving them a written contract or
sign, and made an express pact with them.'* Jeffrey Burton
Russell considers that in this Bull 'the Inquisition was trying,
with some success, to extend its own jurisdiction over sorcery by
identifying it with heresy'.[36] Thus the two particular enemies of
John XXII, *fraticelli* and sorcerers, became the main target of the
Inquisition during his pontificate, and the laws which were to be
used in the future against sorcerers and for witchcraft were
given their final form.

Again, what is interesting in the next few years is the Pope's
concern with magical practices amongst the clergy, which to
judge from the cases mentioned in his letters must have been
widely practised. We read of a Benedictine monk practising
alchemy, divination and necromancy,[37] a canon of Saint-
Caprais d'Agen who is accused of demon worship,[38] the prior of
Saint-Sulpice in Tarn who is accused of making wax images for
sympathetic magic and also invoking demons,[39] and of a
Cistercian monk accused of experimenting with the invocation
of demons.[40] But the effects of John's persecution were often
the opposite of those desired, as we have seen in the case of
Cecco d'Ascoli: 'the stimulus which his proclamations had given
to the trade of the magician continued to extend it (e.g., sorcery)
and render it profitable'.[41] This is the first indication of a
phenomenon which was later to develop enormous dimensions,
when later inquisitors codified sorcery and witchcraft with
almost diabolical precision and enabled aspiring magicians to
use their works as practical guides to witchcraft.

John XXII's persecutions were short-lived, and he himself put
an end to them by a further Bull in 1330 – when he ordered the
archbishops of Toulouse and Narbonne, and the inquisitors of
Toulouse and Carcassonne, to conclude all sorcery and witch

---

*'. . . *demonibus immolant vel ipsos adorant aut homagium ipsis faciunt dando eis in signum
cartam scriptam seu aliud quodcumque, vel qui expressa pacta obligatoria faciunt cum eisdem'.*
Vidal, *Bullaire*, p. 61.

trials in hand and not begin new ones.[42] With this Bull the series of politically motivated witch trials ceased: they 'had aroused widespread attention, and may have aggravated general concern about witchcraft, but may also have made people sceptical about accusations that arose specifically from political or personal motives'.[43] Shortly afterwards, in 1334, John XXII died, to be succeeded in the unusually short time of sixteen days by his former colleague Benedict XII. With the new Pope, the focus of trials for witchcraft and sorcery shifted from important or politically involved suspects to ordinary village witches and local sorcerers. There was also a tendency to try suspected sorcerers in ecclesiastical or secular courts in the next few years, even inside France.[44]

Heretical Mysticism: Beguines, Beghards and Free Spirits

The same discontent with the Church that had inspired such men as St Bernard of Clairvaux and St Francis, and later pushed the *fraticelli* towards their demands for absolute poverty, was also evident in the spread of mysticism, 'not purely as a personal outlook but as a social ideal'.[45] This social ideal was perhaps most fully realized by the Beguines, who made their first appearance in Liège around 1210 and who became an important movement in northern Europe by the middle of the thirteenth century. They were unusual in being predominantly a woman's movement – with a less important male counterpart in the Beghards – which had no Rule and no authority from the Holy See, but whose members took an oath of chastity and led a common life in convents like other religious. Their lives were taken up by devotion to God, in search of ecstatic and visionary experiences.[46] The Beguines were much admired by such figures as Matthew Paris and Robert Grosseteste, and in the thirteenth century were largely accepted by the Church. It appears to have been their real or imagined association with the *fraticelli** in southern France that later incurred the suspicion of the papacy.[47]

The Beguines reached their maximum strength in the opening years of the fourteenth century, in which the profound paradox of their existence was made crudely visible by zealous Popes and the work of the Inquisition. A rapid succession of

*For example, in a letter of 30 December 1317 John XXII speaks of *fraticelli, bizochi* and Beguines as synonyms (Vidal, *Bullaire*, p. 39).

papal Bulls and letters concerning heretical mysticism often demonstrated a terminological confusion similar to that we have seen in the case of the Cathars. Once again a thin, precarious and often shifting line separated orthodoxy from heresy. On the one hand, the Beguine St Mechthild of Magdeburg (*c.* 1210-1280), authoress of the visionary work *The Flowing Light of the Godhead*, was recognized as a mystic – although she 'displayed clear signs of psychological disturbance';[48] on the other, the Beguine Marguerite Porete of Hainault, authoress of the *Mirror of Simple Souls*, a dialogue of the progress of the soul through seven states of grace, was tried by the inquisitor Guillaume de Paris and burnt for heretical mysticism in 1310.[49] There seems to be very little difference, if any, between these two women and their beliefs. Lambert explains this apparent injustice as follows: 'Mystics, of whom Porete is a fair, though not distinguished example, were describing rare states and treating great mysteries, that lay near the limits of ordinary language: they used paradoxical, even shocking, phrases in trying to convey their meaning.'[50]

Even more curious is the case of the so-called heresy of the Free Spirit, which demonstrates the strange consequences to which the personal convictions of inquisitors could lead. Recent scholarship has argued convincingly that as a sect the Free Spirit did not exist, and that the heresy which goes under this name can at most be attributed to individuals who were more or less involved in mystical practices not much different to those of the Beguines.[51] At the Council of Vienne the existence of a sect of Free Spirits was proclaimed, and was therefore real. The Free Spirits were said to live amongst the Beguines and Beghards, who were themselves suppressed officially by the same Council. What appears to have happened is that papal fears of antinomian heresies, coupled with inquisitorial zeal, created heresies to satisfy a need for new heresies. After such a long period of terror of the Cathars, perhaps their eventual extermination seemed too good to be true?

The case illustrates how a large and well-organized international institution such as the Inquisition had become at that moment will always create a task for itself. The fears and ideas of inquisitors were received sympathetically by two Popes who alone spanned half a century, John XXII and Benedict XII. Thus the attack against the *fraticelli* implied similar persecutions of Beguines and Free Spirits. Large numbers of them were burned at the stake in Narbonne, Lunel, Lodève, Béziers, Capestang, Pézenas, Carcassonne and Toulouse from 1319 to 1322.[52] In that latter year John XXII ordered the French archbishops to enquire into the beliefs of the Beguines, and distinguish between the 'good' and the 'bad' ones.[53] But the taint of heresy remained with them after this brief but vigorous period of persecution.

In 1364, Pope Urban V caused Germany – where the Inquisition did not operate at that time – to be divided into four provinces for the purpose of dealing with the Beguines and Beghards. Thorough investigations were carried out with the aim of discovering the existence of groups of Free Spirits.[54] These persecutions began to diminish towards the end of the century, and disappeared altogether in the fifteenth century. In his review of these mystical groups, Lambert concludes that there was a movement of radical mysticism that 'went at least to the limits of orthodoxy in its views of the possibility of union with God in this life, and was indifferent, if not hostile to the sacraments and to the mediating role of the Church'.[55]

The Inquisition was thus actively engaged in suppressing what could hardly be described as heresies at all, and had only a minor role in the political trials of the fourteenth century. This strange and paradoxical period of activity – when it was powerful but had only pseudo-heretical movements to deal with – represented the death throes of the medieval Inquisition, which by the end of the fifteenth century was as ineffective in France as it was in Italy. Only one great challenge awaited it in fifteenth-century France; for the most part the Inquisition had little to do, and its chief problem was the lack of revenue to sustain its organization.

The Trial of Joan of Arc

The final challenge of the Inquisition in France was the trial of Joan of Arc, although it presented anomalies which are reminiscent of those in the Templar trial. Once again, neither arrest nor trial was conceived by the Inquisition. The inquisitor at Rouen was in fact brought into the trial after preliminary hearings had started. It was possibly the most openly and exclusively political trial in which the Inquisition ever played a part.

For Joan's death was a political necessity. Later interpretations have been romantically tinted by the strange aura that surrounds the 'Maid of Orléans', and there is no clearer instance of the fabrication of charges of witchcraft in the history of the Inquisition. As far as the English imagination is concerned, Shakespeare must bear much of the responsibility for creating a compelling figure of Joan as witch. When his Joan of Arc cries desperately in *Henry VI, Part I:*

> Now help me, ye charming spells, and periapts;
> And ye choice spirits that admonish me . . .

and the Duke of York describes her as an 'ugly witch', a 'hag' or an 'enchantress', and commands in glorious language:

> Break thou in pieces, and consume to ashes,
> Thou foul accursed minister of hell!

as she burns, Shakespeare fuels the legend for purely dramatic reasons. For Joan of Arc as an agent of the devil was necessitated by his own plot.

The reality was quite different. W. S. Scott has neatly summarized the circumstances:

When Jeanne d'Arc set out from Vaucouleurs in February 1429, the English were everywhere victorious: in occupation of the greater part of the country north of the Loire, including Paris and Rheims, their army was engaged in besieging Orleans. Surrounded by unscrupulous advisers, his coffers empty, and his legitimacy denied by his own mother, the Dauphin's fortunes were at their lowest ebb.

At the time of Jeanne's capture at Compiègne fifteen months later, the picture had changed completely. Orleans had been relieved; the invader had suffered a series of major defeats; much of the occupied territory had been liberated; and Charles had been crowned at Rheims. That Jeanne should be brought to trial was a political necessity to her enemies: not only must it be shown that the Dauphin's coronation was invalid, but for the morale of the English army it was essential to prove that the Armagnac successes had a diabolic source.[56]

The trial was promoted by Cauchon, Bishop of Beauvais, who was also one of the two judges at the trial – together with the later co-opted inquisitor of Rouen, Jean Le Maître. Cauchon was a declared enemy of Joan of Arc, and was personally responsible for choosing the prosecutor and sixty assessors who made up the court. Throughout the preliminary hearings and full trial, any assessor who made objections was instantly dismissed from his post by Cauchon, and often imprisoned to make sure that he could not continue to put forward such objections.

Before the Inquisition became involved – at Cauchon's instigation – the personality and enmity of the Bishop had already conditioned this trial and its outcome. The French historian Lucien Fabre has provided an excellent sketch of the character of Cauchon which will help us to understand the political machinations behind the trial:

> We shall never understand the trial of Joan of Arc unless we first understand Cauchon. He was one of those rare and genuinely terrifying persons, one of those dominant and masterful characters, who in the days of the struggle between Empire and Papacy might have found employment in either camp, and would have brought to the service of Pope or Emperor the same self-confidence, the same complete indifference to ideals, the same craving for power, the same vigour, and the same bad faith. At the time of Joan's trial, the Bishop of Beauvais had his eyes greedily fixed on the Archbishopric of Rouen, which was then vacant, and a Cardinal's hat; and such was the state of the Papacy and the attitude of the Councils in those years that he aspired even higher. All he needed was the support of the greatest King of the West and of its greatest Duke* when the time for the next Conclave came round. What other Cardinal than Cauchon would these temporal sovereigns be able to suggest?
>
> In 1430 he was sixty years of age and well on the way to success and fortune. The least obstacle in his way irritated him profoundly, and more than any other this Armagnac Maid, who had so obviously been born to end her life at the stake.[57]

This assessment of Cauchon's character and ambitions is borne out by the Bishop's actions during the long trial.

After eight months of imprisonment, the trial of Joan of Arc began with a six-day public examination inside the castle of

*i.e., the King of England and the Duke of Bedford.

Rouen. This was followed by fresh interrogations in her cell, manipulated by Cauchon: of sixty assessors accredited to the trial, never more than six were present at any hearing and only fourteen of the total of sixty were called upon.[58] Then began the Trial in Ordinary, at which Joan began her irrevocable slide into what Fabre called 'the prosecutor's infernal labyrinth of words'.[59] The first of the seventy articles of indictment declared that Bishop Cauchon was competent to try her: if Joan agreed, then she practically arranged her own execution; if she objected and failed to accept Cauchon's jurisdiction, she would be tried as a heretic. In an important sense, therefore, the remaining sixty-nine charges were irrelevant; the elaborate accusations of making a pact with the devil, uttering heretical propositions, an initiation into sorcery during childhood, and dressing as a man, were superfluous.

The deputy-inquisitor, Jean Le Maître, played a minor role in these proceedings. On 19 February 1431, at the second Council of Formal Preliminaries, his absence is remarked upon and the Bishop orders him to be summoned. Two days later, Le Maître answered this summons as follows: '. . . that he was only commissioned in the city and diocese of Rouen; and since the trial was held before the bishop, not as Ordinary of the diocese of Rouen, but as of borrowed jurisdiction, he was doubtful as to joining in the matter . . . nevertheless, in order that the trial should not be null and void, as for the unburdening of his conscience, he was content to be present at the trial since he had inquisitorial powers'.[60] A letter from the Inquisitor-General on 4 March ordered the clearly reluctant Le Maître to act as vicar 'in connection with a certain woman of the name of Jeanne, commonly called the Maid'.[61] According to Quicherat, in his introduction to the trial transcripts, Jean Le Maître took part in the trial from 13 March. But the final trial document opens with a resounding declaration that places equal responsibility on Bishop Cauchon and Jean Le Maître.[62]

This distortion is also apparent in the last climactic days of Joan's trial, and life. When Joan of Arc signed an abjuration on 24 May, and was sentenced to life imprisonment, the inquisitor visited her in her cell and obtained assurances from her that she would relinquish her male attire. In the following days she was maltreated and repeated attempts were made by English soldiers to rape her; on the 28th she refused to wear female dress, and claimed to have heard her 'voices' again. At that point she was considered to have relapsed into heresy. But the confused circumstances of her death, and the undue haste, are quite different from the usual dignified proceedings of the Inquisition. Clearly the relapse was engineered just as the whole trial had been. She was excommunicated at seven o'clock on the morning of 30 May 1431, and burned as quickly as was decently possible on the same morning.

But her trial and execution had an important sequel, in which the Inquisition played a key role. In 1449, King Charles VII of France entered the city of Rouen, recently liberated from foreign rule, and ordered a re-trial of Joan of Arc, arguing that 'we wish to know the truth of this matter and to learn the manner in which the proceedings were conducted'.[63] It is clear that Charles was in no doubt about her innocence, and that he – like many citizens of Rouen who testified in the rehabilitation trial – was firmly convinced that the English had been responsible. Henry Lea comments cynically that he ordered the enquiry because 'it ill comported with the dignity of a King of France to owe his throne to a witch condemned and burned by the Church'.[64] Charles had been indicated as the true heir to the French throne by Joan, who had allied her cause to the young Dauphin from the beginning of her dramatic military career over twenty years earlier.

The Inquisitor-General of France, the Dominican Jean Bréhal, was persuaded to take the initiative in proceedings to annul the previous trial. An ecclesiastical enquiry opened in 1452, to establish the precise causes and circumstances of the original trial, but the real re-trial began in 1455. This time the whole matter was personally supervised by the Inquisitor-General, and the re-trial opened impressively inside the cathedral of Notre Dame at Paris in the presence of Bréhal and two of the three special commissioners appointed by the Pope. The cathedral was packed and the trial proceedings state that 'everyone present shouted with her'[65] as the opening ceremony almost degenerated into a riot in support of Joan of Arc.

It is important to compare the reluctant participation of Jean Le Maître with the constant support and encouragement provided by Bréhal in the rehabilitation trial. For over a year he presided at the trial, and played a fundamental part in the detailed theological arguments. After giving an extremely meticulous account of his role, Régine Pernoud comments as follows:

> Bréhal's work has not always been accepted at its true value . . . In reality, if one takes the trouble to read through it even cursorily, one sees that one is dealing with a work perfectly satisfying to the intellect in its rigorous logic. Every doubtful or controversial point, either in Joan's answers or in the judge's allegations, is made a subject for methodical discussions based on the teaching of the Fathers and Doctors of the Church, from whom the work contains more than nine hundred quotations; and the same holds true for points of law and procedure.[66]

Bréhal's triumph, consecrated by the Archbishop of Reim's official pronouncement of the decision of the court on 7 July 1456, shows us the high intellectual standards that were to be found in the top ranks of the Inquisition. But ironically the quashing of the condemnation of Joan of Arc, and the complete rehabilitation which eventually led to her canonization in 1920, was the last important act of the Inquisition in France. After more than two centuries of violent repression, the Inquisition's swan-song was the overturning of a condemnation for heresy for which it held no real responsibility. Such a stance would have been inconceivable in earlier times. In Charles Lightbody's words, the 'rehabilitation of Joan of Arc might perhaps be described as the death blow of the Inquisition in France, despite the efforts of the judges of the Rehabilitation to spare that institution insofar as possible . . .'.[67]

Heresy did not cease in France in the fifteenth century, but the Inquisition no longer had a political *raison d'être* that guaranteed it the support of secular authorities.

PART TWO:
THE DECLINE OF HERESY AND THE INSTITUTIONALIZATION OF WITCHCRAFT

7. The Decline of the Medieval Inquisition

The medieval Inquisition achieved maximum efficiency and power in the mid thirteenth century, at the height of the Church's battle against Catharism. From its inception around 1230 to about 1270 it was fully engaged in searching out and trying Cathars, and at the same time perfecting its techniques, manuals and the relevant legislation. Then, in the last thirty years of that century, there was a marked increase in trials of posthumously suspected heretics and wealthy heretics – with great financial benefits for inquisitors and the Church itself.

From 1300 onwards, we have seen that there was another subtle shift in the Inquisition's interests, towards the religious themselves. The dramatic opening of this phase was with the trial of the Templars, but at the same time in Italy the Inquisition was fully occupied with the *fraticelli*. This new phase seems to have reached a natural saturation point towards the middle of the fourteenth century, after which few trials of religious took place. There had been a brief phase when it appeared that the medieval Inquisition inspired by John XXII would turn against sorcerers and witches, but that was followed by a lull – and only later by a steady increase in the number of witch trials.

The first hundred years of the existence of the Inquisition can therefore be seen to follow closely the temporal and political exigencies of the time, first those of the Church but later those of the State as secular rulers recognized the enormous potential

of such a highly efficient and loyal police organization. Guiraud
argues that if the Inquisition still functioned in 1430,
condemning Joan of Arc in France and the *fraticelli* in Italy, 'it
was not from itself or the Church that it derived its life, but from
the civil power, which had taken it over in order to make use of it
for its own ends as an instrument of domination'.[1] He quotes
Bishop Cauchon of Beauvais as saying to Joan: 'The King has
ordered me to try you, and I will do so.'[2] Although this is
perhaps not strictly true, since Cauchon did not require such an
order, it does indicate a new chain of command in heresy trials.
The King commanded a Bishop, and then the Bishop co-opted
an Inquisitor; this is the exact reverse of procedure two hundred
years before.

Similarly, Lea emphasizes the political impulse behind
inquisitorial actions when he argues that 'it was in their
character as Italian Princes that the popes found the supreme
utility of the Holy Office.'[3] The lesson that an accusation of
heresy was a simple and sure method of destroying enemies and
rivals was soon learned, and the virtual destruction of the
powerful Colonna family in Rome by Boniface VIII and the
Visconti in Milan by John XXII illustrate the ease with which
Popes used this new weapon. It was not confined to the Church
and the Inquisition: as early as 1324 secular and ecclesiastical
authorities in Ireland adopted this weapon in the trial of Dame
Alice Kyteler, who was accused of diabolism, invocation and
sorcery. But the real cause of these allegations was a feud
between powerful aristocratic families in Ireland.[4]

Since according to St Thomas Aquinas opposition to Church
authority was deemed heretical *per se*, there was often no need to
invent elaborate accusations and finance expensive trials. Later,
such potential revolutionary forces as Cola di Rienzo in Rome
and Savonarola in Florence were easily suppressed by means of
similar accusations – and with the assistance of the Inquisition.

Yet this political employment of the Inquisition's power was
sporadic, sometimes dramatized from our present-day historical
perspective because of the importance of the victims. More than
a century separated the spectacular trials of the Templars and
Joan of Arc, but we perceive them as contemporary events and
mention them in a single sentence. The fact is that operations of
the Inquisition concerning ordinary heretics – peasants, minor
clergy or women – diminished greatly after the middle of the

fourteenth century. Already in 1334 a new laxity was evident at a trial in the central Italian town of Rieti. A local *fraticello* called Paolo Zoppo was tried for obscene practices, but the trial was never brought to its conclusion because the people and secular authorities of Rieti sided with Paolo. The inquisitor was forced to flee from the town, but there was no official reaction on the part of Church or Inquisition.[5]

Numerous examples exist to demonstrate the gradual decay of the Inquisition in the fifteenth century. An excellent instance which proves the diminution of the terror that once held sway over the people occurred in Pisa in 1409, when the Inquisition was forced to burn a man called Andreani for the crime of publicly and repeatedly ridiculing the Holy Office.[6] In 1461, the inquisitor at Bologna was sent to teach theology in Rome because his services were never required, and in the same city ten years later the inquisitor Brother Simone of Novara was so unprepared when he actually caught a heretic that he had to send urgently to Rome for instructions on how to deal with such a case.[7] Later, it is noteworthy that when the effigy of Martin Luther was burned at Rome in 1521, together with his books, the Inquisition played no part at all in the ceremony.

That the Inquisition was ineffective is also shown by the fact that travelling Waldensian pastors regularly visited heretics who had fled to Apulia throughout the fifteenth century. 'Everywhere they met friends acquainted with their secret passwords, and in spite of ecclesiastical vigilance there existed a subterranean network of heresy disguised under outward conformity.'[8] The constant presence of sorcery and magical phenomena in Italy and France, visible as sporadic trials brought them momentarily to the surface, suggests that other parallel networks flourished. Although no documents record this presence at a popular level, it is clear that in this period the Inquisition lost its physical grip on the people of southern Europe. At the same time the terror which dominated the collective imagination diminished; the Inquisition was no longer feared as it had once been.

The only category that had reason to fear the Inquisition was that of sorcerers and witches; but their persecution belongs to a period later than that of the medieval Inquisition as we have defined it. Examples of witch trials occur in the first century of the Inquisition's history, but it was only after the publication of a new series of inquisitorial manuals and theoretical treatises at the end of the fifteenth century that the great witch hunts began. Those hunts and panics fall outside the story of the Medieval Inquisition, which was founded to combat Catharism and related heresies; they are more closely associated with the revived and quite distinct institution that evolved at the time of the Counter-Reformation.

8. Heresy, Sorcery and Witchcraft

Recent research into the history of witchcraft and the witch trials has analysed terminological confusions, the hypothetical derivations of witchcraft from heresy or from sorcery, and the precise dates of the phenomenon known as the European Witch Craze. Yet in general terms it is evident that the origins of the witch persecutions of the sixteenth, seventeenth and eighteenth centuries are to be found in the late Middle Ages, and that the Inquisition was deeply involved with the development of complex notions of witchcraft – whether or not one accepts the nineteenth-century 'liberal' idea of witchcraft as an invention of the Inquisition. The essential characteristics of what is commonly called witchcraft – a combination of *maleficium*, night-flights, sabbat, and pact with the Devil – were assembled in the period that ran from 1320 to 1486, and the Inquisition was responsible at least in part for this assemblage and for the great increase in witch trials at the end of the fifteenth century.

Sorcery and the Church

We have seen that from the earliest years of Christianity, sorcery was associated both with Christ himself and with the performance of miracles. This sorcery within Christianity was derived from Jewish magic, which was more often straight-forward divination than *maleficium*; the word sorcery comes from Latin *sortilegium*, meaning the reading of lots, which is close to the idea of divination.[1] A medieval theologian like

Alexander of Hales distinguished between divination, or *divinatio*, and evil-doing, or *maleficium* – that is between what are misleadingly called high magic and low magic.*[2] St Augustine accepted that sorcerers were capable of performing certain miracles that Christians and saints could not perform, and never doubted that miracles were in fact operated by means of magic.[3] Even St Thomas Aquinas, who accepted the power of magic as fully as his illustrious predecessor, dealt with the distinction between magic and miracle in terms of divination: magic was for him performed by the means of herbs and other physical bodies, and employed figures, characters, images, rites and constellations.[4] Aquinas was here speaking of the ancient pseudo-science of divination – which was responsible for the practice of attributing special powers to sacred objects such as relics.

Thus the influence of so-called high magic on theologians and the Church was always very great: Roger Bacon, the Franciscan philosopher and natural scientist, failed to draw a firm line between science and magic. He wrote of 'magical sciences'.[5] Albertus Magnus was known to his contemporaries as an expert on alchemy and astrology, rather than as the teacher of Thomas Aquinas; in an important passage he defended the Magi from accusations of diabolical, evil or superstitious occult arts.[6]

Pagan survivals and accretions characterized the early history of Christianity. Redwald, the King of East Anglia, was said to have two altars in his temple, one for worshipping the true God and one for offering sacrifices to demons.[7] From the eighth century the Church attempted to eradicate pagan observances and sorcery, but isolated examples in the following centuries demonstrate the continuation of these practices. By the end of the twelfth century, however, the 'repression of sorcery seems to have been well-nigh abandoned by both secular and ecclesiastical authorities'.[8] It was no longer considered a direct threat to the Church.

In Spain, where the earliest European universities had been established with strong Islamic influence, the practice of sorcery

*Anglo comments: 'Scholarship has tended to separate the witch from the magician, and to treat, as discrete, low magic and higher magic. But witchcraft beliefs arose from the blurring of such distinctions and from a cosmic vision which saw witch and magus operating within a single system.' (*Evident Authority*, p. 4.)

was widespread. At the University of Cordoba in the thirteenth century, there were daily lectures by professors of astrology, necromancy, pyromancy and geomancy.[9] In 1220, the Archbishop of Santiago, Pedro Muñoz, was dismissed from his post and sent into a hermitage by Pope Honorius III because of his fame as a necromancer, and the Castilian King Alfonso the Wise included astrology as one of the seven liberal arts in his civil code of 1260.[10] Under his rule, occult sciences were rewarded or punished according to whether they were employed for good or for evil.

Both popular and learned traditions of sorcery were more or less accepted alongside Christian practice, as indeed they still are today in many areas. The use of love magic to bring about or cancel a love affair, or weather magic to cause local changes in rainfall, does not seem to have presented any threat to the Church. There was a relaxed atmosphere after earlier persecutions – when for instance the Emperors Nero and Caracalla executed their subjects for the relatively innocuous custom of wearing amulets. The medieval Church itself was perceived as a 'vast reservoir of magical power, capable of being deployed for a variety of secular purposes . . . Almost any object associated with ecclesiastical ritual could assume a special aura in the eyes of the people.'[11]

The major difficulty inherent in witchcraft studies is to discover how this relatively harmless presence of sorcery within and parallel to the medieval Church suddenly erupted into a phenomenon of enormous dimensions that terrorized much of Europe for nearly three centuries.

Sorcery into Witchcraft

Sorcery and heresy both existed in varying degrees throughout Western Europe in the Middle Ages, but during the fourteenth century they became causally linked by theorists in such a way that sorcery was seen as the consequence of certain forms of heresy. In this way was created a 'double crime whose sides were equally horrifying and reprehensible. This dual nature helps explain why witchcraft was regarded as a peculiarly terrible thing . . .'.[12] We have already seen that sorcery only came within the Inquisition's jurisdiction when heresy was involved.

The roots of the development of a new concept of witchcraft have been traced to about 1320, when John XXII took steps to deal with the questions of magic and demons. The initial persecution of sorcerers began then, together with a series of theoretical treatises on witchcraft. Yet Richard Kieckhefer has convincingly demonstrated that the number of witch trials began to increase even before theoretical works could influence the courts,[13] and there appears to be no connection between the politically inspired trials we have examined, ancient traditions of witchcraft, and scholastic or inquisitorial writings on witchcraft. Above all, the presence of the Devil – which is essential to later theories of witchcraft – is extremely rare in early trials. Usually, the charges are based on traditional sorcery, and may have passed without notice had there not been political motives for pressing them.

Many important elements of later witchcraft trials are missing, and it would require nearly two hundred years of additions before the concept of witchcraft was fully developed. Kieckhefer has divided the crucial years of this process into four periods that correspond roughly with the chronologies of other historians: 1300-1330; 1330-1375; 1375-1435; 1435-1500.* The reasons for these divisions can be seen clearly in the distribution of witch trials reported in his 'Calendar of Witch Trials'.[14]

In Kieckhefer's second period the main charges were still of sorcery, with diabolism rarely mentioned. The most notable difference is the absence of political trials. He suggests that they 'had aroused widespread attention, and may have aggravated general concern about witchcraft, but may also have made people sceptical about accusations that arose specifically from political or personal motives'.[15] There was in this period a marked decline in the number of trials, with the records immensely complicated by the previously accepted forgeries of Étienne-Léon Lamothe-Langon, author of the *Histoire de l'Inquisition en France*, published in Paris in 1829. Both Kieckhefer and Norman Cohn have convincingly demonstrated that the figures for trials and burnings given by Lamothe-Langon have distorted the history of witchcraft – and histories of the Inquisition.[16] What had seemed to be a marked increase in burnings for witchcraft in south-west France, and the

---

*Jeffrey Burton Russell divides the same period as follows: 1300-1360; 1360-1427; 1427-1486 (*Witchcraft in the Middle Ages*, pp. 167-265). In general terms these and other chronological divisions are similar, with minor details selected to provide slight modifications.

introduction of surprisingly early sabbats, are now replaced by a period of relative calm. Typical cases are that of the Carmelite Pierre Recordi, tried at Carcassonne in 1329 for love-magic, invocation and diabolism and imprisoned for life by the Inquisition.[17] On the basis of Kieckhefer's Calendar there were forty-eight trials in Europe from 1330 to 1375. Once the ten trials cited from Lamothe-Langon and no other source are omitted – and they are the most spectacular, with regular mass burnings by the Inquisition – the Inquisition is given as the competent tribunal in only one case, when an unspecified number of suspects was tried 'presumably by inquisitor' at Como in 1360. The municipal courts of France, Germany, Austria, England and Italy were responsible for most of the trials, and the picture is quite different without Lamothe-Langon's figures. This absence of the Inquisition may have been the result of a decided cooling of inquisitorial enthusiasm after John XXII's letter of 1330.

In the third period, from 1375 to 1435, two important changes took place that are of interest in the history of the Inquisition: there was a general increase in the number of trials for witchcraft, and a particular intensification of trials for diabolism. Kieckhefer suggests that the latter fact derives from the adoption of inquisitorial techniques and practices in municipal courts towards the end of the fourteenth century. It was also the period of the establishment of the Inquisition in Germany. But the crucial fact, emphasized by Kieckhefer, was that informers were no longer required to substantiate their accusations in municipal courts. Before the introduction of this inquisitorial refinement it was 'particularly dangerous to accuse someone of sorcery or of witchcraft generally',[18] since it was difficult to prove such charges. This danger can be illustrated by a fifteenth-century case in which the ancient practice was revived: the accuser was unable to prove to the court's satisfaction his claim that a woman had practised weather-magic. As a result, he was himself drowned for making a false accusation.[19]

Witch trials spread from France and Germany into Italy and Switzerland in this period, but its most distinctive feature is the increasing frequency of charges of diabolism. This is only partly due to the increasing number of treatises on witchcraft, and more the result of a general fear of magic that appears to have been developing – enhanced by the great series of plagues at the end of the fourteenth century.[20] A further factor was the adoption of twenty-eight articles concerning witchcraft by the theological faculty of the University of Paris on 19 September 1398. These articles 'became a standard for all demonologists, and were regarded as an unanswerable argument to sceptics who questioned the reality of the wickedness of the arts of magic'.[21] They affirmed the reality of witchcraft, and the necessity of a pact with the Devil for the successful practice of magic. Russell has argued that this decision was the result of a general fear of a threat to Christian society,[22] an attempt to transfer to certain defenceless sections of society – such as heretics, Jews and witches – the collective fears and traumas that haunted Western Europe. It was after the adoption of the twenty-eight articles that demonological treatises proliferated.

The last of Kieckhefer's periods, from 1435 to 1500, is the most important and most complex. As William E. Monter has observed, while only thirteen treatises on witchcraft were published between 1320 and 1420, in the much shorter period from about 1435 to 1486 there was a total of twenty-eight.[23] In approximately the same period Russell has estimated that there were over a hundred significant witch trials – although many of the people were still accused of simple sorcery.[24] New elements began to appear and dominate the trials: the riding out of witches to their meetings; the predominance of shape-shifting to help witches – with the Devil or demons appearing as goats, wolves, cats, dogs, pigs, sheep, other animals and birds; detailed physical descriptions that delineate the prototype of the modern iconography of the Devil. A further important element was the introduction of the almost universally practised assembly of witches, usually at night and in groups numbering into the hundreds.[25] Attendance at such an assembly was now considered sufficient to convict a suspected witch.

It should, however, be noted that the concept of pact was relatively unimportant throughout the fifteenth century, and that the term 'sabbat' was uncommon. There is a single mention of a parody of church services, but little to suggest the existence of anything like a black mass – which 'was for the most part a literary invention of the nineteenth-century occultists'.[26] But two features of later witch trials do appear: the pervasiveness of ritual feasting and sexual orgies, and the ritual murder of children.

Towards the end of the fifteenth century there was both an increasing frequency of witch trials everywhere in Europe and increasing theoretical complexity. The concept of witchcraft was being constantly elaborated. The period from 1435 to 1500 closes with two of the most significant monuments in the history of witchcraft: the papal Bull *Summis desiderantes affectibus* of 1484, which is often taken to mark the beginning of the great persecutions, and the publication of the *Malleus Maleficarum,* which provided a complex demonological model for future thinking about witchcraft.

St Thomas Aquinas

Witchcraft was not invented by the Inquisition, as some writers have claimed.[27] But although the idea of witchcraft was at least as ancient as the famous *canon episcopi* of the early tenth century, it was clearly susceptible to later elaboration, as we have seen in this brief survey of fifteenth-century trials. This elaboration was initially the work of scholastic theologians, such as the Dominican philosopher Aquinas; it was on the theological substructure of his work that treatises began to appear in the 1320s, although the full force of his authority was not felt until much later.

In the all-embracing scheme of the *Summa Theologica,* Aquinas found frequent need to mention ideas associated with magic, since they were so closely bound into the essence of Christian thought by an ancient process of contamination. Thus we find him suggesting that divination, which he usually refers to as a 'superstition', can be provoked by the Devil.[28] Yet in discussing why it is not possible to consult demons in order to know the future,[29] and the possible motives for diabolical possession,[30] Aquinas does not treat the explicit problems of witchcraft that were later to cause controversy. His crucial statement, which was to serve as fodder for later theoreticians, is an express condemnation of both implicit and explicit pacts with the Devil or demons. It is so important that a translation of the relevant paragraphs is given here:

Thus the so-called *astronomical* images also owe their efficacy to diabolical intervention. This is indicated by the fact that on these it is necessary to inscribe *characters* which by nature perform no operation: in fact the figure is never the principle of a natural operation. But between *astronomical* and necromantic images there is a difference, that in these latter there are explicit invocations and appearances of the Demon – and they therefore enter in pacts expressly made with the Devil, while in the others such appearances come from the symbols of certain figures, or characters, from merely tacit pacts.

The dominion of His Divine Majesty, to which demons are also subject, implies that God may use them as he wishes. On the other hand, man has not received dominion over the demons, to use them as he wishes: but he must engage in declared war with them. Thus it is in no way licit for man to invoke aid from demons with either tacit or explicit agreements.[31]

Following this unambiguous statement, any magical practice or belief necessarily represented apostasy from the Christian faith. Midelfort glosses this crucial step as follows: 'A modern Jesuit scholar has labelled this step the "moral-theological mistake in the judgement of superstition". It was the crucial link that allowed the Inquisition to shift its attention from outright heretics to magicians and sorcerers, and inquisitors often cited Aquinas between 1323 and 1327 when attacking the invocation of spirits as heresy.'[32]

Aquinas also enshrines orthodox approval of inquisitorial methods when he asserts that *correctio*, or punishment, is a spiritual good when it is aimed at the improvement of a brother Christian,[33] or that to eliminate or impede evil in a person is equivalent to procuring good for him.[34] In this way both theoretical and moral justification for the Inquisition can be derived from the *Summa Theologica*, and there is a certain pleasing symmetry in this fact. The Mendicant Orders had made a great contribution to the suppression of heresy through scholarship, the Franciscans through their important teaching role in the new universities and the Dominicans through their great theologians. In the person of Aquinas, the dual functions of repression and convincing theological argument were perfectly synthesized. Modern scholars like Lambert are right when they stress that the history of the Inquisition is not in itself sufficient to explain the decline of heresy: '... the peaceful countermeasures of the Church and the internal difficulties of Catharism are also relevant'.[35]

The separate Dominican streams of violent physical repression and theological argument merged in the inquisitorial persecution of witchcraft. The dichotomy that had existed between, say, Robert le Bougre and St Thomas Aquinas, or between Guillaume de Paris and Bernard Gui, dissipated as witchcraft was institutionalized in the course of the fifteenth century. It is this fact which may explain the extraordinary virulence of the witch-hunts, and the difficulty of putting an end to a phenomenon which had been so brilliantly and authoritatively created. The power and guile of the essentially Dominican anti-witch Inquisition helped to fix in the popular imagination an irrational concept that might otherwise have played a minor role in European history.

The Role of the Inquisition

It is difficult to ascertain with precision the role of the Inquisition in the phase from 1320 to 1486 of the great witch hunts. Documents are scarce, and historians disagree over many details. Yet consensus seems to be possible on two fundamental matters: that books and manuals written by inquisitors played an important part in the development of the 'craze', and that the use of such inquisitorial techniques as the torture of suspects also contributed to the final elaboration of the concept of witchcraft.

In an early fourteenth-century manual such as that of Bernard Gui, the space devoted to sorcery is limited. The forms of interrogation occupy three pages of text and Gui does not go beyond the traditional problems of sorcery – especially concerning divination.* He directs inquisitors to interrogate suspects on such matters as the prediction of future events, the theft of hosts and holy oil, the baptism of wax images, and other traditional features of sorcery. Only on one occasion does he approach the terminology of later witchcraft, when he asks whether the suspect knows anything of the women who – it is said – ride out at night (*vadunt de nocte*).[36] The lack of the vocabulary of witchcraft in Gui's manual supports Kieckhefer's hypothesis that there is little basis for a concept of witchcraft in popular tradition. Horsley has demonstrated convincingly that there is 'apparently little *popular terminological* basis for a clear designation of a concept of witchcraft'.[37]

---

*His language was echoed by an article in the Vatican newspaper *Osservatore Romano* of 18 January 1984 criticizing horoscopes, palmistry and cartomancy. The Franciscan author did not want Catholics 'to put their faith at risk'.

Other fourteenth-century inquisitors and Dominican writers discussed the matter with a similar absence of witchcraft terminology. Nicholas Eymerich, in his work *Against Those Who Call Up Demons* of 1369, and the Spanish Dominican Raymond of Tarrega, author of a book entitled *On The Invocation of Demons*, both argued that demons could only operate with God's tolerance – and thus took the sting out of critics of witchcraft. This was a surprisingly moderate stance, and Russell has in fact asserted that 'while courts grew harsher the theoretical treatises that dealt with witchcraft were noticeably more liberal'.[38]

It was in the fifteenth century, when trials multiplied and the full weight of Aquinas's doctrines came to bear on theologians, that the literature of witchcraft began to take on the connotations known to us through the *Malleus Maleficarum*. Russell, in his List of Theorists of Witchcraft from 1430 to 1486 gives twenty-two works. An analysis is interesting: of twenty-two titles, six are cited as having been written by inquisitors and four by Dominicans; some of the others may also be by inquisitors. But the quality and importance of these works – especially if the *Malleus Maleficarum* is added to them – dominates the field. The six works by inquisitors are as follows:

1. Johann Nider, *Formicarius*, written about 1435-7 (first printed at Basel in 1470, with further editions until 1692).

2. Raphael of Pornasio, *De arte magica*, about 1450 (never printed).

3. Anonymous Savoyard, *Errores Gazariorum*,* about 1450 (never printed).

4. Jean Vineti, *Tractatus contra demonum invocatores*, about 1450 (never printed).

5. Nicholas Jacquier, *Flagellum haereticorum fascinariorum*, written in 1458, and published at Frankfurt in 1581.

6. Bernard of Como, *Tractatus de Strigiis*, published in Rome in 1584, with further editions until 1596[39]

But inquisitors were learned and often perceptive men, and these works do not all bear the venom of the *Malleus*

---

*Gazariorum derives from *Gazarus*, meaning Cathar: cf. Russell, *Witchcraft*, p. 15, n.

Maleficarum. There was still space for healthy scepticism. In
the case of Raphael of Pornasio, for instance, Thorndike has
shown how 'he admits the existence of a considerable scepticism
as to the truth of magic, and displays a relatively tolerant attitude
towards his opponents and readiness to hear their arguments,
which may seem surprising to those who have been taught to
regard every inquisitor as a dogmatic bigot'.[40] Another
inquisitor, Franciscus Florentius or Paduanus, who Thorndike
describes as 'liberal', is actually quite respectful in his attitude
towards astrology – citing Albumasar and approving of the use
of astrology by doctors. He approves of the doctrines of Peter of
Abano, who had earlier been tried by the Inquisition for heresy,
and asserts that it is lawful to *study* magic as long as one does not
practise it.[41] He appears, as late as 1472-3, when his book *De
quorundam astrologorum parvipendendis indiciis* was written, to
have possessed neither the spirit of persecution nor an interest
in witch-hunting.

Generalizations about the attitudes of inquisitors towards
witchcraft are therefore dangerous. Although the works listed
above clearly played an important role in the elaboration of
witchcraft theory, the intellectual contribution of inquisitors
should not be exaggerated. Thorndike concludes that the fact
that an inquisitor like Franciscus Florentius could write about
astrology, magic, divination and popular superstition at such a
late date 'suggests that in the broad field of occult science and
superstition in the fifteenth century the witchcraft delusion did
not occupy so prominent a place as some have been inclined to
accord it'.[42]

But the very fact that the Inquisition took witchcraft seriously
and attempted to exterminate it was accepted by many people as
evidence of the truth and efficacy of magic. The trials
demonstrated that it was a reality, and the attribution of heresy
to sorcerers put a premium on their activities: 'The sorcerer was
the more in request because people were more than ever
convinced that his claims were well founded'.[43] Inquisitorial
efficiency, and the increased efficiency of secular courts which
had adopted inquisitorial techniques, firmly placed the reality of
witchcraft in the European consciousness. It is in this sense that
the accumulation of theoretical treatises and manuals may be
said to have had an enormous influence on the witchcraft
persecutions.

The Use of Torture

Torture was essential to the success of witch trials. The increased use of it, which had become a 'matter of course' in such trials as those of Artois in 1459-1461, was a key factor underlining the spread of witchcraft.[44] Secular courts also introduced torture into witch trials in the mid fifteenth century.

There are many instances of the distorting effect of torture. Horsley, referring to the records for Lucerne and Austria, asserts that when left to speak for themselves, peasants – who constituted the greatest proportion of suspects – merely accused their neighbours generically of *maleficium*: 'It is especially striking that there is little or no mention of the Devil in these depositions. Night-flying, cannibalism, sabbat, and the pact with the Devil are introduced into such trials only by the witch hunters – or by victims in fearful anticipation of, or painful subjection to, various degrees of torture.'[45] He concludes that the wise women and other people accused of witchcraft were not witches in the sense defined by demonologists: it was only after torture that they 'may have come to believe in the witch hunters' definition of themselves as night-flying witches in pact with Satan.'[46]

Although Kieckhefer stresses the fact that it would be easy to overstate the influence of torture, since many people appear to have confessed freely, he himself provides a detailed illustration of the phenomenon. In 1477, at Villars-Chabod, a woman called Antonia repeatedly denied that she was guilty of witchcraft, even when the inquisitor warned her of the consequences and allowed her three days to tell him the truth. After this pause in her interrogation an interlocutory sentence was passed, and Antonia was taken away to be tortured on the strappado. Half an hour on that instrument was not enough to obtain a confession, and she protested her innocence; but after two further days of torture on the strappado Antonia finally confessed to having engaged in diabolism. It seems that such a period enabled her to invent a sufficiently convincing description of her 'diabolical' activities. The case of Antonia lends weight to the supposition that 'more often than not the extent of the confessions appears to have been directly proportional to the length of the torture'.[47]

Medieval doctrines of penance continued to influence procedure. The *Malleus Maleficarum* states that immediate confession would allow the judge to give mercy to a suspected witch,[48] but this system was open to abuse. At a trial in Arras from 1459 to 1462, where twelve out of thirty-four people accused of diabolism were burned at the stake, suspects were threatened with death if they refused to incriminate themselves.[49] At a trial in Zürich in 1487, a woman was tried by the municipal court for diabolism and sorcery. She confessed when the judge assured her that in doing so she would not be executed; the judge kept his word. She confessed freely, and was sentenced to life imprisonment in a 'narrow cell with no windows, and with only a hatch on the ceiling through which she could be given one meal a day'.[50] When death eventually ended this temporary respite, the same judge ordered her corpse to be burned. Thus the advantages of confession were, in practice, minimal – since it was the eternal damnation implicit in this posthumous burning that inculcated fear – and one can imagine that her fate was carefully noticed by friends and observers.

Although this example is not from an inquisitorial court, it is easy to imagine similar false promises being made as the fervour for witch-hunting grew. There is obviously only a minimal difference between actual physical torture, the threat of torture, and this kind of psychological torture. The fact of free confessions must not be accepted too readily for the same reason, since the degree of resistance to torture – whether physical or psychological – is notoriously variable. Many suspects would have been sufficiently terrorized at the thought of the *possibility* of torture that came to them at the moment of arrest; they entered the statistics as free confessors. It therefore seems reasonable to conclude that torture did play a significant rôle in fifteenth-century witch trials, and by extension in the development of the concept of witchcraft.

The Malleus Maleficarum

This work was in a sense the culmination of late medieval notions of witchcraft, drawn upon by future demonologists and attacked by later critics. It contained as a prefatory justification the Bull of Innocent VIII *Summis desiderantes affectibus*, which had been issued at the request of its authors, Henry Kramer and Jakob Sprenger, and which ordained their masterpiece of witchcraft theory with papal authority. In Russell's words, 'it established once and for all that the Inquisition against witches had full papal approval and thereby opened the door for the bloodbaths of the following century'.[51] The title, 'The Hammer of Witches', derived from the epithet we have seen applied to Robert le Bougre and Bernard of Caux – the Hammer of Heretics.

In conception and structure it is a linear descendant of the *Processus inquisitionis* and Peñafort's *Directory*. But it is much more complex, and far longer. It is also written within a world view informed by scholastic philosophy: the method – question, argument and then conclusions – is that of the *Summa Theologica*. The *Malleus* contrived to link the *maleficium* of popular sorcery with heresy through the agency of the Christian concept of the Devil, and also shifted the blame for sorcery onto women with exaggerated and misogynistic force. It created the popular view of the witch as a woman* that survives today; in that respect it was truly a seminal work. The authors' purpose was clear:

> Witchcraft was a vast and vile conspiracy against the Faith; it was on the increase; witches were depopulating the whole of Christendom; and, through the impotence of the secular courts, these creatures remained unpunished. The *Malleus* was written to demonstrate precisely what witches were doing, and how they could be stopped. It first establishes the truth of the existence of witchcraft and its heretical nature; then elucidates the principal evils practised by witches and demons; and finally lays down formal rules for initiating legal action against witches, securing their conviction, and passing sentence upon them.[52]

The authors set out to prove the reality of witchcraft, arguing that even those crimes which cannot be said to be objectively real are illusions provoked by the Devil at the request of witches. Witchcraft was perceived by them as treason against God, and thus the most horrible of crimes deserving the most exemplary punishment. All previous details of witchcraft are assembled in this work by two leading Dominican inquisitors – Kramer having had wide experience of witch trials – and formed the model for later theories. But it is worth noting, as Russell points out, that the authors do not mention 'familiar spirits, the

---

*Eugenio Battisti has shown how the iconography of the witch changed dramatically in the last years of the fifteenth century, with deformations and conscious association of the Devil (*L'Antirinascimento*, pp. 148-153). The process can be seen clearly in the works of Dürer.

obscene kiss, sabbat orgies, or the devil's mark, which all become common in succeeding centuries'.[53]

This work was written shortly after the invention of printing and benefited from a diffusion that no earlier manual had enjoyed; there were at least eight editions before 1500. It has often been argued that the printing press 'dealt a mortal blow' to the Inquisition, and that its inarrestable decline dates from the introduction of printing.[54] But it would seem to be more accurate to state that the existence of such manuals in printed form augmented the Inquisition's power by cancelling the distinction between learned and popular traditions. Although the *Malleus* may not have been read by the creators of 'popular' tradition, there is no doubt that it found its way throughout Europe at all social levels by means of oral diffusion. There is evidence to show that literacy was far more widespread in the early sixteenth century than is often thought,[55] but in any case the verbal distortions typical of the oral dissemination of ideas contributed to the new status of witchcraft.

With Thomist thoroughness the authors created a *summa* of witchcraft theory that was never to be completely superseded. But it is fair to say that beyond what Anglo calls the 'scholastic pornography'[56] and the almost criminal mental aberrations of Henry Kramer, the *Malleus* is replete with original and interesting observations that are at times surprisingly close to modern ideas. For example, a present-day scholar like Kieckhefer concludes that in the period from 1300 to 1500 three types of trial predominated: the trial of sorcerers additionally accused of diabolism; trials of folk doctors such as herbalists or wise women additionally accused of witchcraft; and trials resulting from jealousy or anger – often within tight family groups.[57] In what Charles Williams justly describes as a 'flash of realism', Kramer and Sprenger are capable of asserting that 'the most prolific source of witchcraft is the quarrelling between unmarried women and their lovers'.[58]

The *Malleus* is full of circular arguments, and riddled by examples of the fallacy of authority; when they cannot convince their critics Kramer and Sprenger seem to set out to stupefy them with examples and authorities. It is a seriously flawed work, yet it shaped the future. Before it was written, both sorcery and witchcraft existed but had not been responsible for the deaths of tens of thousands of people. Kramer, Sprenger, the Dominicans and the Inquisition must bear much of the blame for the appalling consequences of its publication.

PART THREE:
SPAIN AND THE REBIRTH
OF THE INQUISITION

9. The Foundation of the Spanish Inquisition: 1478

At the moment of the Inquisition's maximum weakness in Italy, France and Germany, and before the witch-craze reached its full dimensions, a new and quite different form of Inquisition was founded by Ferdinand and Isabella of Spain. There were three main reasons behind this foundation: a political decision to achieve religious conformity in Spain, the failure to do so by enforcing conversion of the Jewish and Moorish population, and a profound fear that insincere converts would contaminate the Christian faith.[1]

Since the thirteenth century, Spain had been divided into three main areas: the Kingdom of Castile (which had recently incorporated the old Kingdom of Léon and the Moslem cities of Cordoba and Seville), the Kingdom of Aragón (which was enlarged in that century by the additions of Catalonia, Valencia and the Balearic Islands), and Granada, the last stronghold of the Moslems on the Iberian peninsula. From 1232, when Gregory IX had sent the Bull *Declinante* to the Archbishop of Tarragona, there had been an Inquisition in Aragón. It seems that this Bull was issued on the insistence of Raymond of Peñafort, who was the inspirer of Gregory's policy of persecution and therefore the spiritual father of the Inquisition.[2] Under the Dominican inquisitor Nicholas Eymerich the Aragonese Inquisition had known another moment of notoriety, but by the late fifteenth century it was largely inactive. In the Kingdom of Castile there had never been an Inquisition, although under Alfonso the Wise a crusade against the infidels had been arranged with the blessing of Innocent III.[3]

The history of the Spanish Inquisition and the history of modern Spain itself are inextricably linked, and the first premise necessary for each of them was the unification of the old kingdoms of Castile and Aragon. This occurred in the brief space of five years, when Isabella succeeded to the throne of Castile in 1474, and her husband Ferdinand succeeded to that of Aragón in 1479. The new Inquisition was one of the immediate consequences of this process of unification and was conceived from the beginning more as a political weapon than its medieval counterpart. It was authorized by Sixtus IV in 1478 to examine the genuineness of Jewish *conversos*, or recent converts to Christianity. It was thus a weapon of the Castilian aristocracy in their bid to resolve the 'Jewish problem', which had existed in Spain for centuries and which had – they argued – recently come to a head. It is not an exaggeration to state that without this 'Jewish problem' there would have been no Spanish Inquisition,[4] and much of its history was dedicated to the suppression of the Jews – and rather less to the Moors. It was thus very much a political tribunal with racialist overtones.

But, paradoxically, it was the great religious tolerance of medieval Spain that had allowed the Jews to succeed and become prominent members of society.[5] This tolerance itself created ideal conditions, which in turn led to resentment amongst the traditional nobility. It can be seen in the fact of Spanish Christians freely converting to Islam in the southern regions, and in the continual influx of Jews as the result of persecution in other countries. However, as early as the seventh century the Spanish Jews had been persecuted, and they had themselves looked on the arrival of the Moslems with relief – in the hope that future persecution would be directed against the newest arrivals. In 1235 the Council of Arles had introduced the wearing of a yellow circular patch for easy identification of Jews, but the climax had come in 1391 when there had been massacres all over the country. In June of that year, there had been 4,000 deaths in Seville alone.[6] Thus, a hundred years before the establishment of the Inquisition in Castile, the category of *conversos* came into being as tens of thousands of Jews converted to Christianity to avoid a similar fate. From the beginning their sincerity was questioned, and the events of the 1490s derived

ultimately from the persistence of such doubt amongst the
Castilian aristocracy. They had intermarried with Spaniards of
all social classes and races and achieved considerable financial
power and social status, holding important positions in both
Church and State.

The foundation of the Inquisition was a logical corollary of
the policy of consolidation enacted by Ferdinand and Isabella.
That policy turned the perspective of Spanish political vision
inwards, together with the essentially incestuous world-view of
the ruling classes that supported the new King and Queen. The
Jews were thought to represent a genuine threat to the power of
this ruling élite – much as the Cathars had appeared to threaten
the Roman Church – and a full-fledged Inquisition throughout
Spain was seen as a means of reasserting the predominance of
the aristocracy. In 1483, the *Consejo de la Suprema y General
Inquisición* was created as part of a general bureaucratic
reorganization by Queen Isabella. It was first designed to
function within the Kingdom of Castile under the newly
appointed Inquisitor-General, Fray Tomàs de Torquemada;
then, since an Inquisition already existed in Aragón, all that was
required was the additional papal appointment of Torquemada
as Inquisitor-General in Aragón, Valencia and Catalonia. This
was made by Sixtus IV on 17 October 1483. Permanent
tribunals were set up in Saragoza, Barcelona and Valencia,
though not without protests from the Cortes, nobles and people.
In this way was created the only organization which at that time
possessed equal powers and importance everywhere in Spain.

The Inquisition was ready to play a vital role in the most
significant year of modern Spanish history. In 1492, three events
that transformed Spain and marked the beginning of her history
as a united country occurred within months of each other; they
also provided the base for her enormous power in succeeding
centuries. The year opened with the taking of Granada on 2
January, after nine years of battle. Ferdinand and Isabella set up
their royal house in the Alhambra by joining the palace of
Comares, the official seat of the Sultans of Granada, with the
Palace of the Lions, which had been their private residence.
This symbolic action marked the end of centuries of Moslem
rule in southern and western Spain. Then, on 31 March,
inspired by the successful expulsion of the rulers of Granada

and no longer dependent on their financial support, the King and Queen of Spain gave the Jewish population exactly four months to decide whether they wished to leave the country or remain and convert to Christianity. Between 165,000 and 400,000 Jews left Spain before the end of July, many of them losing their livelihood and paying exorbitant taxes to port officials as they departed; as many as 50,000 decided to stay.[7] Finally, came the announcement of Columbus's discovery of America* – made, ironically, with the help of Jewish finance – which was soon to become of fundamental importance for the power and wealth of Spain, and for the Church and the Inquisition.

Organization

The Spanish Inquisition was loosely based on the organization of its medieval predecessor, with additions and changes made to suit the particular needs of Ferdinand and Isabella. As the power of the medieval Inquisition at its peak – in Italy from 1270 to 1300 and in France from 1309 to about 1330 – was in direct proportion to the efficiency of its organization, so that of the Spanish Inquisition was from the beginning the result of an almost legendary efficiency.

This derived initially from the administrative division of Spain by Ferdinand and Isabella under five Councils: the Council of State, the Council of Finance, the Council of Castile, the Council of Aragón, and finally the Council of the Inquisition – more commonly known as the *Suprema*.[8] In allowing such power to the Spanish Inquisition, Sixtus IV – possibly flattered by the importance assigned to religion within the State – created the circumstances that placed the new Inquisition outside papal jurisdiction. This was the most characteristic difference between the Spanish and other Inquisitions.

The *Suprema* was organized and controlled by the office of the Inquisitor-General, and its power depended to a large extent on the personality of this figure. Hence the particular stamp placed on the entire history of the Spanish Inquisition by its first head, Torquemada. He elaborated the first set of rules, called

---

*The official send-off of Columbus by Queen Isabella was performed in the newly-conquered Alhambra, overlooking the city of Granada. In this way, the two events are intimately linked.

the *Instrucciónes Antiguas,** on the basis of his own experience
and personal authority in 1484, with later additions as new
circumstances arose in 1485, 1488 and 1498.[9] New tribunals
were also created to measure: between 1480 and the 1520s
about twenty-two temporary ones were formed in addition to the
twelve permanent tribunals of Castile and four of Aragón.[10] The
permanent tribunals had a large staff to facilitate the work of two
inquisitors, who were to be masters of theology and at least forty
years old – although this limit was later reduced to thirty. There
was an *alguazil*, or constable responsible for arrests, *calificadores*,
or assessors of the evidence, and a *fiscal*, or prosecutor – whose
role indicates that the Spanish Inquisition adopted the
procedure of *accusatio* rather than *inquisitio*; in addition there
were large numbers of subordinates such as gaolers, chaplains,
clerks, notaries and familiars. The whole organization was
supervised by *visitadores*, or travelling inspectors, who reported
back to the *Suprema* on the functioning of provincial
inquisitions. This structure is not dissimilar to that of a large
medieval inquisition, save for the presence and function of the
fiscal.

   The main difference lies in the sophisticated capillary
organization and the numbers of people involved. The familiars,
often spies and informers, were largely responsible for
spreading fear of the Inquisition through their lawlessness and
arrogance; yet Henry Kamen observes that 'even a brief survey
of the records of the Inquisition shows that the majority of the
denunciations presented to the tribunal were made by ordinary
people, neighbours, travelling companions, acquaintances'.[11] It
would appear that the familiars offended more by their
numerical presence than by their actions. It is estimated that in
the sixteenth century in Toledo there were 805, in Granada
805, and in Santiago 1,009, men whose posts were often bought
and sold, and could be hereditary.

   This army of familiars incurred heavy financial obligations
for the Inquisition, which was never a wealthy organization and
had to pay salaries from the proceeds of confiscated property
and investment income. Kamen shows with a breakdown
of salaries and income how the Inquisition at Cordoba only
just managed to break even in 1578.[12] Yet vast sums of money

*These were amended and amplified by the *Instrucciónes Nuevas* of 1561.

passed through the Inquisition, gathered and sent to the
Suprema by individual tribunals and then returned in the form of
expenses and salaries. Economic difficulties clearly derived from
the enormous number of people required to sustain the
Inquisition's ever-increasing activities. In 1647, for instance, the
tribunal of Palma counted as many as 150 functionaries –
without including familiars – and Turberville was led to argue
that the number of these functionaries seemed to increase as the
work of the Inquisition diminished.[13] But even at the beginning,
the numbers were high. Llorente, one of the first historians of
the Inquisition and himself an ex-Secretary of the tribunal,
claimed that 'Ferdinand and Isabella permitted Torquemada to
be escorted during his journeys by fifty familiars of the
Inquisition on horseback, and two hundred others on foot.'[14]

Financial difficulties were mitigated by numerous privileges
accorded to both inquisitors and familiars. Inquisitors were
assured free board and lodging during their travels, and the
right to purchase food at specially reduced prices. Equally
important was the right for both categories to bear arms. This
may have been justifiable in certain dangerous circumstances,
but it also caused great resentment, since it enabled large
numbers of often ruthless men to wander the countryside doing
more or less as they pleased. This situation was further
exacerbated by the privilege extended to all dependents of the
Inquisition with regard to secular courts, which could not try
familiars as they were judged to be outside the jurisdiction of the
courts. Such a ruling brought complaints against the Inquisition,
especially in Aragón. But although a series of monarchs,
including Ferdinand himself and the Emperor Charles V,
attempted to abrogate these privileges, and even managed in
1553 to obtain an agreement that familiars should be subject to
the jurisdiction of secular courts for all but the least serious
crimes, this position of excessive privilege was never completely
undermined.[15]

But the distinguishing characteristic of the Spanish Inquisition in its early years remained its allegiance to the throne.
Behind the Inquisitor-General and the *Suprema* stood the figure
of the King of Spain, and only in a subsidiary and often
polemical position the Pope.

'To amaze the Patient': Secrecy and the Inquisition

A further important difference between the Spanish Inquisition and its predecessors is the enormous quantity of documents, contemporary accounts and printed materials available, although much of this was distorted by the exigencies of political propaganda against Spain and personal malice. Nevertheless, a much clearer picture of its activities can be obtained from these accounts – making the necessary allowances – than we could piece together from medieval documents. Some features of procedure are, for example, presented in the following account:

The depositions of the witnesses are shown to defendant, with names of witnesses suppressed. Everything is read distorted and contorted – with so many obscurities and circumlocutions and with the wording so vague, as to seem the language of any creature other than a rational being. In the deposition formulas specially noticeable are the holy wiles: when they say 'He heard from a certain person whom he has named', it is to be understood that it is defendant himself from whom he heard it! When the prisoner has answered as well as he can, his advocate opportunely appears. In the presence of the Inquisitors he indicates to the prisoner the evidence by which he is hardest pressed, and the one remedy left – a shrewd guess at his assailant, with a view to consideration of possible exceptions against him; he advises him to try, for some days, to recall to memory those with whom he may chance to have had feud – because, if enmity can be established through legitimate investigation, this one exception will repel any man from giving evidence in this tribunal; he warns him that he can deny evidence that is not sufficiently consistent. This is the utmost assistance which a prisoner can expect from his advocate; and thus he is bidden to be sent back to his prison. Three or four days later he is called to audience, and is asked if he can remember and explain anything – the advocate inquiring if he has made any guess at the witnesses or the delators. Prisoner brings forward what he can remember – begging them to see whether by chance his delators are among these or those between whom and him enmity once, or at that time, existed. If he has not guessed correctly, not only is his reply wasted, but also the three or four days trouble of guessing – and the accusation remains unshaken. But should it chance that he guesses right, the advocate asks him what exceptions he can use against the persons named by him, and intimates not very openly – since he may not do it more plainly – that he has guessed right. The exceptions set forth, and the witnesses named by whom defendant will prove them, after prisoner has been

allowed to repose for some months in his prison at the fathers'
arbitrament, they summon him again to the contest; and the
Inquisitor tells him that the witnesses named by him have been
heard – so that he should see whether he has anything to say for
himself, or whether he wishes to conclude. Defendant concluding,
the Fiscal also concludes; and afterwards the Inquisitors, with the
assessors and the consultors, pass sentence – when the theologians,
monks, and clerks, have weighed whatever defendant has said
bearing on doctrine and the Faith. The marks of their more than
leonine claws are confiscation of property, perpetual or temporary
imprisonment, a mud-coloured garment commonly called *sambenito*,
perpetual infamy to all posterity.[16]

In this remarkable summary, the main features of inquisitorial
procedure are evident. The reader is struck by the author's
insistence on the secrecy of witnesses, and by the 'holy wiles'
with which the inquisitors set to work. But it is interesting to
note, in contrast with medieval practice, the presence of an
advocate, who makes some attempt to defend the prisoner –
although his 'utmost assistance' amounts to little in practical
terms. The singularity of an interrogation carried out as if it
were a guessing game is also striking, and again the stress on the
idea of a 'feud' is fascinating. It reinforces the idea – advanced
by Kieckhefer for witchcraft, and by Kamen for the Spanish
Inquisition – that gossip and revenge were the main causes of
the strife and suffering under the Inquisition, since a feud with a
stranger is a contradiction in terms.

Such a document, allowing for its bias in the last lines, gives a
vivid and accurate picture of the workings of the Inquisition in
Spain. It has indeed been given an exaggerated image by
anti-Spanish propaganda, both in England and in Rome in the
late sixteenth century; but this passage underlines the fact that
although 'in some respects we can modify the picture of a cruel
and merciless Inquisition, what cannot be explained away is the
atmosphere that prevailed prior to arrest and condemnation'.[17]
That atmosphere was charged by secrecy, as in the case of the
unnamed accusers; secrecy was prolonged throughout the trial
and even during the process of torture.

An anonymous Englishman writing about 1600 confirms the
above account, and shows how secrecy was used to create fear:

But if the accused doe not sufficientlie justifie himself, he is condemned to torture. And with his Curate he is constrained to goe, through a place verie hidious, to a rome underground, where he findeth the Judges set. There is ye Executioner, covered with a long black linen robe verie straight like a Sacke, having his head and face covered with a blacke hoode having but two holes before his eies – this done to amaze the Patient, as if a devill came to punish his Misdeeds. If he confesse nothing, they sometimes martyre him more than two howers.[18]

Much later, in a passage of obvious authenticity, Llorente describes how the fiscal might end his interrogation of a prisoner by saying that, in spite of his continued advice to tell the truth, he felt that the prisoner was being reticent and that he would therefore ask that the accused be 'questioned' – which is to say tortured. He vividly conveys the trembling of suspects in that instant of anxious expectation as they waited for the fiscal to make this request.[19] This underlines the extent to which secrecy and the fear it engendered were the main weapons of the Spanish Inquisition, perhaps even more than the torture itself.

Procedure

As in the medieval Inquisition, the procedure began with the announcement of a period of grace, which was first issued in an 'Edict of Grace' and in later years in a more generic 'Edict of Faith'. Heretics were asked to come forward or to denounce others known to them; this remained the basic method of finding suspected heretics. People were denounced for such varied activities as smiling at the mention of the Virgin Mary, eating meat on a day of abstinence, or non-heretical offences such as urinating against the walls of a church and private assertions to a man's wife that he did not believe fornication was a sin.[20] Many people were led to denounce themselves or confess out of fear that a friend or neighbour might do so later anyway; such fears, counter-denunciations and chain reactions within small communities clearly increased the awe in which the Inquisition was held. In Seville, self-denunciation became a mass phenomenon and the prisons of the Inquisition were 'filled to overflowing'.[21]

This practice brought the risk of false testimony, cast doubts upon the trustworthiness of witnesses, and easily allowed minor infringements to be swollen into heresy. All these features were in turn augmented by secrecy concerning the witnesses to a trial, and the consequent 'guessing game' during interrogations. One of the side-effects of this secrecy was that accusations had to be formulated in such a way that they would not lead to immediate identification by the prisoner of the person who had denounced him, and prisoners were often unable to understand the precise nature of charges made against them. Once they had failed to guess the identity of the accuser, they had to try to recall any occasion on which they had committed some action that might be open to interpretations of heresy. The prisoner was thus lost in a labyrinth of paranoia.

Even the most trivial denunciations were taken seriously. Henry Kamen gives the following example: 'When, for example, Doctor Jorge Enrique, physician to the Duke of Alva, died in 1622, secret witnesses claimed that his body had been buried according to Jewish rites. The consequence was that all the Enrique family, relatives and household were thrown into prison and kept there for two years until their acquittal for lack of evidence.'[22]

But while secrecy characterized the operations of the Inquisition as far as the outsider was concerned, so that its methods and procedure were not fully known to anyone not directly involved, the tiniest details of administrative, financial and legal organization were recorded with exceptional care. Much of the power of the Spanish Inquisition derived from its mass of accumulated archival material, which provided an effective control over much of the Spanish population. Many of these archives were destroyed when Napoleon took Spain, but sufficient quantities have survived to provide an immensely detailed picture of the workings of the Inquisition.

Theoretically, the *calificadores* made an assessment of evidence before a suspect was arrested, although these examinations were in fact reserved for cases where there were complex theological matters to be resolved; when clear-cut cases of Judaism or relapsed Moorish or Jewish converts were concerned, this stage was eliminated.[23] In practice this preliminary measure was nearly always neglected, or deliberately overlooked for convenience. The result was that often prisoners 'sat in inquisitorial gaols without any charge ever having been produced against them'.[24] But cases of long imprisonment before trial were rare, since the organization of the Spanish Inquisition ensured that any abuses would eventually come to the attention of the *Suprema* and necessary action would be taken.

When a preliminary assessment had been made, suspects were arrested and imprisoned. At the moment of arrest the *alguazil* was accompanied by a notary, who made an inventory of the possessions of the suspect that could then be utilized in the case of a sentence of confiscation.[25] It was therefore impossible to avoid confiscation by hiding or selling the prisoner's property before his trial took place.

Then the suspect, at any time of the day or night, was taken to the prison of the Inquisition. Here again, propaganda and legend have made conditions seem much worse than they really were. Although it is true that in some prisons the death rate from disease was high, inquisitorial prisons were no worse than others at that time. There were in fact frequent cases of prisoners who sought transfer *to* the prisons of the Inquisition. Kamen gives two instances: a friar made heretical statements in order to obtain a transfer from a secular prison at Valladolid in 1629; in 1675, a priest claimed to be a judaizer in order to be removed from the episcopal prison in which he was held. Much later, in 1820, the prison authorities of Cordoba complained about the conditions of the municipal prison, and asked that its prisoners could be moved to the 'safe, clean and spacious' inquisitorial prison.[26] Yet, as so often in the history of the Inquisition, there was a strange anomaly: the permanent prisons, or *casa di penitencia*, were perhaps envied, but those used for suspects during their interrogation, the *cárceles secretas*, were far more severe in order to assist in the breaking down of suspects. Here, the noises, dark dungeons and terrors associated with the Inquisition would be more usual.[27]

Poor prisoners were provided with food by the Inquisition, while others were allowed to buy their own provisions – as in French and Italian inquisitorial prisons. Bread, wine and meat were the items most commonly bought, but oil, chocolate, eggs and bacon also appear in the records of prisoners' purchases. In addition, shirts, slippers, blankets and other articles of basic comfort were provided or could be bought. The Augustinian mystic and poet Luis de León was able to obtain writing paper and ink, and passed the four years of his imprisonment composing one of his most important works.*[28] Complaints about treatment were no more frequent than in any other penal system, and one feature peculiar to the Spanish Inquisition probably accounts for many of the exaggerated stories about its prisons: when prisoners eventually left a prison of the Inquisition they were forced to swear never to reveal anything they had seen or experienced inside it. One can easily imagine that the terror of returning into the hands of the Inquisition made such an oath relatively easy to keep. The example of Giuseppe Pignata, although he was a prisoner of the Inquisition in Rome, is pertinent: months after a dramatic escape from the prison of the Inquisition, and safe in Amsterdam, he refused to discuss his experiences in prison 'since the terror of the Holy Office is so firmly impressed in his spirit that he trembles only to think about it'.[29]

Torture

The use of torture was subject to the same rules applied in the medieval Inquisition after Clement V's reforms. A prisoner could only be tortured once, so that it was necessary for the inquisitor to state clearly at the end of each session that torture was being suspended – rather than ended – so that records speak of the continuation of torture and never fresh tortures.[30] Similarly, the instructions concerning the presence of the inquisitor and a priest during torture of a suspect were flexible. Article XVIII of Torquemada's *Copilación de las instructiones del Officio de la Sancta Inquisición* states that 'when any person is put to the torture the inquisitors and the ordinary should be present – or, at least, some of them. But when this is for any reason impossible, then the person entrusted to question should be a learned and faithful man.'[31] This extremely ambiguous formula, a 'learned and faithful' man (*hombre entendido y fiel*), is an evident loop-hole designed for abuse of the rules. But Lea observes that 'the popular impression that the inquisitorial torture-chamber was the scene of exceptional refinement in cruelty, of specially

---

*He was imprisoned from 1572 to 1576, and was again denounced to the Inquisition in 1580 and 1582. He was accused of lack of respect for the saints who validated the Vulgate, and his belief that the Jews had not corrupted the text of the Bible. His arrest and trial were in some ways political but also reflected an ideological conflict of great importance.

ingenious modes of inflicting agony, and of peculiar persistence in extorting confessions, is an error due to sensational writers who have exploited credulity'.[32] He estimates that between 1575 and 1610 about 32 per cent of prisoners whose offences made them liable to torture were actually tortured.[33]*

Torture was carried out by a public executioner in the presence of an inquisitor, a representative of the local bishop, and often a doctor. Few victims appear to have died under torture, and cases of permanent injury or loss of limb were relatively rare. There was no particular torture unique to the Spanish Inquisition, and the three most common methods were in fact akin to those used by the medieval Inquisition. There was the *garrucha*, similar to the strappado or pulley-torture, the *toca*, which was the ordeal of water, and the *potro*, which was a form of the rack.[34] The use and variety of torture instruments have been shown to have been much more conservative than once imagined, and free confession in the torture chamber was often sufficient to avoid torture altogether.

Evidently, prison conditions and the ferocity of torture varied from inquisition to inquisition. It always seems to have been the case, even in the centrally organized Spanish Inquisition, that the personality and zeal of individual inquisitors were the determining factors. There are also numerous examples of prisoners being mutilated, losing toes or fingers, and having their limbs broken; but the sight of the instruments of torture in 'a rome underground' after passing in procession through 'a place verie hidious' was often enough. If not, then the mildest degree of torture could obtain a confession, and only the most obstinate prisoner would receive the full treatment. For a modern sensibility, perhaps the worst aspect of inquisitorial torture was its use on witnesses who contradicted themselves while giving testimony, or retracted accusations they had made earlier; in that case, all means available were used to discover the truth.

And appalling accounts of torture by the Spanish Inquisition, with accuracy and detail that suggest veracity, do exist. As Turberville has observed, perhaps the most moving testimony in

*Recent research confirms such an estimate. Monter says that "mediterranean Inquisitions" were far less bloody than secular courts (*Ritual, Myth and Magic*, p. 62). Studies such as Pérez Villanueva, *La Inquisición Española. Nueva Visión, nuevos horizontes* (Madrid, 1980) and Benassar Bartolomé, (Ed) *L'Inquisition Espagnole* (Paris, 1979) have stimulated a re-evaluation.

the literature of the Inquisition are the detailed *memoranda*, in which official notaries faithfully recorded every shout, cry and complaint in a dry almost legal language that was written with no desire to shock but does so by its chilling realism.[35] These *memoranda* confirm the many first-hand accounts by victims of the Inquisition who later published a record of their experiences. The differences and similarities between these two kinds of source material can best be illustrated by comparing two examples: the first taken from the Inquisition's own record of a torture; the second from the account of William Lithgow, a Scotsman who was tortured by the Inquisition at Malaga in 1620.

In 1568, a woman was arrested on the grounds of not eating pork and changing her linen on Saturdays; these innocuous activities had led to an accusation of her being Jewish. This is the record of her torture:

> She was ordered to be placed on the *potro*. She said, 'Señores, why will you not tell me what I have to say? Señor, put me on the ground – have I not said that I did it all?' She was told to tell it. She said, 'I don't remember – take me away – I did what the witnesses say.' She was told to tell in detail what the witnesses said. She said, 'Señor, as I have told you, I do not know for certain. I have said that I did all that the witnesses say. Señores, release me, for I do not remember it.' She was told to tell it. She said, 'Señores, it does not help me to say that I did it and I have admitted that what I have done has brought me to this suffering – Señor, you know the truth – Señores, for God's sake have mercy on me. Oh, Señor, take these things from my arms – Señor, release me, they are killing me.' She was tied on the *potro* with the cords, she was admonished to tell the truth, and the *garrotes* were ordered to be tightened. She said, 'Señores, do you not see how these people are killing me? I did it – for God's sake let me go.'[36]

The dry and precise records point up the drama of a woman imprisoned and tortured on grounds that would no longer justify the merest suggestion of heresy or crime. It is a terrifying document.

William Lithgow's first-person account is equally terrifying, but with a different timbre heightened by his obvious hatred for his tormentors. These extracts will give some idea of the working methods of the torturers, with Lithgow's comments and criticisms omitted:

I was by the executioner stripped to the skin, brought to the rack, and then mounted by him on the top of it, where soon after I was hung by the bare shoulders with two small cords, which went under both my arms, running on two rings of iron that were fixed in the wall above my head. Thus being hoisted to the appointed height, the tormentor descended below, and drawing down my legs, through the two sides of the three-planked rack, he tied a cord about each of my ankles and then ascending upon the rack he drew the cords upward, and bending forward with main force my two knees against the two planks, the sinews of my hams burst asunder, and the lids of my knees being crushed, and the cords made fast, I hung so demained for a large hour.

... Then the tormentor, laying the right arme above the left, and the crown upmost, did cast a cord over both arms seven distant times: and then lying down upon his back, and setting both his feet on my hollow pinched belly, he charged and drew violently with his hands, making my womb suffer the force of his feet, till the seven several cords combined in one place of my arme (and cutting the crown, sinews, and flesh to their bare bones) did pull in my fingers close to the palm of my hands; the left hand of which is lame so still and will be for ever.

... Then by command of the Justice, was my trembling body laid above, and along, upon the face of the rack, with my head downward, inclosed within a circled hole; my belly upmost, and my heels upward toward the top of the rack, my legs and arms being drawn asunder, were fastened with pins and cords to both sides of the outward planks; for now I was to receive my main torments ...

Lithgow was then racked, and recounts the process with the same minute details of ropes and planks. When this was finished, he was subjected to the water torture:

Then the tormentor having charged the first passage above my body (making fast by a device each torture as they were multiplied), he went to an earthen jar standing full of water, a little beneath my head: from whence carrying a pot full of water, in the bottom whereof there was an incised hole, which being stopped by his thumb, till it came to my mouth, he did pour it in my belly; the measure being a Spanish *sombre* which is an English pottle;* the first and second devices I gladly received, such was the scorching drought of my tormenting pain, and likewise I had drunk none for three days before. But afterward, at the third charge perceiving

*About four pints.

these measures of water to be inflicted upon me as tortures, O strangling tortures! I closed my lips again-standing that eager crudelity. Whereat the Alcaide enraged, set my teeth asunder with a pair of iron cadges, detaining them there, at every several turn, both mainly and manually . . .[37]

Yet William Lithgow survived these, and other, tortures, and managed to return home after being imprisoned as a suspected spy in the Inquisition's prison at Malaga.

It must be remembered that the Spanish Inquisition was certainly no worse than contemporary secular courts in other countries – including England – and no more vicious in its application of torture than the Inquisition in earlier centuries in France and Italy.* The record is biased by seventeenth- and eighteenth-century works with such titles as *A Review of the Bloody Tribunal or The Horrid Cruelties of the Inquisition, The Inquisition Revealed,* or more blatantly propagandistic titles like *The History of Romanism* and *A Master Key to Popery.* Similar books inspired and elaborated a legend of violence and torture far worse than the reality of the Inquisition. Though it is undeniable that a good deal of torture took place during the long history of the Spanish tribunal, most serious contemporary historians present a fairer and more balanced interpretation of the Spanish Inquisition, with greater emphasis on the fascinating administrative aspects of the tribunal or its overall effect upon the history and culture of Spain.

Trial, Sentence and Auto de Fe

Since the arrest of a suspected heretic took place after the *calificadores* had made their assessment of the evidence – at least in theory – the prisoner was virtually declared guilty at the very moment of his arrest. The purpose of interrogation was not so much to prove the suspect's guilt as to obtain a confession, after which appropriate penance could be assigned. Furthermore, 'the main task of the tribunal was to act not as a court of justice but as a disciplinary body called into existence to meet a national

---

*Cf. John Evelyn's diary entry as he arrived in the State of Milan in 1646: 'At approach of the city, some of our company, in dread of the Inquisition (severer here than in all Spain), thought of throwing away some Protestant books and papers.'

emergency'.[38] This again stresses the fundamentally political nature of the Spanish Inquisition.

There was really no trial in the modern sense of the term but rather an extended interrogation. Indeed, the prisoner, once in the Inquisition's grasp, was kept in ignorance of the reasons behind his arrest and imprisonment – often for months or years. There was no precise charge, and therefore little possibility of making a plausible defence. The prisoner was simply advised 'to search his conscience, confess the truth, and trust to the mercy of the tribunal'.[39] He was required to confess to a crime that he attempted desperately to imagine, and had little chance of matching the preliminary care and thoroughness of the Inquisition's case against him. This passage from Simanca's *De Catholicis Institutionibus* of 1584 exemplifies such care: 'Much is to be explored in witnesses – condition, rank, poverty, riches, friendship, enmity, sex, age, etc., That Inquisitors should play the part of advocates is most just . . .'.[40] One of the great ironies of the procedure of the Spanish Inquisition is that more care, and advocacy, was practised in the case of witnesses than in that of the suspects themselves. Once the witnesses and their testimony were accepted by the *calificadores*, the accused might be considered already convicted.

Finally, however, the prisoner was informed of charges and given a much edited version of the case against him – omitting, for instance, any details that might enable him to guess the identity of the witnesses against him. Thus the guessing game continued. There were theoretically several ways of avoiding conviction: a prisoner could call his own witnesses to testify in his favour, he could object on personal grounds against his judges, or he could plead such mitigating circumstances as drunkenness, insanity or extreme youth at the time of the supposed crime.[41] There were also defence lawyers, known as *abogados de los presos*, who began as independent lawyers but who during the course of the sixteenth century became full-time officials of the Inquisition. Later, they were obviously distrusted by prisoners of the tribunal and there was little they could really do to assist their 'clients'.

When the seemingly interminable series of interrogations, audiences and waiting periods eventually came to an end, sentence could be pronounced. A special jury known as the *consulta de fe* was formed, consisting of the inquisitors, an episcopal representative, and – where necessary – experts in theology and law.[42] But as the Inquisition became increasingly centralized, difficult decisions were taken by the *Suprema* itself – and always had been in cases where there was disagreement between the inquisitor and consultors.

The condemned heretic would have to appear in an *auto de fe*, at which the penalties were officially announced. This could be a private *auto particular* for lighter offences, or the public form called the *auto publica*, which is much better known. Sentences were closely parallel to those of the medieval Inquisition that we have already analysed. The following list will give some idea of sentences and the proportions between them; it is compiled from the records of the Inquisition at Toledo at two distinct periods of its history:[43]

	1575-1610	*1648-1794*
Reconciliation	207	445
Sanbenito	186	183
Confiscation	185	417
Imprisonment	175	243
Exile from locality	167	566
Scourging	133	92
Galleys	91	98
Relaxation in person	15	8
Relaxation in effigy	18	63
Reprimand	56	467
Acquittals	51	6
Dismissed and suspended	128	104

These figures provide several interesting insights into the working of the Spanish Inquisition. It should first be noted, however, that the sentence of 'Reconciliation', equivalent to the medieval penance, implied a further sentence – usually confiscation and often imprisonment.

The *sanbenito* was the Spanish name for the signs of infamy, a variant of the yellow-crossed garment of the medieval Inquisition. Two new punishments in this list are scourging and the galleys. Ferdinand himself was responsible for the introduction of the galleys, and 'thereby found himself a cheap source of labour without having to resort to open slavery'.[44] But this sentence was used sparingly and prisoners were rarely given more than ten years in the galleys, while secular courts in the same period often gave life sentences. The sentence of scourging was more common, and involved public whipping through the streets either on foot or on an ass. No distinction was made between the sexes: in Valencia in 1607 a man of eighty-six and a girl of thirteen each received a hundred lashes.[45] This was the usual number, while two hundred was the maximum. But the handing out of multiple sentences using the lash was quite frequent: in 1672, Alonso Ribero was sentenced to four years' exile, six years in the galleys and 100 lashes; Francisco de Alarcon was sentenced to five years' exile, five years in the galleys and a fine.[46] Later, the galleys were simply floating prisons moored or anchored at sea or in a river port.

The ultimate penalty, again as in the medieval Inquisition, was the stake, reserved for unrepentant or relapsed heretics. The inquisitors attempted to the last moment to convince even relapsed heretics to confess and save their lives. If this last-minute confession took place during the *auto de fe*, they were given the benefit of strangulation before burning; if they did not confess even then, they were burned alive. But as the list for Toledo clearly shows, more heretics were burned in effigy than in person – some because they had managed to evade the Inquisition by fleeing, and others because they had died during imprisonment. The figures given for actual execution at the stake are low: only fifteen cases from 1575 to 1610, and eight from 1648 to 1794. Henry Kamen explains that 'the relative frequency of burnings in the first savage years of the Inquisition disappeared in the eighteenth century, and in the twenty-nine years of the reigns of Charles III and Charles IV only four people were burnt'.[47]

The burnings took place within the *auto de fe*, and it was perhaps their spectacular nature that impressed them upon the minds of so many travellers who watched them. They usually took place on a feast day in the presence of king or nobles, and followed a public procession, a mass, sermon and the reconciliation of sinners. The most celebrated *autos de fe* were held in the elegant *Plaza Mayor*, a square in the centre of Madrid, in the presence of the king and his court. A contemporary description of the *auto de fe* of 1690 will illustrate the pomp, grandeur and excitement:

The officers of the Inquisition, preceded by trumpets, kettle-drums and their banner, marched on the 30th of May, in cavalcade, to the palace of the great square, where they declared by proclamation that on the 30th June the sentence of the prisoners would be put in execution. There had not been a spectacle of this kind at Madrid for several years before, for which reason it was expected by the inhabitants with as much impatience as a day of the greatest festivity and triumph. When the day appointed arrived, a prodigious number of people appeared, dressed as splendid as their respective circumstances would admit. In the great square was raised a high scaffold; and thither, from seven in the morning until the evening, were brought criminals of both sexes; all the Inquisitions in the kingdom sending their prisoners to Madrid. Twenty men and women out of these prisoners, with one renegade Mahometan, were ordered to be burned; fifty Jews and Jewesses, having never before been imprisoned, were sentenced to a long confinement, and to wear a yellow cap; and ten others, indicted for bigamy, witchcraft and other crimes, were sentenced to be whipped and then sent to the galleys: these last wore large pasteboard caps, with inscriptions on them, having a halter about their necks, and torches in their hands. On this solemn occasion the whole court of Spain was present. The grand inquisitor's chair was placed in a sort of tribunal far above that of the king. The nobles here acted the part of the sheriffs' officers in England, leading such criminals as were to be burned, and holding them when fast bound with thick cords; the rest of the criminals were conducted by the familiars of the Inquisition.

At the place of execution there are so many stakes set as there are prisoners to be burned, a large quantity of dry furze being set about them. The stakes of the Protestants, or, as the inquisitors call them, the professed, are about four yards high, and have each a small board, whereon the prisoner is seated within half a yard of the top. The professed then go up a ladder betwixt two priests, who attend them the whole day of execution. When they come even with the aforementioned board, they turn about to the people, and the priests spend near a quarter of an hour in exhorting them to be reconciled to the see of Rome. On their refusing, the priests come down, and the executioner ascending, turns the professed from off the ladder upon the seat, chains their bodies close to the stakes, and leaves them. Then the priests go up a second time to renew their exhortations; and if they find them ineffectual, usually tell them at parting, that 'they leave them to the Devil, who is standing at their elbow ready to receive their souls, and carry them with him into the flames of hell-fire, as soon as they are out of their bodies'. A general shout is then raised, and when the priests get off the ladder, the universal cry is: 'Let the dogs' beards be made!' (which implies, singe their beards). This is accordingly performed by means of flaming furzes, thrust against their faces with long poles. This barbarity is repeated till their faces are burnt, and is accompanied with loud acclamations. Fire is then set to the furzes, and the criminals are consumed.

The intrepidity of the twenty-one men and women in suffering the horrid death was truly astonishing; some thrust their hands and feet into the flames with the most dauntless fortitude; and all of them yielded to their fate with such resolution that many of the amazed spectators lamented that such heroic souls had not been more enlightened. The near situation of the king to the criminals rendered their dying groans very audible to him; he could not, however, be absent from this dreadful scene, as it is esteemed a religious one, and his coronation oath obliges him to give a sanction by his presence to all the acts of the tribunal.[48]

The detail is more profuse in this example, but it must have been little different from the holocausts of Robert le Bougre and was certainly no more thorough than the destruction of the body of John Hus.

The Spanish Inquisition caused great suffering, thousands of deaths, and serious economic and cultural effects on the history of Spain. But it must not be forgotten that Spain enjoyed her greatest moment of power and prestige during the centuries in which the Inquisition was at full spate. The colonies were established, literature, music and painting flourished – especially from about 1550 to 1700 – and modern Spain was created. Some authors say that 2,000 people were executed by 1490, and 4,000 by 1520, but after that date burnings declined. It is likely that hundreds more died in succeeding centuries, but even the exaggerated claim of Llorente does not go beyond 32,000. This is commonly accepted as an absurdly high estimate and pales beside the figures for deaths at the stake in the witchhunts elsewhere in Europe during the same period.

Compared to the maniacal enthusiasm of such as the French inquisitor Nicolas Remy, who was said to have burned 800 women in one day,[49] the activities of the Spanish Inquisition no longer shock. Only the work of Torquemada, in the first violent period of expulsions and repression, might be compared to such fury.

A reliable recent estimate by E. William Monter, based on

newly analysed documents and the latest Spanish scholarly research, suggests that of 150,000 people tried between 1550 and 1800 by the Spanish Inquisition only 3,000 were actually put to death.[50] Such scholarly revision clearly places the history of that tribunal in a totally different perspective.

The negative aspects of the Spanish Inquisition cannot be denied, but it must be considered rather in its rôle in Spanish cultural history than for voyeuristic sensationalism. The terror was real, but Spain survived and grew.

10. Reform and the Roman Inquisition

With the Bull *Licet ab initio,* issued on 21 July 1542, Pope Paul III created a new papal Inquisition quite distinct from the earlier tribunal in Italy and clearly inspired by the recent success of the Spanish Inquisition. The prime mover of the new organization was Cardinal Giovanni Pietro Carafa, (1476-1559), a zealous ex-Dominican and one of the most extraordinary men of the sixteenth-century Roman Church. His long career was intimately linked with reform movements within the Church and the fight against heresies deriving from the Reformation. As instigator of the new Inquisition, its patron when he later became Pope Paul IV, and spiritual patron when the man he had chosen to head the Inquisition became in his turn Pope as Pius V, the early years of the tribunal are irrevocably bound to his own life.

Carafa had participated in the founding of the Oratory of Divine Love, a 'voluntary association dedicated to austerity of life and charitable occupations',[1] as early as 1517 – shortly before the Protestant Reformation was fired by Luther's theses. Thus he belonged to an earlier tradition of reform and protest, 'although it is obvious that under the impact of the Reformation the movement changed character: it became at once more purposeful and gradually more intolerant'.[2] When the desired reforms received no papal backing, Carafa and his friends continued to work in their dioceses. Together with St Cajetan of Tiene, in 1524 he founded an order of clerks regular. Carafa was at that time Bishop of the Abruzzi town of Chieti (in Latin:

Theatinum) and the movement became known as the Theatines, working in collaboration with the secular clergy although its members took holy vows.[3] Within a few years this new order spread throughout Italy, and later almost reached an agreement to merge with the Jesuits. The Theatines produced more than two hundred bishops, thereby providing a solid and influential power base for the founder of this nursery of ecclesiastical dignitaries. Such an order was symptomatic of a general reawakening of monastic orders, and many others were founded in the same period.

The real power of Carafa began, however, when he persuaded Paul III to refound the Inquisition. From the beginning of his pontificate in 1534 that Pope had worked towards reform, founding new congregations to supervise the conduct of the Roman clergy and to enquire into the administration of the Papal States. Soon afterwards he elevated Giovanni Pietro Carafa to Cardinal, and then appointed a papal commission for reform in which Carafa was one of the leading members – together with Cardinal Pole. In January 1538, this commission presented a report proposing reforms within the Church: 'They laid down the moral and intellectual qualifications needed for admission to the Holy Orders; they imposed upon all clerics, from the humblest curate to the most elevated member of the Sacred College, a manner of life suitable to the duties of their state . . .'.[4] Important clauses from this report were later included in the decrees of the Council of Trent – which was also summoned by Paul III.

In 1540 the Pope granted recognition to the Society of Jesus, and in 1542 to the Capuchins – a breakaway movement from the Franciscans that in many ways echoed the ideas of the *fraticelli*. But his two most significant innovations were the foundation of the Roman Inquisition and the first attempt to create an Index of prohibited printed books deemed likely to propagate false teachings. In both these initiatives Carafa played an important part.

At the beginning, the new Roman Inquisition consisted of six Cardinals, twenty-seven counsellors and three theological experts. Cardinal Carafa was president of the tribunal, and chose members of his own Dominican order to carry out the work of inquisitors. It was designed to operate everywhere in Europe, but for the moment its work was mainly devoted to

Italy. Carafa's austere personality was reflected in the rigour with which the Inquisition began working; in only a few years it managed to create an awe-inspiring reputation in Rome.

But the new Holy Office – as it was more commonly known to Romans – really came into its own with the election of Carafa as Paul IV in 1555, at almost eighty years of age and after two brief pontificates which separated him from his friend Paul III. The Inquisition became his chief weapon of reform, and the ongoing Council of Trent was temporarily forgotten. The Venetian Ambassador in Rome wrote that 'The Pope's violence is always great, but in the matter of the Inquisition it is really indescribable. On Thursday, the day appointed for its meetings, nothing on earth could prevent him from attending. I remember the day when the Spaniards occupied Anagni: all Rome was running to arms, trembling for its life and property; but Paul IV calmly went off to preside over the Holy Office, dealing point by point with the agenda, just as though there were no enemy at the gate.'[5]

Paul IV's zeal made him extremely unpopular with his own subjects in the Papal States. He alienated men of learning with the harsh Index of 1559, and the people generally by his quixotic attempt to conquer Naples – which resulted in an ignominious defeat at the hands of the Duke of Alba, the Spanish vice-regent. The Inquisition enjoyed unlimited powers during his pontificate, and the Dominican inquisitors worked quickly and efficiently against the slightest semblance of heresy. The Pope had the inquisitors' informers spy on the private morals of the people of Rome, and insisted on exemplary punishments for the most minor offences. A contemporary chronicler wrote of him that his head 'might be compared to the Vesuvius of his native city, since he was ardent in all his actions, wrathful, hard, and inflexible, undoubtedly moved by an incredible zeal for religion, but a zeal often lacking in prudence, and breaking out in eruptions of excessive severity'.[6]

His unpopularity may be judged from the fact that on the night of his death there were riots in the city of Rome. As he lay dying, the people stormed through the streets, releasing up to four hundred condemned men from the city's prisons by force. The prison of the Inquisition, which stood to the right of Bernini's colonnade as one looks out from St Peter's, was also sacked, with the liberation of seventy-two prisoners. Then the crowds made for the Dominican convent of S. Maria sopra Minerva, headquarters of the Inquisition and the church where Paul IV was later buried.* Further riots were only prevented by the presence of a Roman nobleman, Marcantonio Colonna, whose word the people respected.[7] Within seventeen years of the re-foundation of the Inquisition, its dying instigator was humiliated by the subjects of the Papal States.

The Censorship of Books

Events leading up to the Reformation had illustrated the enormous power of the printed word. A list of prohibited books was issued in Rome in the same year as the foundation of the new Inquisition, and before 1559 had been followed by others in Louvain, Paris, Venice, Lucca, Milan, Florence, Valladolid and Toledo.[8] But there was as yet no attempt at the compilation of a centralized list with papal authority, so the books that were banned varied widely from list to list – reflecting local concerns.

The tradition of banning and burning books held to threaten the faith already had a long history within the Church, as we have seen. It is usually thought to date from the banning of an unauthenticated life of St Paul by the Council of Ephesus in AD 150. There had been many individual cases: in 1140, Innocent II ordered the burning of the writings of Peter Abelard; in 1230, Gregory IX ordered the burning of copies of the Talmud; and in 1256 Alexander IV ordered the burning of a treatise by William of St Amour which criticized the Mendicant Orders.[9] But the situation changed dramatically in 1543 when heavy penalties were imposed on those who sold the books banned by episcopal lists, and Cardinal Carafa ordered that no book could be printed without permission from the Inquisition. Carafa and Paul III fully recognized the power of the printed word; that Pope utilized the power when he invited Cardinals Aleandro and Contarini to 'write a work that would instruct preachers in the proper method of expounding Christian doctrine to the various classes of society'.[10]

*An *avviso* in the Vatican Secret Archive describes the scene as follows: 'At this hour, that is, at midnight, a courier has arrived with the news of the death of the Pope. This has given great joy to all. Those who had had statues made of him were to break them into pieces as soon as they knew he was dead. Then they set free from prison all those who were there because of the Inquisition, burning documents and court records'. (Ambrosini, *Secret Archives*, p. 183).

One of the new features of the 1559 Index, evident in its full title *Index Auctorum et Librorum Prohibitorum,* was the simultaneous banning of books and authors. This was an important innovation, and had far-reaching consequences. In some cases a single book was chosen to be banned as the result of unorthodox views expounded in it, but in other cases an author's entire work was banned – most notably in the case of Erasmus. The long-term effect was that in all future Indices some authors had their 'Works' on the list, including books that could not possibly be interpreted as dangerous to the Church or offensive to its doctrines.*

In 1564, this preliminary attempt was consolidated and expanded by another Index issued at the end of the Council of Trent. The so-called Tridentine Index was granted even greater authority since it had been drawn up by a general council of the Church. It was to be the basis of all future lists. In March 1571, Pius V created a special Congregation of the Index and full control passed from the Inquisition. But the *Magister* of the papal palace, who was always a Dominican, was standing counsel of both the Inquisition and the new Congregation of the Index; thus a certain continuity was maintained, and the Inquisition served as a police force to enforce decisions made by the Index. Inquisitors were called upon to examine books and pass them for publication, and, as we shall see, the Index again passed into the full control of the Inquisition in 1917.

Apart from Spain, which by this time ran an independent Index, the Tridentine Index was fully approved and accepted by Belgium, Bavaria, Portugal and Italy; France and Germany accepted rather half-heartedly. The ten fundamental rules that formed the basis of all future Indices were as follows:

1. All books condemned before 1515 not in this Index were condemned in any case.

2. Books of heresiarchs were completely forbidden.

3. Translations of ecclesiastical writers were permitted if they contained nothing contrary to sound doctrine.

---

*An *avviso* from the Vatican suggests another effect: "The Index of prohibited books that has just been printed gives everyone a good deal to talk about and think about, especially the booksellers, who see themselves half bankrupted." (Ambrosini, *Secret Archives*, p. 184).

4. Permission from inquisitor or bishop was required in order to read translations of the Bible.

5. Books edited by heretics could be read after correction.

6. Books concerning controversies between contemporary heretics and Catholics in the vulgar tongue were subject to the same rules as Bible translations.

7. Obscene books and lascivious books were to be banned (ancient texts could be read for their style, but not by the young).

8. Books which were good but with heretical portions could be allowed after correction by Catholic divines.

9. Books of geomancy, hydromancy, necromancy, etc., or treating of sorcery in any way, were utterly rejected.

10. The Index established the procedure for vetting the books.[11]

Examples of authors who were completely banned, apart from Erasmus, are Savonarola, Machiavelli and Boccaccio.* Passages from many famous Italian authors were to be removed or corrected; and even Dante was censored. The passage in his *De Monarchia*, Book II, in which he argues that Imperial authority derives from God and not from the Pope, was to be excised.[12] But on the whole this Index was more tolerant than later ones, and more so than the Spanish Index. Its main concern was with books in Italian or likely to be of interest to readers in Rome; foreign authors were mainly untouched by it – except for writers whose works supported Protestantism in any way.

Censorship was not universally accepted, however, even within Italy, and Paul F. Grendler has recently shown the extent to which the Venetian printing industry was bolstered by the severity of the Inquisition in Rome itself.[13] Venice became the centre of book production in Europe in the second half of the

*Peter M. Brown has argued that corrections to the *Decameron* are not necessarily attributable to the Inquisition. The work was banned in 1559, but allowed to be published after correction in 1564, with only the parts offensive to the Church removed (stories about priests). The completely different version published in 1582 was the result of the moral criteria of literary criticism: Lionardo Salviati, a critic and philologist, was responsible for obtaining and carrying out the second revision (cf. *I veri promotori della Rassettatura del 'Decameron'*, pp. 315-16). In a near-contemporary satire, Traiano Boccalini refers to Salviati as the 'assassin' of the Decameron (*Pietra del Paragone Politico, tratto dal Monte Parnaso*, Impresso in Cosmopoli per Ambros Teler, 1615, p. 73).

sixteenth century, together with cities in Switzerland and Germany beyond the control of the Inquisition. In England, at the same time, censorship was political rather than ecclesiastical.* An amusing and unexpected use of the lists of prohibited books was made by Thomas James in a treatise on the Index written in 1627; he recommended the Bodleian Library in Oxford to use the Index as a purchasing guide to unexpurgated copies of banned books, and thus assisted in the preservation of works that might otherwise have been forgotten.[14] It was indeed fortunate that much of northern Europe was more or less immune to decrees issuing from Rome: 'If the Inquisition had been in a position to carry on throughout Europe, or even throughout the catholic States, a censorship as effective as that put into force in Spain, the extermination of books would have been so considerable that there would have been brought about a serious break between the literatures of the centuries.'[15]

As it happened, the most disastrous effect was on the development of scientific thought in Italy; the lead which Italian scientists and philosophers had achieved during the Renaissance was truncated and never recovered. In 1616 the Congregation of the Index banned Copernicus's *De Revolutionibus Orbium Coelestium*, and three years later Kepler's *Epitome astronomiae Copernicae*. We shall see how the Inquisition attempted to censor Galileo's ideas, and Thorndike has shown how many scientific careers were destroyed by the combined operations of Index and Inquisition. The burning of Giordano Bruno in Rome in 1600 symbolizes this attitude, although the precise nature of the charges against him is not clear.[16]

At first, the banning, amendment and correction of books was a sweeping and often random exercise; the conditional *donec corrigatur*, or 'prohibited until corrected', was used eccentrically and often for no good reason. There was little time for subtle distinctions. But during the pontificate of Pius V the bans 'became implacably severe. Pompeop De' Monti in 1566, Mario Galeotta and Pietro Carnesecchi in 1568, Aonio Paleario in 1560 – one by one the victims were sent to the gallows or the stake.'[17]

---

*Although John Dee's fears were not political. He wrote: 'Saturday night I dremed that I was deade, and afterwards my bowels wer taken out I walked and talked with diverse, and among other with the Lord Thresorer who was com to my house to burn my bokes when I was dead, and I thought he looked sourly on me'. (*The Private Diary of Dr John Dee*, London: The Camden Society, 1842, pp. 17-18.)

Continuity was assured even beyond Carafa: Pius V had been a Dominican and protégé of Carafa, and later Head of the Inquisition under Paul IV; his successor as pope was Sixtus V (1585-1590), a Franciscan who as a Cardinal had been a member of the newly formed Congregation of the Index. As soon as he was elected to the Holy See, he set about the preparation of a new Index. Thus, as in the thirteenth century, a series of powerful Popes exercised immense power through the Inquisition. Paul III has often in fact been compared to Innocent III, and the orthodoxy that these sixteenth-century Popes established through the Council of Trent survives with minor amendments to this day – much as that created by Gregory IX, Innocent IV and St Thomas Aquinas had survived intact until the sixteenth century.

Milton poured scorn on the Index of Prohibited Books in his great pamphlet for the freedom of the Press:

> After which time the Popes of Rome, engrossing what they pleased of political rule into their own hands, extended their dominion over men's eyes, as they had before over their judgements, burning and prohibiting to be read what they fancied not . . . until the Council of Trent and the Spanish Inquisition engendering together brought forth or perfected those Catalogues and expurging Indexes that rake through the entrails of many an old good author, with a violation worse than any could be offered to his tomb. Nor did they stay in matters heretical, but any subject that was not to their palate, they either condemned in a prohibition, or had it straight into the new Purgatory of an Index. To fill up the measure of that encroachment their last invention was to ordain that no book, pamphlet, or paper should be printed (as if St Peter had bequeathed them the keys of the press also out of paradise) unless it were approved and licensed under the hands of two or three glutton friars.[18]

This passage provides a marvellously lively example of the tone of propaganda against the Inquisition, and in fact Milton is not quite fair in this case. The Index was not as harsh as he makes out, and in examples given later we shall see that it was mainly concerned with expressly theological – and often controversial – works.

In 1917, with the decree *Motu Proprio de attribuenda Sancto Officio Censura Librorum* published as a preface to the newly edited Index of that year, Pope Benedict XV ordered the transfer of the work of censorship back to the Holy Office.[19] The last edition of the Index was published in 1948, with a supplement in 1959. Many people still living recall the lists of additional books which were affixed to church doors periodically throughout Italy until the Index was finally suspended in 1966. Thus, although for much of its history the Index was formally separated from the Inquisition, it began and ended its existence with the Holy Office – and was never far from the control of that parent organization.

Paolo Veronese and the Venetian Inquisition

The same reforming zeal that caused the expurgation of Boccaccio's *Decameron* found another target in painting. Again, it was Carafa as Paul IV who led the way: in 1558 he ordered that the nudes painted by Michelangelo on the ceiling of the Sistine Chapel were to be covered; 'the eviction of pagan statues from the Vatican Palace by Pius V was yet another manifestation of the same spirit; and this campaign of prudery was afterwards carried to such lengths that Pope Innocent X had a charming new-born Infant Jesus, by Guercino, covered with a shirt.'[20] These pagan statues formed the basis of the collection now in the Capitoline Museum in Rome, although some were saved for the Church when Sixtus V 'converted' them to Christianity. In a celebrated work that was to become the theoretical basis for Baroque architecture, Carlo Borromeo was forced to justify the use of columns by arguing that they were essential for 'structural durability';[21] otherwise, they might well have been banned as being of pagan origin.

Outside Rome, the work of the Inquisition was carried out and supervised by papal nuncios. In Malta, for instance, the Pope's diplomatic representative was the inquisitor: from 1574 to 1798 a series of sixty-two Italian inquisitors exercised effective religious and disciplinary control over the lives of the Knights of Malta.[22] The post was much sought after as a sure prelude to higher promotion. Appointees to the position of nuncio-inquisitor included ex-governors of papal cities, vice-legates and even bishops. At least one Maltese inquisitor, Fabio Chigi, reached the Holy See as Alexander VII in 1655.[23]

In Venice, even before the refoundation of the Inquisition, we find Clement VII in 1533 ordering Girolamo Aleandro, his nuncio in that city, to arrest and try a Lutheran heretic* and send the documents to Rome.[24] Paul III showed constant concern about the presence of heretics in Venice, Padua and Vicenza, which were geographically exposed to Lutheran and other Protestant influences from the north. The Inquisition at Aquileia, near Trieste, was actively involved in suppressing Lutheranism at the end of the century. Carafa had written a special report on the heretical practices of certain members of the Franciscan brotherhood in the diocese in 1532.[25] After 1542, when the new Roman Inquisition began to function, one of the papal nuncio's main concerns was the diffusion of heretical publications, both those printed in Venice itself and those printed in Italian at Basle – which filtered into Italy through the Venetian Republic. The nuncio Giovanni della Casa had compiled the local list of prohibited books mentioned above, and he frequently wrote to Rome demanding an authoritative list with the backing of the Holy See. Then, on 22 April 1547, the new Venetian Inquisition was established by the Doge, and began to function regularly – though not without great difficulty.

The main problem was that the Inquisition at Venice had three masters, each of whom attempted to exercise control over its work. The nuncio and inquisitor, who were at first Franciscans but from 1560 Dominicans appointed by apostolic brief, represented Rome; the Patriarch or vicar-general represented the Diocese of Venice; and three Venetian noblemen called the *Tre Savii sopra l'Eresia* or *Assistenti*, present at all trials, represented the Venetian State.[26] The Republic was loath to surrender its independence, and was particularly jealous as far as its own citizens were concerned; many cases were resolved by the parallel Venetian Inquisition, a much less severe tribunal, and the Republic often refused to hand over its prisoners to Rome.[27] Thus it has been argued that 'the Inquisition in Venice was an embodiment of compromise, devoted to regulations if not forestalling conflict . . .'.[28]

By virtue of its trading role, Venice was a melting pot of Jews, Greeks, Catholics, Protestants, Moslems, Lutherans, Anabaptists and Huguenots. So the Inquisition became chiefly concerned 'with offences involving a clear public interest'[29]

---

*This man is worth noting, since he was the Pallavicino whom Benvenuto Cellini met in prison at Castel Sant'Angelo in Rome, and describes in his autobiography (Part II, chapter 1).

rather than with personal religious convictions. Yet the lack of restrictions in Venice should not be exaggerated. While it is true that the Republic later offered a safe refuge to Galileo, it is also true that Giordano Bruno made a fatal misjudgement when he decided that it would be safe to re-enter Italy after many years wandering and accepted an invitation to reside in Venice. He was arrested and tried there, although he was subsequently burned in Rome.[30] In fact the Venetian Republic co-operated with the Roman Inquisition to a considerable degree until the 1590s.

Before that date, there was a famous trial in Venice involving one of her most celebrated painters, Paolo Veronese, which had as important an effect on painting as the case of Galileo later had on scientific thought. Veronese had made a large canvas of the *Feast in the House of Levi*, now in the Academy Museum in Venice, in which he had placed dogs, dwarfs, a fool, a parrot, men with German weapons, and a man with a bleeding nose. The Inquisition considered these elements to represent an affront to the Church and to decency, since such details are not mentioned in the biblical story of Levi and were not – according to them – suitable subjects for religious paintings. Although such accusations may seem strange to us today, the interrogation of Veronese is fascinating for the pernickety thoroughness it illustrates in inquisitorial minds.

After questioning Veronese about the details of the painting, including the fool, the bleeding nose and other figures, the transcript of his trial continues:

Q. Did any one commission you to paint Germans, buffoons, and similar things in that picture?

A. No, milords, but I received the commission to decorate the picture as I saw fit. It is large and, it seemed to me, it could hold many pictures.

Q. Are not the decorations which you painters are accustomed to add to paintings or pictures supposed to be suitable and proper to the subject and the principal figures or are they for pleasure – simply what comes to your imagination without any discretion or judiciousness?

A. I paint pictures as I see fit and as well my talent permits.

Q. Does it seem fitting at the Last Supper of the Lord to paint buffoons, drunkards, Germans, dwarfs and similar vulgarities?

A. No, milords.

Q. Do you know that in Germany and other places infected with heresy it is customary with various pictures full of scurrilousness and similar inventions to mock, vituperate, and scorn the things of the Holy Catholic Church in order to teach bad doctrines to foolish and ignorant people?

A. Yes that is wrong; but I return to what I have said, that I am obliged to follow what my superiors have done.

Q. What have your superiors done? Have they perhaps done similar things?

A. Michelangelo in Rome in the Pontifical Chapel painted Our Lord, Jesus Christ, His Mother, St John, St Peter, and the Heavenly Host. These are all represented in the nude – even the Virgin Mary – and in different poses with little reverence.

Q. Do you not know that in painting the Last Judgement in which no garments or similar things are presumed, it was not necessary to paint garments, and that in those figures there is nothing which is not spiritual? There are neither buffoons, dogs, weapons, or similar buffoonery. And does it seem because of this or some other example that you did right to have painted this picture in the way you did and do you want to maintain that it is good and decent?[31]

Veronese was fortunate. He was admonished and ordered to eliminate the details that had given offence, within three months from the date of his trial and at his own expense. This strange failure to deal with the root of the problem as seen by the Inquisition was emphasized by Sir Anthony Blunt: 'It is typical of the methods of the Counter-Reformation that the Inquisition in this case was satisfied with certain changes of detail which left the painting exactly as worldly in feeling as it was before.'[32]

This paradoxical combination of power and lack of power, of apparent ruthlessness but real inability to do anything, characterizes the sixteenth-century Inquisition in Italy. The complex local conditions of Venice highlight the paradox.

The Trial of Galileo

The episode of the two trials of Galileo is one of the most remarkable and most misunderstood in the history of the Inquisition. The ramifications, aftershocks and lengthy process of rehabilitation by the Church are not yet exhausted.*

Galileo's difficulties with the Church began when he refused to heed a warning to treat the movement of the earth hypothetically, and insisted on its real motion. In doing so, he was held to have offended the Scriptures and a recent study has shown how he was eventually embroiled in a complex theological issue.[33] But from the beginning Galileo seems to have suffered from the petty jealousies of friars of several Orders. He had himself, in a letter to Pietro Dini, written at Florence in May 1615, explained with exemplary logic how it would be possible to reconcile the ideas of Copernicus with the Scriptures: 'The way in which I could quickly and surely demonstrate that Copernicus's position is not contrary to the Scriptures would be to show with a thousand proofs that it is true, and that the opposite cannot hold good; thus, since two truths cannot contradict each other, it is necessary that both his theory and the Scriptures are in agreement.' But he then goes on to state that it would not in any case be worth trying to convince 'peripatetics' who were incapable of the most elementary reasoning.[34] This disdain, and his increasing conviction that he was the object of a monkish conspiracy, were at least in part the reasons for his trouble. Much later, in a conversation that he did not expect to be reported, the Jesuit astronomer Christoph Grenberger said: 'If Galileo had only known how to retain the favour of the Jesuits, he would have stood in renown before the world, he would have been spared all his misfortunes, and he could have written what he pleased about everything, even about the motion of the earth.'[35]

But Galileo's character was not conciliatory, and from this position derived the admonition of his first trial. It was issued by

*Scientists at a conference on Galileo in the Vatican in May 1983 expected the rehabilitation to be announced by John Paul II. But the Pope limited himself to admitting, on 10 May, the Church's responsibility in the birth of 'serious incomprehension, the consequences of misunderstanding or errors, that only patient and humble revisions will be able to dissipate'. In July 1984, the commission appointed by the same Pope in 1980 to resolve the 'Galileo case' had not yet reported on its findings.

the Inquisition on 24 February 1616 with the title *Censura facta in S.^{to} Officio Urbis*; Galileo's assertions that 'the sun is at the centre of the world' and that 'the earth is not at the centre of the world' were presented, and then rejected as absurd, heretical and against the Scriptures.[36] He was warned not to propagate such doctrines or defend them either in words or in writing, although this prohibition has been the object of much controversy. Von Gebler concluded that '1. Galileo did not receive any prohibition, except the cardinal's [i.e., Bellarmine, who had previously warned Galileo] admonition not to defend or hold the Copernican doctrine; 2. Entire silence on the subject was therefore not enjoined upon him.'[37]

Galileo did, however, pass this first stage of his dealings with the Inquisition relatively unscathed, especially when it is considered that he had been judged by 'a congregation like that of the Holy Office, which is the foundation and base of religion and the most important in Rome', as Piero Guicciardini expressed it in a letter to Galileo's patron Cosimo II, Grand Duke of Tuscany, in the following week.[38] The threat seemed to have passed, particularly when Pope Urban VIII – newly elected and a friend to Galileo – wrote a letter praising him to the Grand Duke in 1624.[39]

But Galileo's obstinate character and his uncompromising search for truth were to drive him inevitably towards a conflict with the Inquisition. At about the time of Urban's praising letter he began work on a new book provisionally entitled *De Fluxu et Reflexu Maris*, or 'On the Ebb and Flow of Tides'. He wrongly believed the tides to be caused by the movement of the earth, but the thesis was sustained on the basis of the Ptolomeic and Copernican systems. This was the work that took most of the next seven years of his life, and was eventually published with the title (in Italian rather than Latin) *Dialogue Concerning the Two Chief World Systems*.

In 1630, he went to Rome with the manuscript of the *Dialogue* to obtain a licence to print it from the Inquisition, and to arrange for its publication by the Accademia dei Lincei. This plan was thwarted by two unexpected factors: the death of the president of the academy, Prince Cesi, and an outbreak of contagious disease which temporarily halted commerce and communications between Rome and Florence. Back in Florence, Galileo arranged to have the book checked by the

Florentine Inquisition. In a letter to Andrea Cioli, he speaks well of the Inquisitor, Brother Jacinto Stefani, 'who reviewed with extreme accuracy and severity (as I had asked) the whole work, noting even some minute errors that should remove any shadow of doubt not only in themselves but in my most malign adversary . . .'.[40] Brother Jacinto even went so far as to insist that the new work be printed.

It appears that at that moment even Niccolò Riccardi, the Dominican professor of theology entrusted with the task of authorising Galileo's manuscript, was in favour of publication, and was only concerned about the 'mode of presentation' of the *Dialogue*. He wished however to retain the original manuscript in order to be able to check eventual proofs.[41] Riccardi wrote that Galileo had been given his *imprimatur,* or 'let it be printed', with necessary amendments and corrections made for publication in Rome. He added that 'I have no greater wish than to serve his Highness the Grand Duke my Lord, but wish to do so in such a way that persons under his protection be immune to any danger in their reputation.'[42] As the result of a misunderstanding that full permission had been given for publication, the book came out in Florence in February 1632.

This appears to be the substance of future accusations against Galileo, rather than the actual contents of the book. In the inquisitorial document summarizing the case before his trial the matter is presented as follows:

In 1630 Galileo brought to the Master of the Sacred Palace his book in manuscript, to be passed for publication; and the Master gave it to Father Raffaele Visconti, his companion and professor of mathematics, and having amended it in several places he was ready to give his faith as normal if the book were printed in Rome.

A letter was written to this Father, who sent his faith, and then we waited; a letter was also written to obtain the original manuscript, to see the corrections made.

The Master of the Sacred Palace, who wished to see the book again and shorten the time necessary, agreed to read it page by page; and so that negotiations could be started with the printer he gave his *imprimatur,* for Rome.

The author went to Florence and requested permission from the Master to print it in that city; this was denied, and he negotiated with the Inquisitor of Florence, washing his hands of the business, and advised him what should be observed in printing it. He left to him the charge of printing or not printing.

He showed the Master of the Sacred Palace a copy of the letter
that he sent to the Inquisitor on this matter, and also a copy of the
reply from the Inquisitor to the Master in which he states that it has
been corrected by Father Stefani, Consultor of the Holy Office.

After this, the Master of the Sacred Palace heard nothing more,
until he saw the book as it was printed in Florence with the
Inquisitor's *imprimatur*, and also the *imprimatur* of Rome.[43]

The document goes on to recall the controversial admonition of
1616, and states that Galileo had 'fraudulently omitted' this fact
when he had requested permission for publication of the
Dialogue. It concludes – and this is the crucial and fatal step –
that the Inquisition should deliberate the method of proceeding
against *both Galileo* and *his book (tam contra personam quam circa
librum)*. When the eight charges which are to be made are given,
one fact stands out immediately: the first charge against him is
that 'he had put the *imprimatur* of Rome without permission
. . .'. Only in the third of the charges does the matter of the sun's
stability or the earth's mobility arise.

The Inquisition therefore played a role quite different from
that often portrayed. It is impossible to avoid the fascinating
hypothesis – substantiated by further evidence during the trial –
that Galileo was brought to court as the result of his double
offence to the Inquisition itself: he ignored the 1616 admonition
(which was given verbally even though the document may have
been falsified later), and he printed the book without obtaining
full permission. With the help of his powerful friends and
patrons, including the Pope, and the desire of everybody
concerned – even Father Stefani – to avoid difficulties, it seems
likely that the *Dialogue* could in fact have been published in a
slightly amended form without the clamour and complications of
the trial. Seen from the point of view of a history of the
Inquisition, the trial of Galileo therefore takes on fresh interest
as an example of its pervasive power.

The remainder of the story of relations between Galileo and
the Inquisition is now more readily intelligible. The real
problem is identified by his friend Filippo Magalotti, in a long
letter written to Mario Guiducci in Florence on 7 August 1632
explaining the case and seeking a possible solution. He wrote:

Moreover, I will do everything possible to discover what happens to Signor Galileo and to help him, as far as I can do so with profit. But it is true that things happen in the greatest secrecy, since it is an affair of the Holy Office; if it were an affair of the Index it would be easier, at least to discover what was going on.[44]

It was now the man, Galileo, who was to be tried by the Inquisition, and the publicity and general comment worsened his case. Stillman Drake has commented: 'Galileo could not be acquitted without damage to the reputation and authority of the Roman Inquisition, so it was privately arranged that he should admit to some wrongdoing and submit his defence, with the understanding that he would be treated leniently.'[45] But his character rendered such an arrangement precarious at best, and in the end he was destroyed by his condemnation. There was really no escape.

The *Dialogue* was withdrawn from circulation in August 1632, and on 23 September Galileo was cited to appear in Rome before the Inquisition. He was then sixty-eight, and a sick man; his letters are full of references to physical disabilities and ailments. He did not wish to travel to Rome, but could not refuse such an order from the Inquisition. Another friend apologized for his inability to offer any assistance:

> I am deeply sorry for your affliction, particularly at such an age, and would like to be able to relieve you with my own blood; but as it is a matter of the Holy Office, things do not proceed with the terms of other Congregations, and for threats of excommunication no information is given and it is useless to try recommendations.[46]

Again, emphasis is placed on the fact that the Inquisition is *different.*

Galileo's last attempt to avoid the journey was to send on 17 December a certificate signed by three leading Florentine doctors, who asserted that he was too ill to make the journey. This only served to anger the Inquisition even more. Antonio Barberini wrote to Clemente Egidi in Florence ten days after the letter was sent:

The fact that Galileo Galileii did not immediately obey the order to come to Rome has been very badly accepted by the Congregation of the Holy Office;* and he should not excuse his absence by reference to the season, since it is his fault that the matter has gone this far; and he does very badly to seek to palliate the Holy Office by pretending to be sick, because his Holiness and these eminent Signori do not wish in any way to tolerate such pretences, nor to allow him to avoid coming here: I pray you to tell him that if he does not obey immediately, a Commissario with doctors will be sent to fetch him and to lead him in chains to the prison of this supreme tribunal, since it is clear that he has abused the good will of that Congregation . . .[47]

Once more, Galileo seems to have been responsible for provoking the inquisitors against him.

His protection was, however, sufficient, even after these warnings, for him to be accommodated inside the Palace of the Inquisition and to keep his personal servant with him. Stories of his physical sufferings are grossly exaggerated. Von Gebler showed convincingly that Galileo only spent twenty-two days in the buildings of the Holy Office, 'in the handsome and commodious apartment of an official of the Inquisition', and that he was never tortured but only 'mentally stretched upon the rack'.[48] Sentence was passed on 22 June 1633, and it suggests that he might have avoided the trial by conforming immediately to the desires of the tribunal. After reminding him of his offences with respect to the Inquisition, 'that have greatly aggravated your offence', Galileo was sentenced 'to the formal prison of this Holy Office for as long as we deem necessary; and as a salutary penance we order you to say the seven penitential psalms once a week for three years . . .'.[49]

But Galileo was still no ordinary prisoner. He was allowed to return to Florence and continue working for the rest of his life under house arrest. On 20 March 1638, a letter from the Florentine inquisitor mitigated the sentence to the extent that Galileo was allowed to attend mass at a church near to his home.[50] Thus his difficult relations with the Inquisition eventually came to an end, blind and seventy-four years old, and only four years before his death. Two years earlier he had taken

*The Inquisitor-General, Cardinal Guido Bentivoglio, had been a student of Galileo's in Padua; it is fascinating to speculate what deep-rooted grudges he may have borne towards Galileo (cf. Paschini, *Vita e Opere,* p. 534).

great care in publishing a new book, *Two New Sciences*, in Amsterdam, out of range of the Inquisition's power to prohibit or impede publication. His work was not removed from the Index until 1822.

The spectacle of Galileo abjuring before the tribunal of the Holy Office on his knees, denying the movement of the earth in which he firmly and consistently believed and publicly claiming to curse and detest his 'errors', is a sad one. The falsity of this abjuration is transparent, and must have seemed so to his friends and contemporaries. But too much was against him: 'Not just physics, not merely fundamentalist exegesis, but centuries of acceptance by everyone or nearly everyone, that the sun really moved and the earth did not.'[51] It was possibly Galileo's personality that forced the issue into the open; it seems certain that his personality and consequent provocation of the Inquisition were the reasons behind his humiliating treatment.

At any event, the widely diffused notion that Galileo was condemned for his views on astronomy does not bear careful examination. A recent and carefully documented study by the Italian historian Pietro Redondi, *Galileo Eretico* (1983), has demolished the possibility of holding such a view. His important discovery in the archives of the Roman Inquisition – revealed in an enthralling account of the problems of gaining access to the document, and the consequent detective work involved in interpreting it – of a document containing a secret accusation against Galileo leads to another conclusion, and substantiates the claim of Christoph Grenberger cited above. The real offence of Galileo, according to Redondi's fascinating hypothesis, was to raise the ire of the Jesuits by violating the tridentine dogma of the Eucharist with his atomistic ideas. It was a subtle philosophical issue.

Galileo had violated the fundamental counsel of Father Pereira, expressed in his manual of natural philosophy *De communibus omnium rerum naturalium principiis* (1576), to aim constantly to 'unite philosophy and the scriptures . . . against the modern cunning of modern heretics.'[52] The precise accusation in the document discovered and published by Redondi states that Galileo's atoms were material and his doctrine therefore incompatible with the existence of "Eucharistic accidents" sanctioned by the second canon of the XIIIth session of the

Council of Trent.[53] The philosophical, and theological, issue is as follows:

> An important 'experimental' principal of philosophical and theological value was the miraculous permanence of heat, colour, taste, odour and other sensible accidents of the bread and wine after the consacration which transformed their substance into the body and blood of Christ. If we interpret those accidents, as the *Saggiatore* would have us do, that is with the 'minimum particles' of matter, then even after the consecration they will be particles of the communion bread and produce those sensations.[54]

Thus material particles of bread would be present in the consecrated host: a clearly dangerous doctrine.

Yet Redondi's discovery does not modify the basic argument of this chapter – that Galileo was in an important sense condemned as the result of continued offences against the Inquisition, and *not* for his scientific theories. The two hypotheses sustain one another against the traditional explanation, and it is remarkable to what degree a careful reading of the documents of the case – and the shrewd comments made by Galileo's friends and contemporaries – controverts that explanation. It is also fascinating to recognize the clear echo of the importance of the doctrine of transubstantiation in thirteenth-century inquisitorial trials.

In July 1984 a new edition of trial documents, based on the archives of the Holy Office, the Index and the Vatican Secret Archive, was published (*I Documenti del Processo di Galileo Galilei*, Ed. Sergio M. Pagano, Rome: Pontificia Academia delle Scienze, 1984). Although the full trial transcripts were lost, probably when the Vatican archives were transferred to Paris by Napoleon, this edition contains six previously unpublished decrees of the Inquisition and shows that an anonymous cardinal rather than the Jesuits was responsible for the initial charge against Galileo. The hypothesis outlined in this section remains unaltered by these slight corrections.

In an important sense, which can never diminish his scientific achievement, the trial of Galileo is more fascinating for the insights it provides into the working of the Inquisition. It was again proved to be an efficient, implacable and powerful tribunal of the faith, from whose methodical work and political omnipotence – and from whose secret procedures – no man could escape unscathed once its wrath was aroused. No matter who he was, and what connections he might have.

The Escape of Giuseppe Pignata

Yet prisoners did occasionally manage to flee, and the same implacability is demonstrated by the detailed account that Giuseppe Pignata wrote of his escape from the Inquisition's prison at Rome in 1693. His story also provides unexpected glimpses of prison conditions at the end of the seventeenth century.

Prisoners were gathered together in a large hall for a Congregation of the Visit at the two principal feast days of Christmas and Easter, and Pignata remarks that when his friends met him there during the twenty-two months preceding his sentence they were astonished to see that he had *put on weight*.[55] This suggests that conditions were better than we might otherwise expect, and other observations suggest that extra comforts were readily available for those who could bribe the guards. Pignata was an excellent artist, and was asked to make a portrait of a guard's beloved, whom he had never seen; the result was so good – according to the delighted guard – that he managed to obtain in exchange a penknife.[56]

He then needed to modify the penknife for his task. 'It was the custom', he relates, 'that the first Father Companion of the Inquisitor visited the prisoners every week to see if they lacked anything, and to provide a sad consolation to the poor afflicted with his good words.'[55] One day, Pignata supplicated the Father Companion to give him a girdle for a hernia that he had contracted whilst being tortured. The prison surgeon visited him, and examined Pignata's body where 'by nature I am bigger to one side than to the other'. As a result he obtained a small brazier with which he planned to make a tool to bore through the vaulted ceiling of his cell.

After several months of patient work – balanced on a precarious pile of tables and chairs – he succeeded in making the hole and made an escape with the use of knotted sheets. The story of how he hid from the Inquisition spies who searched all over Rome for him in torrential rain, of his near starvation and terrible exhaustion, makes a minor classic of escape stories. His main concern was to reach the frontier of the Kingdom of Naples, which resolutely defended its territory against incursions by the Inquisition.* Every mountain pass between the Papal States and the Abruzzi region of the Kingdom of Naples was heavily guarded by police and spies. But Pignata, guided by the servant of a loyal friend through a series of traps and narrow escapes, eventually reached a ditch that marked the frontier. Nothing could be more eloquent than Pignata's own description of this event:

> Once on the other side of the ditch, I threw myself to my knees to give thanks to God for having allowed me to set foot in this Canaan that I had so long desired. I kissed and re-kissed the earth a hundred times with my eyes full of tears and my heart full of joy. And Francesco, seeing me, could do nothing else but imitate me. Then I said a *Te Deum*, and we set off.[58]

Pignata's terror belonged to the seventeenth century. Soon afterwards the Roman Inquisition began to lose the immense power it had wielded since the revival instigated by Carafa. There were no more dramatic trials like that of Galileo, and no more spectacular burnings like that of Giordano Bruno. The immediate drama of the Counter-Reformation was forgotten, and the Roman Inquisition gradually declined throughout the eighteenth century – parallel to the decline of the Spanish Inquisition.

Elsewhere in Europe, the forces of the Inquisition in the seventeenth century were mainly concentrated on the persecution of witches.

*Naples had steadfastly resisted the establishment of the new Inquisition. In 1510, the people had rebelled against the news that it was to be introduced by the Spanish rulers. In 1544, Charles V again tried, but the idea was rejected by the Neapolitan nobles – who feared that the vice-regent, Don Pedro of Toledo, would utilize it to suppress his personal enemies and revenge past wrongs. Heretics captured in Naples were sometimes sent to Rome (Pasquale Liberatore, *Della Polizia Ecclesiastica nel Regno delle due Sicilie*, Naples, 1852, pp. 139-140).

11. The Witch Craze and the Inquisition

It has been reliably estimated that between 200,000 and 1,000,000 people, mainly women, died during the witch craze in Europe in the sixteenth and seventeenth centuries.[1] Thus witchcraft, once it had been institutionalized by the Inquisition, was an important element of the history of that period – although with an uneven influence due to the erratic geographical distribution of the phenomenon. But neither the Inquisition itself nor the rapid spread of demonological texts as the result of the invention of printing can explain the huge increase in cases of witchcraft.

The most notable feature of the witch craze is the appearance of the sabbat at the end of the fifteenth century.[2] It is a curious fact that after hundreds of years of sorcery and witchcraft this new and complex element should appear together with the beginnings of modern scientific thought. Hugh Trevor-Roper summarized this remarkable fact:

The merest glance at any report by the acknowledged experts of the time reveals an alarming state of affairs. By their own confession, thousands of old women – and not only old women – had made secret pacts with the Devil, who had now emerged as a great spiritual potentate, the Prince of Darkness, bent on recovering his lost empire. Every night these ill-advised ladies were anointing themselves with 'devil's grease', made out of the fat of murdered infants, and, thus lubricated, were slipping through cracks and keyholes and up chimneys, mounting on broomsticks or spindles or airborne goats, and flying off on a long and inexpressibly wearisome aerial journey to a diabolical rendezvous, the witches' sabbat. In every country there were hundreds of such sabbats, more numerous and more crowded than race-meetings or fairs.[3]

From the first specific reference to a sabbat in 1475,[4] these meetings multiplied until within a century hundreds of sites were known throughout Western Europe. The most fantastic occurrences became accepted as literally true because they were recognized as such by both ecclesiastical and secular tribunals.

The sabbat took place at night, usually at midnight and on a Thursday, although later no particular day was set aside; sites included woods, fields, cemeteries, ruins, and even the interiors of houses or ruined churches. There was no universal form, although a standardized procedure tended to formulate the same questions in trials carried out by the Inquisition, so that the answers – suggested and channelled by the questions – bear a marked similarity and consistency. Once again, Trevor-Roper has presented a vivid picture of what happened when the witch – usually a woman – presented herself at the sabbat:

> First, she was surprised to observe nearly all her friends and neighbours, whom she had not previously suspected to be witches. With them there were scores of demons, their paramours, to whom they bound themselves by the infernal pact; and above all, dominating them all, was the imperious master of ceremonies, the god of their worship, the Devil himself, who sometimes appeared as a big, black, bearded man, more often as a stinking goat, occasionally as a great toad. Those present recognized their master. They all joined to worship the Devil and danced around him to the sound of macabre music made with curious instruments – horses' skulls, oak-logs, human bones, etc. Then they kissed him in homage, under the tail if he were a goat, on the lips if he were a toad. After which, at the word or command from him, they threw themselves into promiscuous sexual orgies or settled down to a feast of such viands as tempted their national imagination.[5]

This factor of national differences was of great importance, for there was never a universal model for the sabbat or any of the other manifestations of the witch craze. Distinctive national styles of witchcraft emerged as the craze went on, especially in those countries where a new and distinct nationalism was developing. Broadly speaking, in England, where the Inquisition did not exist, scholarly research emphasizes *maleficium*, with a virtual absence of full sabbats and devil-worship; in France, the trials of women possessed by the Devil are stressed; in Spain, emphasis was on non-harmful magic of the traditional kind; the sabbat was most pronounced in Germany and Switzerland.

The Inquisition, and the influence of the *Malleus Maleficarum*, significantly emphasized the participation of women in the sabbat. But Monter's observation that, as far as the Jura was concerned, these women 'often had a fund of arcane knowledge of herbs and special formulae which could be used to cure as well as to harm – and perhaps to introduce, in a drugged sleep, some excitement into their monotonous and wretched lives'[6] tends to minimize the possible influence of the Inquisition. Other recent scholars such as Caro Baroja have sought to stress the importance of drugs such as deadly nightshade and henbane* in the witches's concoctions.[7]

The most surprising feature of geographical distribution is the almost total absence of the sabbat and related phenomena in Spain. It appears that the inquisitors there, so ruthless in their pursuit of Jews and Moors, were not easily hoodwinked into accepting the existence of a conspiracy by the Devil. As early as 1526, the *Suprema* ordered an inquiry into witchcraft, deciding that witches reconciled to the Church may have suffered delusions and were not therefore to be handed over to the secular arm.[8] Doubt was even cast on the authority of the *Malleus*. But the most interesting evidence of all was contained in what Charles Williams justly described as 'one of the great documents of the Church',[9] a report made by the Inquisitor Alonzo Salazar de Frias on a potential outbreak of witchcraft in Navarre in 1612. He carried out an extraordinarily accurate examination of the claims of 1,802 people who had confessed under an Edict of Grace. Chemists checked so-called magical ointments, and doctors checked the virginity of women who claimed to have had intercourse with the Devil or demons. It was discovered that a sabbat was supposed to have taken place at

---

*Mental attitudes, prejudices and sympathies clearly condition one's point of view concerning the use of drugs: O. Snell, a doctor, and W. E. Peuckert experimented with traditional unguents. Snell, convinced that witches' tales were the result of mental illness or hysteria, suffered a bad headache; Peuckert, who believed in the reality of the sabbat, had hallucinations identical to those described by witches in their trials (cf. Ginzburg, *I Benandanti*, p. 27, n.).

a site on which the secretaries of the Inquisition were positioned at the same time.

In conclusion, Salazar de Frias wrote: 'I have not found even indications from which to infer that a single act of witchcraft has really occurred, whether as to going to *aquelarres* [i.e., sabbats], being present at them, inflicting injuries, or other of the asserted facts.' Even more remarkably, he went on to argue as follows:

> I also feel certain that, under present conditions, there is no need of fresh edicts or the prolongation of those existing, but rather that, in the diseased state of the public mind, every agitation of the matter is harmful and increases the evil. I deduce the importance of silence and reserve from the experience that there were neither witches nor bewitched until they were talked or written about.[10]

Thus, with this extremely perceptive and intelligent report, the witch craze was truncated in Spain at exactly the moment when it reached its climax elsewhere. Salazar de Frias clearly recognized the detrimental effect of the *Malleus*, and the effect such writings could have on the popular imagination as they filtered through; his lucidity serves as a reminder of the complexity of the Inquisition's role in the history of witchcraft.

He was not alone in expressing such rational views in the midst of the witch craze. Johann Wier, for example, wrote in his *De Praestigiis Daemonum*, published at Basle in 1564, that 'witches were persons whose minds had been deranged and imaginations corrupted by demons, but that they were not responsible for their actions and confessions any more than the insane, and that they were guilty neither of heresy nor entering voluntarily into pacts with the Devil'.[11] It would be possible to argue that in this case the 'demons' were in fact the inquisitors who channelled the thoughts and fears of 'witches' into pre-established responses, and demonologists who produced the ever more sophisticated versions of witchcraft with all their pseudo-intellectual paraphernalia.

The Benandanti

A curious illustration of the way in which the Inquisition managed to manipulate the minds of people is provided by Carlo Ginzburg's account of the *Benandanti* of Friuli, in north-eastern Italy.

In 1575 a strange fertility cult came to the notice of the Franciscan inquisitor of the Diocese of Aquileia, Brother Giulio d'Assisi. A man called Paolo Gasparutto explained to him the existence of certain unusual witches 'who are good, called vagabonds and in their language *benandanti*', 'who prevent evil' in contrast to other witches.[12] The *benandanti*, literally 'those who walk well, or go well', are presented from the beginning as a harmless sect; there is no mention of the Devil, although some features of their behaviour vaguely reminded the inquisitor of the sabbat. Their activities consisted in 'fighting, playing, leaping, and riding various animals', while the women 'beat the men accompanying them – who held bunches of fennel in their hands – with millet branches'.[13] This ceremony represented a battle between the *benandanti* and the witches, and took place four times a year on the Thursdays that fell between Ember Days.* The battle was described as taking place in spirit, and not in the body; but at first the inquisitor did not accept the existence of these agrarian rites, and as the result of the scepticism of a local nobleman the *benandanti* were forgotten for five years.

When he was interrogated again by the new inquisitor, Brother Felice da Montefalco, in 1580, Paolo Gasparutto affirmed that he too had forgotten about his previous declarations and strongly denied having heard of 'Lutherans' in his area. The inquisitor imprisoned him as the result of continual denials. Another *benandante* was found, and he indicated in his confession the true nature of the sect: Battista Moduco claimed that he went to the meetings to defend the faith of Christ, that he did not know any heretics, and that their fights with the witches were important because 'if we win, that year will have a good harvest, and if we lose there will be shortages'.[14] He claimed that there were sometimes as many as 5,000 present at these meetings, but his evidence clearly suggested the simple survival of a widespread and perhaps ancient fertility cult. It existed in the areas of Verona, Vicenza and Gorizia in addition to Moduco's own area.

Then a gradual transformation of this harmless sect began.

*The 1095 Council of Placentia appointed as Ember Days the Wednesday, Friday and Saturday which followed the first Sunday of Lent, Pentecost, the 14th of September, and the 13th of December or Advent (*OED*; Ginzburg, *I Benandanti*, p. 4). These four periods of fasting and prayer (the *quatuor tempora*) correspond to the four seasons.

Under further interrogation in the Inquisition's prison at Udine, Gasparutto invented the story of an angel coated in gold who had told him to go with the *benandanti*.[15] This new feature, possibly invented by the frightened prisoner to escape the unpleasant situation into which he found himself being precipitated, had the opposite effect to that intended. It alerted the inquisitor: here was a patent suggestion of diabolism, and a hypothetical link between the games of the *benandanti* and the activities of a sabbat.

The time gap between the two interrogations was three months, from 28 June to 24 September 1580. From the moment of that fatal invention the inquisitor, who had previously listened passively to Gasparutto's stories, began to take an active interest in the questioning – steering the questions so that the prisoner's replies conformed with a pre-established thesis. Ginzburg comments:

> The inquisitor had managed to divert Gasparutto's testimony into his own patterns and theological co-ordinates: the meetings of the *benandanti* and witches were nothing but a sabbat, and the 'society' of *benandanti* was itself diabolical, even though it falsely claimed to be under divine protection and to fight with the help of an angel. In the face of the inquisitor's ever more pressing demands Gasparutto's certainty seems to vacillate, as if the reality in which he believed had suddenly changed its aspect and slipped from his grasp. Some days later he would declare to Brother Felice: 'I believe that the apparition of the angel was the devil who tempted me, since you have told me that he can transform himself into an angel.'[16]

The transcripts published by Ginzburg provide fascinating proof of the thesis that inquisitors channelled testimony to their own ends: 'I believe that the apparition of the angel was the devil ... since *you have told me* ...'.

Gasparutto was no match for the wiles of Brother Felice, and slid into further trouble as the trial proceeded. It ended with a relatively light sentence of six months imprisonment and a series of penances; but in the trial of another *benandante*, Toffolo di Buri, in 1583, the suspect affirmed that the *benandanti* also combatted witches who 'with the art of the Devil eat the flesh of little children',[17] so that they could be perceived as opposing witchcraft. The Inquisition had however established by that time that the sect existed, that it was governed by a 'captain' with a pseudo-military organization, that both men and women were enrolled at about the age of twenty, and that they could leave after a period of between ten and twenty years.

From the time of these early trials until about 1620 no further trials of the *benandanti* were brought to a conclusion, and there was a strange truce created by mutual incomprehension between them and their inquisitorial opponents – who were fully occupied with outbreaks of Lutheranism. But new features slowly appeared, and by the beginning of the century it was accepted that the *benandanti* were able to recognize witches and cure the evils they brought about. This was an almost certain indication that they were themselves witches – from the Inquisition's point of view.

The process was slow. It was not until 1634, after a series of 850 trials and charges made to the Inquisition at Aquileia and Concordia, that the sabbat was first mentioned.[18] But the end result was remarkable: people who in 1610 opposed witchcraft and fought against local witches had by 1640 become fully-fledged witches themselves. The trial of a *benandante* called Giovanni Sion in 1634 produced a detailed description of participation at a sabbat that 'corresponded in general outline to that recurrent in all the demonological treatises'.[19] Sion asserted the reality of his involvement in the sabbat and stressed his physical participation, describing the unguents used beforehand and naming other witches present. No clearer example exists of what Kieckhefer called the 'imposition of learned notions' on popular culture by the Inquisition.

The trial of another *benandante* called Michele Soppe in 1649 is even more detailed and explicit.[20] In response to the inquisitor's demand whether he had made a pact with the Devil, Soppe replies simply: 'Yes, Sir.' He admits to having renounced God, and kneeling to worship the Devil in the form of an ass. With the Devil's help he had entered houses in the form of a cat and murdered children; he provides the macabre details of how he sucked up their blood with 'diabolical art'.[21] Thus the *benandanti* had turned full circle from witch-hunters to witches. Jeffrey Burton Russell has observed that 'No firmer bit of evidence has ever been presented that witchcraft existed, that it was largely the product of elements of folk belief and practice, and that the role of the Inquisition was not to invent witchcraft, but to impose upon others its own definition of witchcraft.'[22] As the reality of witchcraft had previously been 'proved' by the free use of torture during interrogations,* in the case of the *benandanti* it had been imposed on a numerous sect in the course of half a century.

But the *Benandanti* did not suffer the same persecutions as witches in other parts of Europe. Trials were lengthy and incomplete, and sentences were usually confined to brief imprisonment and penances. The good sense of inquisitors in Spain was beginning to make itself felt in Rome. In the case of Michele Soppe, Cardinal Francesco Barberini – nephew of Urban VIII – wrote to the inquisitor at Aquileia: 'Reverend Father, the crimes of Michele Soppe are extremely serious, but the most severe sentence cannot be passed against him unless the bodies of the children he claims to have killed are found.'[23] The Cardinal went on with words taken from the 1620 tract *Instructio pro formandus processibus in causis strigum malficiorum et sortilegiorum*, which contained a series of instructions on how to proceed against witches based on the opinions of Salazar de Frias. This *Instructio,* which was published in 1655, insisted on the need for medical examinations to prove the reality of crimes supposed to have been committed by witches. Its wide influence in seventeenth-century Italy helps to explain the relatively light treatment of the *benandanti* and also the sharp decline in witch trials in the second half of the century.

Who were the witches?

We have seen how the Inquisition was involved in the institutionalization of witchcraft in the late fifteenth century, and how it was capable of creating witchcraft where it did not exist by means of torture, clever questioning and psychological pressure. It is equally important to understand the practical effects of inquisitorial activity by asking two further questions: who were the witches, and what were the effects of this persecution on European society?

As Richard A. Horsley has pointed out, 'although professional historians of witchcraft are aware that the official concept of

---

*The case of Nicolas Remy is curious. This zealous inquisitor became so obsessed with magic and witches that he wished to start a crusade against them. In the end, he convinced himself that *he* was a witch and died at the stake on the basis of his own imagined confessions (Reviglio, *L'Inquisizione,* p. 47; cf. Williams, *Witchcraft,* pp. 255-6).

witchcraft was a composite theory formulated out of elements originally pagan but transformed by Christian theological and ecclesiastical interests, they nevertheless fail to distinguish adequately between the official *theory* and the popular realities'.[24] The popular reality was that throughout Europe certain classes of people were commonly considered to be 'witches' of some kind: sociological analyses provided by Monter and Midelfort go some way towards explaining this aspect of the reality of witchcraft, elaborating the thesis that the three categories of sorcerers, folk doctors and wise women, involving cases of jealousy or anger, were behind most charges of witchcraft in Europe up to about 1500. But it is difficult to go beyond such vague staements because definitions and materials vary from place to place. Horsley himself concludes of Austria that 'there is apparently little popular terminological basis for a clear designation of a concept of witchcraft'.[25]

In a chapter on the sociology of witchcraft in the Jura, Monter has provided an analysis of 99 people, 91 women and 8 men, who were executed in Geneva during a small panic in 1571-1572.[26] This offers some precise indications: of the 91 women, 45 were widows and 14 spinsters. More interesting is the break-down of occupations for the 8 men, and the husbands or fathers of the women executed: 14 were labourers, 4 pinmakers, 2 fishermen, 3 carpenters, 2 masons, and 1 each of tailor, passementier, needlemaker, servant, sergemaker, locksmith, ironworker and packer. This substantiates the observation of Thomas that in England the witches were 'poor and usually women'.[27] Monter himself concludes that witchcraft was a magical means of revenge for real or imagined injuries received by people of these social classes: 'If we began by emphasising how often these accused witches were elderly widows or spinsters, we can argue that witchcraft accusations can best be understood as projections of patriarchal social fears onto atypical women, those who lived apart from the direct male control of husbands or fathers. These defenceless and very isolated women became the group most often exposed to charges of witchcraft.'[28]

The social fear sometimes led to the extinction of entire families of women. Luisa Muraro gives the example of Anna Maria Sertora, tried and burned by the Inquisition at Poschiavo in 1675. Nearly three years before, her mother had been executed, and quite probably her cousin – who was tried, although her sentence is missing in the records. In the same year, 1673, an aunt of hers was tried and exiled, and her grandmother had been burned for witchcraft in 1630.[29] The female side of Anna Maria's family therefore represented a real dynasty of witches, at least in the eyes of the local inquisitors.

The percentages of female witches are given by both Monter and Midelfort. In his study of large witch-hunts in south-western Germany, Midelfort lists both men and women executed: in six witch-hunts before 1627, 87 per cent of executed witches were women; in nine hunts after 1627, a slightly lower figure of 76 per cent was recorded.[30] In Monter's wider statistical survey these figures were confirmed: of 5,402 accused witches in England, Castile, Belgium, Finland, Venice, France and Switzerland that he gathered from sixteen samples, the average percentage of women is 78 per cent.[31] Perhaps more interesting is the revelation that the male witches were usually either old and handicapped, ordinary criminals, relatives of female witches, or combinations of all three categories.[32]

The anthropological concept of witchcraft as a 'social strain gauge' appears to be useful in explaining this concentration of relatively poor women and socially handicapped men. It also meets the requirement of dealing with witchcraft as an essentially local or family problem. Marwick's contention that the relationship between accuser and witch is nearly always much closer than that between witch and victim seems as pertinent in the context of medieval European witchcraft as it does in its original Oceanic context. He discerns 'a means of detecting the tension-points of a social structure by the frequency with which attacks of witchcraft and sorcery are believed to occur between persons standing in various relationships'.[33] Fears of socially indigestible groups such as unmarried women created such a 'tension-point', and Midelfort shows how during the Thirty Years War it was the soldier who bore the brunt of social hatred in place of the witch.[34]

Following the period of the War, in the 1630s, there was in fact a gradual decline in the number of witch-hunts. The fact that 'witches' disappeared when the tensions of sixteenth-century Europe began to diminish suggests that they had never really existed. A recent survey of scholarly research on witchcraft by Horsley concludes that 'some, but not many of those tried for witchcraft were sorceresses' and that a 'substantial number of the witches were wise women'.[35] It was on the traditional healers such as wise women and midwives that the full weight of the accusations fell. Horsley goes on: 'It becomes increasingly clear that the realities of popular life and belief do not accord at all with the official concept of witchcraft. The victims of the witch-hunts were *not witches* in the sense of the official demonologists' definition, although once subjected to torture many victims may have come to believe in the witch-hunters's definition of themselves as night-flying witches in pact with Satan.'[36]

Many witches were simply social outcasts, quarrelsome or eccentric old women who were unfairly treated as the result of the misogynistic tendencies of demonologists – first and foremost Henry Kramer. Left alone, peasant societies would never have engendered a 'witch craze'. For centuries the wise women and other healers who worked on the frontiers of magic had existed side by side with the Church even in moments of great tension – plagues, wars, imbalance in population. Intellectual explanations of the witch craze as related to the fortunes of a world view, or the idea of witchcraft as the world mirrored in reverse, seem to be as far from the everyday practice of peasant society as the contemporary learned cultures that lay parallel to them.[37] The only safe generalization is that witchcraft was an immensely complex and varied phenomenon that can really only be understood within small geographical areas and strict limits of time. Norman Cohn remarked in a review of Monter's *Witchcraft in France and Switzerland* that notwithstanding its merits and scholarship the author 'seems hardly to realise how extraordinary the whole business was – and not only by the standards of today but by the standards of any century before the fifteenth'.[38]

What was the responsibility of the Inquisition? We have already seen its importance in developing and honing the concept of witchcraft, and to what an extent inquisitorial procedure changed the course of witch trials in the fifteenth century. Horsley has gone much further in interpreting this influence:

With the institution of the inquisitorial procedure and the conduct of extensive witch trials by secular and ecclesiastical officials, the people's witch beliefs were transformed into a highly effective means of social control. The peasants' witch beliefs thus became functional – if by no means therapeutic – in an utterly different, almost opposite way. Through a period of great tensions, as Europe made the difficult transition from one economic-political system to another, the peasants were induced, through the witch trials, to blame much of their malaise on their local witches and were able to rid themselves of social elements which appeared burdensome or troublesome.[39]

In providing the procedure and much of the manpower for the witch-hunts, the Inquisition clearly bears much of the responsibility. But as a release of social strain witchcraft reached its peak at the maximum moment of wrenching between a medieval world-view and that of a recognizably modern Europe, between the years 1570 and 1630. For this, the Inquisition is only partly to blame.

Furthermore, after the Reformation witch-hunting did not remain the preserve of the Catholic Church. In Hugh Trevor-Roper's words, 'If the Catholic evangelists had launched the craze, the Protestant evangelists would soon revive and extend it.'[40] Protestants adopted the demonology elaborated by the Inquisition and took it with them as they moved through northern Europe. The witch-hunts also occurred where there was no Inquisition, for instance in England. Luther, Zwingli and Calvin believed in the sabbat and night-flights as firmly as any fifteenth-century inquisitor. Yet, without making the error of equating coincidence with causality, it is undeniably true that the decline of the European Witch Craze coincided with the decline of the Inquisition in the eighteenth century.

12. The Apotheosis and Decline of the Spanish Inquisition: 1558–1834

The Spanish Inquisition expanded rapidly as the power of Spain grew. In the Kingdom of Sicily it began operations in 1487 with a Dominican inquisitor, Antonio la Pegna, who was personally chosen by Torquemada. The first Sicilian *auto de fe* took place on 18 August of that year,[1] but from the beginning there were many complaints about methods used to extract confessions and also against familiars.[2] Unsalaried inspectors were forced to make their living from the proceeds of confiscations. After three *autos* in which thirty-five people were burned in August and September of 1513, the Sicilian parliament made a vigorous protest.[3] The proximity of the island to Rome was also problematical: Torquemada's successor as Inquisitor-General, Diego Deza, counselled King Ferdinand to ensure that the Inquisition in Sicily was not left under the authority of Rome.[4] From the end of Spanish dominion of Malta, in 1550, the nuncio-inquisitor there was required by papal order to observe at close hand what the Spanish Inquisition was doing in Sicily.[5] The office of inquisitor in Sicily was considered a stepping-stone to future promotion within the Spanish ecclesiastical hierarchy; many Sicilian inquisitors – there were usually three based in Palermo – later became bishops, and some became Cardinals.

But in Sicily, as in Naples, the people were not afraid to protest. When Ferdinand died in 1516 they rose up against the Vice-Regent and inquisitors, and dispatched an ambassador to

the future Emperor Charles V – then in Flanders – to request
the suppression of the Inquisition in Sicily. Charles replied with
a firm letter soliciting 'the restitution of the said Holy Office in
this realm . . .'.[6] He even wrote directly to the Pope that the
Holy See should not accept complaints about the Inquisition in
Sicily, but should forward them to the Inquisitor-General in
Spain. This zeal was followed by a series of seventeen *autos de fe*
between 1519 and 1534. The maximum period of activity in the
long history of the Sicilian Inquisition was in fact from 1527 to
1529 – when Charles V sacked Rome and laid his claim to the
Roman Church as Holy Roman Emperor.

Under Philip II (1556-1598) the Sicilian Inquisition
continued to function regularly, but with smaller and less
frequent *autos*; from 1586 the Inquisitor was Louis de Paramo, a
Dominican and author of a history of the Inquisition that has
already been cited. But in the seventeenth century it functioned
only spasmodically and the number of prisoners was small.
While in Spain the Inquisition achieved its apotheosis under
Charles II (1665-1700), with the great ceremonial *autos-de-fe* in
Madrid, in Sicily it was almost inactive. The Sicilian Inquisition
was finally abolished in 1782, and some idea of its overall activity
can be gleaned from La Mantia's lists of trials, *autos*, and
inquisitors from 1487 to 1782: in that period, 189 people were
burned at the stake, and 263 burned in effigy.[7] These figures are
fairly typical of Inquisitions beyond the Iberian peninsula.

Soon after the Sicilian Inquisition was established, Ferdinand
tried to introduce one into Sardinia, and in 1505 succeeded in
setting up a permanent tribunal in the Canary Islands – which
had previously come under the jurisdiction of Seville.[8] Many
Jewish fugitives had gone to the Canaries in 1492, and had
created new lives for themselves on an island where the distant
Inquisition did not appear to bother about them. As so often in
the history of the Inquisition, it was the arrival of a single,
particularly zealous and energetic inquisitor at Las Palmas in
1569 that ended this relative calm. He busily sought out
relapsed Moslems and Jews, although much of his work involved
cases of blasphemy and witchcraft. But the Inquisition in the
Canaries echoed its parent organization on the mainland in
persecuting English, Dutch and Flemish heretics.[9] Most were
willing to abjure their Protestant faith in order to escape the
stake, but one man, George Gaspar, refused and was burned

alive in an *auto-de-fe* in 1587.[10] Others were tortured, boats were burned, and the conditions of the prison at Las Palmas became proverbial in English accounts of the Spanish Inquisition.

More important in the long term was the introduction of the Inquisition into Portugal. The people of Lisbon had spontaneously followed the Spanish Inquisition's lead when they executed more than 2,000 Jews in 1506, and King John II of Portugal obtained permission for an independent Inquisition to be founded in 1536 with a Grand Inquisitor and four Inquisitors-Major. It was suspended in 1544 by papal order, but restored in 1548 with offices in Oporto, Coimbra, Lomego, Tomar, Evona and Lisbon. But the story of the Portuguese Inquisition changed dramatically when Philip II of Spain conquered Portugal in 1580. The Spanish Inquisition was established as a parallel institution, with the curious result that Jews who had previously escaped from Spain now attempted to return to the more powerful and richer country – where the Inquisition now concentrated its attention on other matters.[11] In Portugal, fresh zeal stimulated persecutions of a kind which were by then only memories for Spanish exiles.

During the reign of Philip II, in 1571, the Inquisition was also established in Mexico. There, as in the Canaries, many of the victims were foreign travellers, merchants and sailors; the public flogging of such English pirates as Sir John Hawkins and his crew, captured in 1567, was popular with the Spanish inhabitants.* But the Mexican Inquisition continued to function well into the nineteenth century, and it exercised an important political function at the time of the Mexican War of Independence from 1808 to 1815. Miguel Hidalgo, one of the leaders in the fight for independence, was the victim of brutal political repression. He was accused of a series of absurdly contradictory charges – such as being a deist and an atheist, a Jew and a Protestant – and then sentenced in his absence with no chance of defending himself. In 1811 he was eventually captured, and immediately executed.[12] Another revolutionary

---

*John Martin, one of Hawkins' crew and known as "the unluckiest man in the English fleet", was garrotted and burned at the second *auto-de-fe* in Mexico City on 6 March 1575 (see Hair, *An Irishman before the Mexican Inquisition*, p. 298).

leader, Morelos, was deprived of his holy orders and accused of being a follower of Hobbes and Voltaire – the bugbears of the Spanish Inquisition at this time. Once so deprived, he was handed over to the secular authorities for trial.

The whole of Spanish South America came under the control of the Inquisition when a tribunal was established in Lima in 1570, with jurisdiction both in Peru and the rest of the continent. As work increased a subsidiary tribunal was set up in 1610 at Cartagena in Colombia with jurisdiction over New Granada – which included Colombia and present-day Venezuela. But these two South American tribunals were never as active as those in Spain itself: the real task of the Spanish Inquisition remained the suppression and control of Jews and Moors in Spain, with the important adjunct of Portugal.[13]

Examples of popular refusal of the Inquisition were fairly common in Europe. The example of Sicily was echoed with greater success in nearby Naples, where – as we have seen – the population rose in revolt three times against the imposition of the tribunal over them. At the same time, the Inquisition never succeeded in entering successfully into the Duchy of Milan, except for brief and zealous periods. Similarly, attempts to force Catholic supremacy in the Low Countries under Philip II led to violent protests and revolts against the Inquisition.* Protestant forces in Flanders demanded the suppression of the Inquisition there in 1566, and the end of public advertisement against heresy.[14]

Later, as the result of personal enmity between Charles VI, Emperor of Austria, and Philip V of Spain, a new tribunal completely independent of Spain was set up in Vienna, in 1724. Pope Clement XI issued a bull which brought the Inquisition in Sicily under the jurisdiction of this new Supreme Tribunal of Vienna – and Austrian inquisitors and officials for a time exercised their powers in Sicily.[15] This curious episode underlines yet again the openly and often contradictorily political nature of the Spanish Inquisition.

Thus the Inquisition was active throughout the Spanish-speaking world, and made attempts to impose itself on other countries where non-Spanish cultural influences were an

---

*The medieval Inquisition had functioned there from 1232 to 1519. See list of inquisitors in Fredericq, *Corpus Documentorum*, pp. xxxviii-xlviii.

impediment. In triple dress, it functioned as a repressive instrument, a political tool in the hands of the Spanish Kings, and as a bulwark of Catholic faith at a time of great crisis in the Christian world. Much of the complexity of the history of the Spanish Inquisition derives from cases where these three separate functions were enmeshed and confused. Nevertheless it should be remembered that it was never as important or powerful elsewhere as it was on the Iberian peninsula. As the Cathars remained for centuries the *bête noire* of the medieval Inquisition, so the presence of Jews and Moors in Spain remained the primary target of the Spanish Inquisition.

The Censorship of Books and Ideas

As the Inquisition set up an efficient network of repression throughout the Spanish Empire, it also created a kind of *cordon sanitaire* around the Kingdom of Spain. The most effective weapon in this cordon was the censorship of the written word, which was exercised in Spain by its own Inquisition independently of the Congregation of the Index in Rome. As authoritative a person as Alphonso de Castro, chaplain to Philip II, firmly believed that Spain's freedom from heresy was due to the successful prohibition of heretical literature – in contrast to the situation in France, Italy and southern Germany.[16]

The burning of books had been practised on a grand scale in Spain before the existence of an Index. At Salamanca in 1490 more than 6,000 volumes on sorcery and magic had been burned, and in the same year large quantities of Hebrew bibles were destroyed at Seville.[17] But these were spontaneous reactions, and the Inquisition was not at first required to deal with books; Isabella had in fact removed a 10 per cent tax on books called the *alcavada* when she founded the Inquisition.[18] In 1502 a new law concerning the examination and licensing of printed books was introduced in response to a new awareness of their efficacy in spreading ideas. There was ample evidence that books were being printed in Spanish in Germany and then imported illegally; thus all books printed or imported without licence were to be burned.[19] From 1521, Lutheran works were banned, and by the 1540s the Inquisition had a 'rough unofficial Index of its own'.[20] Spanish versions of other Indices appeared during the same decade.

Thoroughgoing censorship of books in Spain began with the

Pragmatic Sanction of 1558, issued a year before the first Roman Index by the Infanta Juana in the name of the absent Philip II. This sanction provided a strict procedure for the censorship of books, and for obtaining licences to print. It was a savage decree: manuscripts were to be checked before and after printing, and booksellers were obliged to display a catalogue of banned books in their shops. The death penalty was specified for the possession of any book condemned by the Inquisition and for the importation of unlicensed books. This decree remained the basis of censorship in Spain until the nineteenth century; as late as 1804 it was insisted that the decree be strictly enforced.[21]

In 1559 Spain declared its autonomy in the matter of issuing licences for readers, and the Inquisition issued instructions on how readers were to be chosen. Permission was given for a specific number of banned books, but even the most highly recommended reader could not obtain a licence for certain authors; in later centuries these included Rousseau, Montesquieu, Mirabeau, Diderot, d'Alambert and Voltaire.[22] Licences were given to scholars so that they could refute heretical ideas, but the life, character and ideas of applicants were checked carefully before they were issued. The only category of reader that was considered automatically eligible was that of inquisitors and bishops. Llorente describes the procedure of selection as follows:

> In Spain the inquisitor obtained secret information on the applicant's conduct, the opinion that was generally held of his manner of discussing religious questions, and his care in fulfilling his duties as a Christian; and even if these reports were favourable to him, it was still difficult to obtain permission to read, and above all to look at banned books. If the inquisitor were favourable, the applicant was invited to provide a written justification for his soliciting of this privilege, on what matter he wished to consult the banned books, what kind of work he proposed to read, and the reasons which had led him to engage in such studies.[23]

The 1559 list of prohibited books 'came out during the high-tide of heresy in Europe, and was consequently directed against heretical works and translations of the Bible in particular'.[24] It implied increased activity at the *Inquisición de los Puertos del Mar*, at the Spanish sea ports, which became busy with careful searches of foreign ships in an attempt to prevent book smuggling. From 1566 the *visitas de navios*, during which commissioners of the Inquisition boarded ships at anchor in Spanish ports to search for banned literature, began to have a negative effect on commercial operations. Pauline Croft has made a study of this part of the inquisitors' task at the port of Seville:

> English books were thought to be entering Spain in 1569 although the tribunal at Seville insisted to the *Suprema* that searches for such literature were conducted with impeccable thoroughness. In 1576 there were suspicions that 'Lutheran' books were being re-exported to Spain from Barbary, while seven years later a diplomatic agent abroad warned the Inquisition of the smuggling of heretical works from Flanders, formerly a major centre of Spanish book production. During the war, the tales in circulation grew even more grandiose; the tribunal reported that it had heard that 45,000 books printed in Holland and Zealand were being steadily infiltrated into Spain, a story that was still current in 1603.[25]

As was to be expected, this intense activity produced absurd and even grotesque results from time to time. An Englishman called Massey and two friends aboard the *Red Lion*, which arrived at Seville in 1575, were sentenced to seven years imprisonment as the result of Massey's possession of a prayerbook entitled *The Treasury of Gladness*.[26]

Further important Indices were issued in 1583 and 1584, with the accumulated expertise of thirty years of censorship. The *cordon sanitaire* was perfected so that it virtually cut Spain off from foreign ideas and influence. Books in Portuguese, German and Flemish were added to the lists. The organization was incredible: a corrector-general collated printed books with manuscripts, with delegates performing the same task in the provinces. The smallest pamphlet of a few words was subjected to the same scrupulous attention as a famous heretical work, and huge numbers of books were burned once judgement had been passed against them. There was an established tradition: Cardinal Ximénez was said to have burned over a million volumes during his campaign to convert the Moors at Granada.[27] Torquemada himself organized a book-burning in his monastery of St Stephen of Salamanca, and similar ceremonies continued throughout the sixteenth century. Book-shops and private libraries were expurgated of prohibited volumes with a zeal that far exceeded the work of the Roman Index. The manpower of the Inquisition increased as such searches intensified towards the end of the century; book production and bookselling suffered rapidly rising costs as the result of constant fines and taxes. Printing was threatened with extinction, and 'learned Spaniards deterred from writing'.[28]

Henry Lea cites an astonishing episode of the Inquisition's thoroughness in a later century. In 1794 a book was published in Philadelphia, and on 24 October of the same year a prohibition order reached Mexico City. Four months later, on 15 February 1795, a priest called Father Feliciano Menenses y Rejon signed in Yucatan a certificate in which he stated that he had read the prohibition to his congregation. With justifiable irony, Lea comments that he had warned 'his little congregation of Indians and half-breeds not to read the dangerous book', and to surrender any copies in their possession.[29] The entire apparatus of one of the most efficient institutions in the Western world was fully occupied with this immense task for centuries, and the work involved is almost inconceivable: as a final example, a single inquisitor spent eight hours a day for four months carrying out the expurgation of a private library.[30]

Various systems of classification were propounded by successive Indices. From 1558 to 1612, for instance, works were divided into the two classes of Latin and vernacular books. Authors banned in the Latin list included Boccaccio and Rabelais, and works considered heretical such as the writings of Tyndale, Latimer, Zwingli, Hus, Abelard, Dante's *Monarchia*, Thomas Cranmer, Machiavelli's *Discourses*, More's *Utopia*, and the works of Cardinal Pole. Spanish works included the translation of Ovid's *Art of Love*, and of Machiavelli. The 1612 Index introduced a classification which divided prohibited works into three categories: authors, all of whose works were banned; single books, classified by author; and anonymous works. The entire corpus of banned books was printed in a single large volume, the *Index librorum prohibitorum et expurgatorum*. Some examples: the first category included Erasmus, Rabelais, Savonarola and Macchiavelli; the second category had Dante's *De Monarchia* and three short passages from the *Divine Comedy* that were to be expurgated, the *Decameron* and Ariosto's *Orlando Furioso*.

Books were constantly added to the Index in supplements, but none was removed. A snowballing effect led to ever larger Indices, and the great editions of 1632 and 1640 superseded earlier editions. The works of Bacon were added to the first category, and Petrarch was to be expurgated – an illustration of the fact that fresh prohibitions were not restricted to contemporary works but could reach backwards into literary history. Apuleius's *Golden Ass* was prohibited, but the works of Kepler and Tycho Brahe were allowed after minor cuts. The most curious episode of the 1640 Index was the removal of a single sentence from Cervantes's *Don Quixote*. It was the apparently innocuous sentence: 'Works of charity performed negligently have neither merit nor value',* taken from Chapter 32 of the Second Part. Although this excision, in Lea's words, 'finds an explanation in the war which the Inquisition was waging against the mystics',[32] there is something bordering on the fastidiously insane in the cutting of fourteen words from a novel of nearly a thousand printed pages. It demonstrates the extent to which potentially dangerous literature had been banned or expurgated by 1640, since there would not have been time for such minor corrections if this were not the case. But the existence of *Don Quixote* also proves that great literature could be written even within the strict conditions of censorship imposed by the Inquisition.

The Spanish Index was more successful in preventing the circulation of foreign books. A supplement published in 1805 banned the works of Pope, Sterne, Adam Smith's *The Wealth of Nations* and Burke's *Reflections on the Revolution in France*.[33] If these names are added to the French authors of the Enlightenment cited above, it will be clear how the Inquisition influenced intellectual life in Spain. The force that produced the great Spanish culture of the sixteenth and seventeenth centuries was entirely nourished from within, and it was that dearth of fresh stimulus that brought the so-called Golden Age to an end. Censorship existed in other countries, but 'nowhere was the imposition of orthodoxy so effective and complete as in the one country where an institution of international dimensions devoted its entire resources to the task'.[34]

Preventive persecution

A subsidiary weapon of the Inquisition in maintaining the *cordon*

'Las obras de charidad que se hazen flaxamente, no tienen merito ni valen nada.'

sanitaire was the persecution of foreigners in person. This was practised at all sea ports on the Spanish coast, and also at important river ports. In Andalucia full-time commissioners, or *comisarios*, received expenses from the Inquisition and often a gratuity on retirement for observing local foreign residents and visiting seamen. These *comisarios* were assisted by familiars and translators, and every four months inquisitors from Seville visited them to check on their work.[35] The English communities were divided between permanent residents – often married to Spanish women – visiting seamen, and young factors gaining experience with merchants before returning to work in London. But this situation was complicated by refugee English and Irish Catholics who had fled the equally fierce persecutions of Elizabeth I; they often worked as translators and interpreters for the Inquisition, and were therefore in ideal positions 'to pursue private vendettas against their countrymen with impunity'.[36]

In 1575, Sir Henry Cobham was sent as ambassador to Philip II to improve conditions for English merchants, in particular with regard to goods confiscated by the Inquisition:[37] In the following year he reached an agreement with the Spanish king which absolved visiting seamen from compulsory church attendance, and provided protection against the Inquisition as long as they did not openly offend the tribunal. But abuses against Englishmen continued and further protests by Sir Henry were of no use since the king by that time had no authority over the Inquisition.

Few Englishmen suffered the full consequences of arrest by the Inquisition. Between 1558 and 1585 only thirty-three were tried by the tribunal of Seville, which was Spain's largest port. From the time of Cobham's agreement the numbers dropped: it seems that they were inflated by means of hyperbole on the part of the Inquisition itself, and by virulent anti-Spanish propaganda by English authors at the time of the attempted invasion of England by the Armada. When war broke out the numbers again increased, but still only fifty-seven Englishmen were imprisoned by the Inquisition at Seville between 1585 and 1604. Most of these cases were for minor instances of 'lack of respect' by visiting seamen. Residents had learned the rules essential for avoiding unpleasant involvement with the Inquisition, but there were many examples like that of the sailor at San Lucar in 1585, 'who on being asked to kiss a model of the baby Jesus, did so with the jesting remark that it was of no more significance than kissing a wall'.[38]

Ships' crews often found themselves in trouble for committing offences that they could not imagine as existing: the entire crew of the *Emmanuel Ede* was imprisoned when the ship's carpenter failed to take his hat off as the Sacrament was carried past him as he worked on board.[39] The *comisarios* went on board to find out whether Protestant services had been performed, which they obviously had been since they were obligatory. Books were confiscated, sailors were arrested. Henry Gottersum, the cook of the *Elizabeth* that anchored at Puerto de Santa Maria in 1574, was burned alive for admitting that he was a convinced Protestant. But it was more common for convicted Englishmen to serve their prison terms in the galleys. Pauline Croft comments: 'On occasion, the imprisonment term was for life, but despite Elizabethan propaganda and popular belief, the death penalty by burning was rarely inflicted. Six Englishmen are recorded as having been relaxed at Seville in the sixteenth century . . .'.[40] She suggests that it was the secretiveness of the Inquisition, widespread fear of it, and the ubiquitousness of the familiars that gave rise to exaggerated accounts of huge numbers of prisoners burned and imprisoned.

In the seventeenth century, arrests of Englishmen declined – especially after it was decreed that the Inquisition itself should bear the costs of searching ships rather than the ships themselves. The ferocity with which the Inquisition expurgated and burned books was a more efficient method of isolating the country, with no danger of diplomatic protest. Propaganda distorted the truth, yet these controls and the legends they created were themselves part of the Inquisition's armoury in maintaining the *cordon sanitaire*.

The Persecution of Freemasons

In the sixteenth century, the battle against foreign heretics was conducted against the Lutherans, and any sect that propagated similar heretical doctrines was quickly eliminated. Later opponents included the Jansenists, particular adversaries of the Jesuits, and the Inquisition continued to work against them even after the Jesuits were expelled from Spain in 1767 for their opposition to Charles III.[41] Ideas emanating from France under the aegis of the Enlightenment were ruthlessly expunged.

When Freemasonry began a rapid expansion in the 1730s, with new Lodges being established all over Europe, it generated a scare within the Catholic Church almost equal to that created by the Cathars centuries before. In Rome, on 28 April 1738, Pope Clement XII issued a decree against Freemasons that was published by the inquisitor Peter Romolatius. Its full title was *The Condemnation of the Society or Conventicles* De Liberi Muratori, *or of the Freemasons, under the penalty of* ipso facto *Excommunication, the Absolution of which is reserved to the Pope alone, except at the point of death.* In this decree Freemasons are picturesquely described as men who 'break as thieves into the house, and, like foxes, endeavour to root up the vineyard',[42] in an almost biblical language that signified that they represented a serious threat to the hegemony of the Catholic Church. The decree continues:

> We will moreover and command, that as well bishops and superior prelates, and other ordinaries of particular places, as the inquisitors of heretical depravity universally deputed, of what state, degree, condition, order, dignity, or pre-eminence soever, proceed and inquire, and restrain and coerce the same, as vehemently suspected of heresy, with condign punishment.[43]

The effects of this decree couched in medieval Church language was immediate: the officer of the Lodge in Rome, which had held its last Lodge meeting on 20 August 1737, was imprisoned by the Inquisition 'as a terror to others';[44] in Florence, a man called Crudeli was arrested, imprisoned and tortured by the Inquisition on charges of having furnished an asylum to a Masonic Lodge.[45] The Spanish Inquisition quickly followed suit, and increased its vigilance over Masons in Spain and Portugal. In 1742 a French Freemason called James Mouton and an Englishman of Swiss birth, John Coustos, were taken in Lisbon. All available resources were thrown against this new enemy at a time of relative inactivity on the part of the Inquisition. When a new Bull renewing the provisions of Clement's decree was issued in 1751, a Spanish inquisitor named Peter Torrubia insinuated himself into the Freemasons. He was initiated in the same year, and remained long enough to acquaint himself fully with Masonic ritual and the names of subscribers to the Lodge. 'Being unable to accuse them of any malpractices, he named for punishment the members of ninety-seven lodges, without any pretext whatever; and as he himself was the accuser, witness and judge, the whole of them were subjected to torture on the rack.'[46]

The greatest charge against the Freemasons was that of being a secret society, and thus suspected of 'occult heresy'.[47] This paradoxical charge, from one of the most secret and therefore literally occult of all organizations,* was behind the provision that 'oaths of secrecy in matters already condemned, are thereby rendered void, and lose their obligation.'[48] Their persecution reflects deep fear and uncertainty within Spanish society rather than any real danger presented by Freemasonry.

The most celebrated Masonic prisoner was the John Coustos, mentioned above, who in 1746 published in London *The Sufferings of John Coustos, for Free-Masonry, and for his refusal to turn Roman Catholic, under the Inquisition at Lisbon*. His account, tinged by hatred of the Inquisition and perhaps exaggerated in view of the small number of Masons thus persecuted, is interesting for many details of inquisitorial procedure at such a late date. Coustos was born in Berne, but was a naturalized Englishman and lived in London for twenty-two years before going to work as a diamond cutter in Portugal. He arrived in Lisbon in 1742, at the height of the persecutions against Freemasons after Clement's decree, and recounts how at first his letters were checked. Then the Inquisition decided 'to seize one of the chief Freemasons in Lisbon',[49] and Coustos, already Master of the Lodge, was chosen together with his friend Alexander James Mouton. First Mouton was arrested, and then Coustos himself was arrested at night on 5 March 1743 at a coffee house. He comments laconically: 'The Portuguese, and many foreigners, are so apprehensive of the sinister incidents which often happen at Lisbon in the night-time, especially to a person who ventures out alone, that few are found in the streets of this city at such a late hour.'

He was searched, and then left in a cell for several days – during which time he was shaved and his hair cut off. Bare-headed, he was taken to the President and four inquisitors

*Interestingly, a contemporary apologist for the Inquisition argued precisely that 'occult paths require an occult Inquisition' (Gian'Antonio Bianchi di Lucca, *Della Potesta e della Chiesa, Trattati due contro le nuove opinioni di Pietro Giannone*, Roma: Nella Stamperia di Pallade, 1745, vol. I, p. 300).

for a preliminary interrogation, providing such information as his name, place of birth, religion and profession. Then the patient degradation was continued as questioning was suspended for three more days. On being recalled before the tribunal, Coustos was asked if he had looked into his conscience and discovered offences committed against the Holy Office in the past. On realizing that he was being charged with Masonic membership, he recited a brief history of the brotherhood. The guile of the inquisitors surfaced when they suggested 'that it was their firm opinion that Masonry could not be founded upon such good principles as I, in my former interrogatories, had affirmed; and that, if this society of Freemasons was so virtuous as I pretended, there was no occasion of their concealing, so very industriously, the secrets of it.'

He was formally charged with being a Freemason, 'this sect being a horrid compound of sacrilege, and many other abominable crimes', and of asserting that Freemasonry was a good in itself, 'wherefore the proctor of the Inquisition requires, that the said prisoner may be prosecuted with the utmost rigour; and, for this purpose, desires the court would exert its whole authority, and even proceed to tortures, to extort from him a confession . . .'. Coustos was then left in his dungeon for six more weeks before appearing in an audience with the Portuguese Inquisitor-General, Cardinal da Cunha. On again refusing to justify his position, he was threatened with torture:

> I hereupon was instantly conveyed to the torture-room, built in the form of a square tower, where no light appeared, but what two candles gave; and, to prevent the dreadful cries and shocking groans of the unhappy victims from reaching the ears of the other prisoners, the doors are lined with a sort of quilt.

Coustos was racked until blood flowed from the places where his body was tied. Then he was left in his cell for a further six weeks before being subjected to the strappado. A further two months and he was taken back to the torture chamber for a new torture:

> The torturers turned twice round my body a thick iron chain, which, crossing upon my stomach, terminated afterwards at my wrists. They next set my back against a thick board, at each extremity whereof was a pulley, through which there run a rope, that catched

the ends of the chains at my wrists. The tormentors then stretching these ropes, by means of a roller, pressed or bruised my stomach, in proportion as the ropes were drawn together. They tortured me on this occasion to such a degree, that my wrists and shoulders were put out of joint.

After this third session, the torture was finished and his wounds were dressed by the prison surgeon.

The continuous process of humiliation and waiting comes across vividly from his account. After a further unspecified time, Coustos was ordered on Saturday 20 June 1744 to prepare himself for the *auto de fe* that would take place the following day. Dressed in a yellow robe with red stripes, accompanied to his left and to his right by familiars, he followed the Dominicans in a procession through the streets of Lisbon. He was sentenced to four years imprisonment in the galleys, which he found a great relief: he and his fellows 'thought ourselves the happiest persons upon the earth' – an understandable relief that can be compared to Pignata's delight on reaching the frontier of Naples. He continues:

The liberty I had of speaking to my friends, after having been deprived of even the sight of them during my tedious, wretched abode in the prison of the Inquisition; the open air I now breathed, with the satisfaction I felt in being freed from the dreadful apprehensions which always overspread my mind, whenever I reflected on the uncertainty of my fate; these circumstances united, made me find the toils of the galley much more supportable.

This emphasizes that it was the apprehension and uncertainty which most afflicted the prisoners of the Inquisition. The psychological torture was far worse than the effects of instruments of physical torture – which shock modern readers.

The worst had now passed. He was able to bribe the guards to gain exemption from the daily work of the galley – carrying water to other prisons. Diplomatic strings were pulled by the British Minister at Lisbon, and a petition for his freedom presented to the King of Portugal. Coustos was released at the end of October 1744, without serving his full sentence. Without awaiting permission, since he feared a reversal of this decision, he fled on board a Dutch ship standing off Lisbon and travelled back to England on it. He was at last free of what he refers to contemptuously as 'that infernal band of friars'.

But the persecution of Masons continued. Fear of them
intensified in the years following Coustos's imprisonment, and
they were even identified with Manichaean or dualist sects –
another distant echo of the Cathars. In 1752 a pamphlet was
published with the title: *Verdadera cronologia de los Maniqueos que
aun existen con el nombre de Franc-masones.*[51] Shortly afterwards,
this paranoia led to the belief that the Freemasons were behind
the French Revolution. According to a contemporary Spanish
historian, Llorente was a Freemason and his motives in
publishing a critical history of the Spanish Inquisition were
therefore suspect:[52] feeling against him was especially strong
since it was thought that the abolition of the Inquisition was part
of a Masonic plot to de-Catholicize Spain. The abolition of the
Holy Office would be the first move in this presumed strategy.

The Abolition of the Spanish Inquisition

The French Revolution marked the beginning of the end for the
Inquisition in Spain. Already by the end of the reign of Philip V
it was 'well on the way to a decline in wealth and numbers'.[53]
Ideas from the Enlightenment filtered through in spite of
censorship: the Count of Aranda, minister to Charles III, was
much influenced by liberal philosophy – an unthinkable position
in an earlier century. An economic boom was pressing changes
in social and political life. Thus, when Murat took Spain in 1808
and placed Joseph Bonaparte on the Spanish throne, the
abolition of the Inquisition was an expected corollary.

But it was neither immediate nor easy, since powerful
conservative forces resisted such a move. Napoleon himself
abolished the Inquisition formally when he arrived in Spain in
December 1808, but it continued to function spasmodically. A
lengthy series of parliamentary debates considered the future of
the Inquisition, and it is in this revolutionary context that fears
of a plot to de-Catholicize Spain must be understood. This
uncertainty is reflected in the events of 1820: the Inquisition was
again abolished after its buildings had been ransacked by the
people in Barcelona and Majorca; then this abolition was
revoked, and 'individual tribunals continued to carry on a
shadowlike existence'.[54] Debates continued in parliament for
years while the Inquisition languished in this 'state of lifeless
suspension'.[55]

It is in this context that Llorente's activities as historian become comprehensible: he had been secretary for the Inquisition from 1789 to 1791, and was given the archives of the Office when Napoleon tried to abolish it in 1808. He destroyed much of the material, and fled to Paris with the remainder. Thus the liberals had no easy target, and they could not easily throw off the shackles of three centuries of repression – although as early as 1813 the Cortes had voted that the Inquisition was incompatible with the new Constitution. The real problem – a legacy of the Inquisition's previous efficiency – was that 'in parliament there was a sense of an inferiority complex in the reformers'.[56]

This was eventually overcome. The debate was renewed and led to the definitive suppression of the Spanish Inquisition on 15 July 1834. The last execution for heresy took place in 1826, when a schoolmaster called Cayetano Ripoll was hanged as an impenitent deist. In a sense, however, the real end of the Inquisition in Spain came on 6 June 1869, when the principle of religious tolerance was made part of the Spanish Constitution.

It was the end of a complex institution that had been designed from the outset as a political weapon in the fight for Spanish purity, and that had worked to the last moment combatting what it took to be the enemies of the Spanish State. It was thus less concerned with religious doctrines than its medieval antecedent in Italy and France. Henry Kamen concludes that: 'the intolerance of the Spanish Inquisition becomes meaningful only if related to a wide complex of historical factors, and the religious issue was not always the most prominent or relevant of these.'[58]

13. Inquisition and Index in the Twentieth Century

For the Catholic Church, the twentieth century opened with a strong conservative reaction against modernism that provided fresh life for an institution that had been falling into decay. One of the instigators of this reaction was Cardinal Merry del Val, the most influential of modern secretaries of the Inquisition – the post equivalent to Inquisitor-General.

Rafael Merry del Val was the son of an English mother and the secretary to the Spanish Legation in London, who later became Ambassador in Rome. He was born in London in 1865, studied at the Jesuit Ushaw College in Durham and the Gregorian University in Rome, and was ordained in the Catholic diocese of Westminster. Once graduated as a Doctor of Philosophy and Theology, he followed the traditional family diplomatic career with the Church after his ordination in 1888. As the son of the Spanish Ambassador he was welcomed in the palaces of the black nobility – families whose noble title derived from the Church – in Rome. Although an Englishwoman, his mother identified herself totally with this ultra-conservative society, many of whose members were descendants of the great papal families of the sixteenth and seventeenth centuries. It is said that she once refused a request to preside over a charitable tea on the grounds that 'I cannot preside over the tea-table, for if a lady of the white world comes up, I couldn't possibly offer her a cup of tea'.[1] The effects of such an upbringing as Merry del Val enjoyed can only be imagined. As early as 1898, at the age of thirty-three, he was appointed consultor to the Congregation of the Index.

He was instrumental in the election of Pius X in 1903. Soon after this he became a member of the Congregation of the Holy Office, and exercised almost total control over the Pope. He was responsible for preventing the ex-President of the United States Theodore Roosevelt from obtaining an audience in 1910, and also blocked the historian Louis Duchesne when he requested an audience after the banning of his *History of the Church*. He was a member of a powerful lobby of conservative Cardinals, which included six of the key position-holders inside the Vatican and the general of the Jesuits – the 'black pope', Father Ludovico Martin. They contrived to convert a Biblical Commission founded by Leo XIII (ironically, the patron of Duchesne) into a militant mouthpiece for their own interests. This commission asserted in 1905 that the books of the Holy Scripture were to be considered absolutely historical, and a year later they upheld the Mosaic authority of the Pentateuch; in 1907, they declared that St John was the author of the fourth Gospel.[2] Under Benedict XV (1914-1922), after a long and successful career in diplomacy and as Secretary of State, Merry del Val was named Secretary of the Supreme Congregation of the Holy Office.

In a sense, his masterpiece as Secretary of the Inquisition was the preface he wrote in 1929 for the 1930 edition of the *Index Librorum Prohibitorum*, which was reprinted in the two final versions of the Index in 1945 and 1948. His thoroughgoing conservatism marks him out as equal to the most zealous of inquisitors; had Merry del Val been born a few centuries earlier it is likely that his zeal would have led him to match the deeds of some of his bloodiest predecessors. But his violence and hatred of the modern, liberal world was confined to words. It would appear to be the result of Merry del Val's pressures that the work of the Index was restored to the Inquisition in 1917.

The preface to the Index opens grandly:

Through the centuries the Holy Church has sustained tremendous persecutions, slowly multiplying the heroes who sealed the Christian faith with their own blood; but today Hell promotes a far more terrible battle against her, sly, bland, and harmful: the wicked printing press. No danger greater than this threatens the integrity of Faith and morals, so the Holy Church will never cease to indicate it to Christians, that they may be aware.[1]

After briefly reviewing the history of censorship, from the nineteenth chapter of the Acts of the Apostles to the Popes who contributed to the origin and development of the Index, Merry del Val goes on to justify this practice with admirable sophistry:

And the Church, constituted by God as infallible master and sure guide of the faithful and for this reason provided with all necessary powers, could not do otherwise: it has the duty and consequently the sacrosanct right to prevent error and corruption – however disguised – from contaminating the flock of Jesus Christ.

Neither can it be said that the banning of noxious books is violation of liberty, war against the light of truth, and that the Index of forbidden books is a permanent outrage against the progress of letters and sciences.

It is first of all manifest that nobody asserts that man is provided with freedom by her Creator more validly than the Catholic Church, and none more than her has defended this gift of God against those who have attempted to negate or diminish it. Only those infected by that plague which goes under the name of liberalism* can see injuries inflicted on free choice in the restraints imposed against libertinism by the legitimate power: as if man were always authorized to do as he wishes because he is master of his own actions.[3]

The author has identified his principal enemy: liberalism. With the same aristocratic disdain he goes on to explain how the function of prohibiting books is one of the pastoral concerns of the Church – with an allusion to what were described as 'pornographic' works by religious conservatives of his day, in practice works such as *Madame Bovary* and Zola's novels.

The preface is fascinating for the insight it provides into the thinking of a twentieth-century inquisitor. Merry del Val concludes eloquently:

Irreligious and immoral books are sometimes written with charming style, often deal with arguments which either adulate carnal passions or flatter the pride of the spirit, and always aim to take root in the minds and hearts of incautious readers by means of studied artifices and captiousness of every kind; it is therefore natural that the

---

*Such vituperation was reciprocal, and by no means invented by the Church: cf. Mill's views on religious persecution in his *Essay on Liberty*, ed. Mary Warnock, Cleveland and New York: Meridian, 1965, pp. 154-155.

Church, as a provident mother, admonishes the faithful with timely prohibitions so that they do not draw their lips to the easy chalices of poison. It is not from fear of the light that the Holy See forbids the reading of certain books, but out of that great zeal with which God enflames it and which does not tolerate the loss of souls – teaching the same experience that man, fallen from the original justice, is strongly inclined towards evil and is consequently in great need of protection and defence.[4]

Such protection, clearly, Cardinal Merry del Val believed himself bound to provide. This remarkable preface was signed 'From the Palace of the Holy Office, the Feast of the Sacred Heart of Jesus, 7th June 1929', by Merry del Val in his role as 'Secretary of the Supreme Holy Congregation of the Holy Office'.[5] It is not a medieval document, but one that remained in force until 1966.

To give an accurate idea of the contents of these twentieth-century Indices, the more than 4,000 works on the 1945 Index have been divided into six categories. Not all the books have been cited, but those of general interest, and particularly those of interest to an English-speaking reader. These books are chosen from works in English, French, Italian, Latin, German, Greek, Arabic, Hebrew, Spanish and Dutch; Giovanni Casati made a statistical analysis in 1936, with the following results concerning the nationality of banned writers: 692 French, 655 Italian, 483 German (including Austrian and Bohemian authors), 143 English, 109 Spanish, with 24 other nationalities and 552 anonymous works.[6] These figures give a good general idea of the contents; the examples given will bring them into closer focus:*

1. *English books on religious matters:* Sixty, mostly controversial and often open attacks against the Catholic Church, although some pro-Catholic titles are included. A typical example is *An Enquiry into the Nature and Place of Hell* (1743).

2. *Books on the Inquisition:* Only five studies are on the Index, among them Llorente's *Histoire*.

---

*Dates given in brackets are those of the original prohibition, *not* necessarily of publication. Titles are as given in the Index.

3. *Complete works banned:* This list provides an interesting history of modern thought as it was perceived to be threatening the Church: Boyle (1698), Bruno (1600), Croce (1934), Dumas (1863), Gentile (1934), Grotius (1757), Hobbes (1649), Hume (1761), Henry More (1696), Proudhon (1852), Voltaire (1752), Zola (1894).

4. *Other works of philosophy:* The general thrust of the above list is further refined by the prohibition of single works that almost represent a history of Western philosophy: Bergson, *Creative Evolution* (1914), Berkeley, *Alciphron* (n.d.), Comte, *Cours de Philosophie Positive* (1864), works of Cudworth (1739), Descartes, *Meditations* and other works (1663: *donec corrig.*), works of Robert Fludd (1625), Kant, *Critique of Pure Reason* (1827), Locke, *Essay Concerning Human Understanding* (1734), seven books of Malebranche (n.d.), Mill, *Principles of Political Economy* (1856), Rousseau, *Du Contract Social* (1766, with four other works), Spinoza, *Tractatus Theologico-politicus* and his posthumous works (1690).

5. *Other English books of interest:* Addison, *Remarks on Several Parts of Italy* (1729), Sir Thomas Browne, *Religio Medici* (n.d.), Erasmus Darwin, *Zoonomia, or the Laws of Organic Life* (1817), Defoe, *History of the Devil* (n.d.), Gibbon, *The History of the Decline and Fall of the Roman Empire* (1783), Goldsmith, *An Abridged History of England* (1823: *donec corrig.*), Marvell, *An Account of the Growth of Popery and Arbitrary Government in England* (1730), Sterne, *A Sentimental Journey* (n.d.).

6. *Other books of general interest:* Albertus Magnus, *De Secretis Mulierum* (1604), Gabriele D'Annunzio, drama and prose (1911), Diderot's *Encyclopédie* (1804), Flaubert, *Madame Bovary* and *Salammbô* (1864), Montaigne, *Essays* (1676), George Sand, novels (1840), Stendhal, stories and novels (1828; 1864).

This sample of prohibited books well illustrates the work of the Index, and indicates – with the works of Flaubert, D'Annunzio, Zola, Benedetto Croce and Henri Bergson – how up to date it was maintained. It is worth emphasising that the contents of the

Index are often exaggerated: on the whole, it was concerned – as the titles given indicate – with books that explicitly controvert matters of Catholic doctrine, and not with pornography or literature unless such books happen to have alerted the Inquisition to their existence by adverse publicity.

From the moment that the Index again became part of the Inquisition's function, it was one of the most important tasks. From 1908, Pius X dropped the word 'inquisition' from the official title of the organization – probably at Merry del Val's instigation – and the Congregation was known simply as the Holy Office (an alternative title since the sixteenth century), as we have seen in the signature to the preface to the 1929 Index. From 1908 the Pope himself usually presided over the Holy Office as Prefect, and the everyday business was carried out by the Cardinals who constituted the permanent members of the tribunal.

The most recent changes took place under Pope Paul VI in the 1960s. He reorganized the Congregation of the Holy Office in 1965 with the title of 'The Sacred Congregation for the Doctrine of the Faith', which it still bears today. This reformed Inquisition is competent in all matters directly or indirectly concerning catholic doctrine or threatening orthodoxy. The following year Cardinal Alfredo Ottaviano, Secretary of this freshly-named but essentially identical organization, was the man responsible for the formal suppression of the Index in June. Yet there were always two distinct aspects of the Index: on the one hand it was responsible for prohibiting books already published that were brought to its notice; and on the other, it was responsible for the correction and amendment of works by Catholic authors submitted before publication. The latter function is still reserved as a right by the Catholic Church in an attempt to regulate the use of books by clergy and faithful. In recent years, examples have been furnished during controversies concerning, for instance, the celibacy of priests, divorce and abortion, and in long-drawn-out theological debates.

An interesting recent example of the continuity of outlook – linking with the persecution of Freemasons in the eighteenth century – was partly the result of the political and financial scandals deriving from the activities of the Italian P2 lodge, which threatened to damage the image of the highly implicated Vatican. At the same time there had been persistent rumours of

Masonic prelates and a general loosening of restrictions on Catholic Freemasons. On 17 February 1981 the Sacred Congregation for the Doctrine of the Faith issued an explicit declaration against Freemasonry, insisting that 'canonical discipline* regarding Freemasonry remains in force and has not been modified in any way, consequently neither excommunication nor the other penalties envisaged have been abrogated'.[7]

Thus, with its image improved and its name twice changed, the Inquisition still exists and functions today under Cardinal Joseph Ratzinger – the heir to a tradition of over seven hundred years.

After an opening to tolerance and a new liberty of thought by John XXIII and John Paul I, Cardinal Joseph Ratzinger was summoned to Rome to cover the theological lacunae of John Paul II and was made Prefect of the Congregation. He is presently engaged in a conservative rear-guard action against the progressive faction of the Church in South America, together with the Opus Dei. In an article in the monthly *30 Giorni* of March 1984, Ratzinger enunciated the theoretical basis of the mass, in his view undermined by the 'theology of liberation' practised by Latin American bishops – whom he accused of Marxist tendencies and political reductionism. Under his guidance the political, anti-Communist, aspect of the Inquisition is again stressed, while Cardinals Sebastian Biaggio and Bernardin Gatin, successive heads of the Congregation of Bishops and both members of Opus Dei, have led a silent campaign in which more than fifty Brazilian bishops have been substituted in the past two years. 'Inspectors' have been sent from Rome to control teaching and discipline in Brazil.

*Excommunication for Freemasons was promulgated in Canon 2335 of 1917 by Merry del Val. This discipline was dropped on 27 November 1983.

14. Conclusion: Some Effects and Influences of the Inquisition

There are several ways in which the Inquisition may be said to have modified the course of history and influenced the cultural development of Western Europe. Many of them have been made explicit, or at least hinted at, in the foregoing chapters, arranged chronologically as a history of the Inquisition. In conclusion, we shall briefly consider some of the most interesting effects and influences in four main categories: Economic, Cultural, Scientific and Political.

Economic influences

Emphasis has already been placed on the negative social and economic effects of the confiscation policy in medieval France and Italy. Apart from the immediate and predominantly local effect of destroying the personal wealth of families in northern and south-western France, there were long-term effects. At the end of a long period of cultural supremacy of the Languedoc, economic collapse caused new investments to be made elsewhere and transferred the focus of medieval urban development to Italy. The cities of Languedoc remained static, while those of northern France, Flanders, England and central Italy flourished. In part, this was the result of other factors, such as the practice of dividing inherited property amongst the heirs and a possibly irreversible decline already in action. But any overall view of economic change in the thirteenth century should take into account the effects of inquisitorial activity.

A more striking example of economic effect may be seen in Spain. The expulsion and persecution of the Jewish population was disastrous, leading to the rapid export of capital and creating a vacuum of expertise in international finance that had negative consequences for at least three centuries. As a society based upon the exigencies of the Castilian nobility gained power, the burden of taxation tended to fall on the poorer people with no Jewish population to make up the needs of the Spanish treasury. At its moment of greatest potential wealth, with money pouring in from the Americas, Spain did not grow richer and the centre of European economic activity developed far away. G. R. Elton has explained this apparently paradoxical fact as follows:

> Thus despite its flourishing wool production, cloth-exports to the Americas, and the constant influx of bullion from the colonies, Spain grew no richer, to the amazement of contemporaries who could not understand the situation at all. Although this generation witnessed some active commercial enterprise in the towns, the social structure of Castile, dominated by a greater and lesser nobility contemptuous of all trade except that of arms, did not permit Spain to benefit permanently from the rain of silver, which, by stimulating progress and profits, promoted marked economic advances elsewhere – in Germany, Antwerp and England in particular.[1]

There are clear indications of commercial activity and prosperity shifting away from the areas in southern Europe that came under the direct control of the Inquisition. It is interesting to note that the money-wise city of Florence was governed by men shrewd enough to object to the policy of confiscation; their city prospered while other late medieval towns declined.

Cultural influences

There has been much discussion about the role of the Inquisition in the decline of the troubadour culture of Languedoc. It is hard to prove direct responsibility, although the immediate cause was the loss of power during the Albigensian Crusade by secular lords who belonged to the troubadour tradition. But the new austerity imposed by the Church at the beginning of the thirteenth century also had great impact on a culture which – if not heretical – was at least partly based on non-Christian sources.[2] An interesting test case is that of the troubadour Fulk of Marseilles: 'A mediocre poet, Fulk recommended himself to the execration of posterity by the perfidious cruelty with which he dealt with the Albigensians and the town of Toulouse.'[3] For most of his early life he had dedicated himself to the usual troubadour pastimes of love, music and poetry, but it appears that in the end he was disgusted by the court loves and betrayals that surrounded him. In 1196, saddened by the death of his lord's wife and the ruin of his protectors, the Count of Toulouse and Alfonso of Aragón, he took holy orders as a Cistercian monk.

The turnabout was both sudden and unusual. A historian of the troubadours has remarked that Fulk 'finished his life as the Bishop of Toulouse, unexpected conclusion of a tumultuous life'.[4] In that role he made his name as a ferocious opponent of heresy, and enters the history of the Inquisition as one of the first people to order the Dominicans specifically to stamp out heresy.[5] Pierre Aubry relates that in the late 1220s, when he had long since ceased to write love poetry, '[Fulk's] contemporaries derived great pleasure from maliciously making some *jongleur* sing in front of him one of the songs that he had written early in his life. On that day, the poor contrite bishop ate only bread and water.'[6]

Fulk of Marseilles bridged the gap between two completely different styles. There is a fine irony in the fact that a troubadour should assist the Inquisition, and thus contribute to the suppression of a tradition of which he was once a part. Henry Lea comments on the general situation that the 'precocious civilization which had promised to lead Europe in the path of culture was gone, and to Italy was transferred the honour of the Renaissance'.[7] The poetry of the troubadours was transmuted by Dante into literary Italian, and a new culture that became the foundation of modern European literature. That such potential should have been destroyed stands as the first negative mark against the forces that produced the Inquisition in thirteenth-century France.

Fortunately, in the second phase of its existence, the Inquisition's zeal in censorship seems to have had little effect on literature beyond Spain and the Papal States. Due to a happy accident of chronology, alternative centres of printing were created by the effect of the Reformation just as the Index was attempting to crack down on book production. Potentially dangerous works could be printed in

Germany, Switzerland and even Venice. It would be foolish to assert that the prohibition of Hobbes or Rousseau had any impact in London or Geneva, but the doctrines of philosophical liberalism they inspired and worked on were held back from Italy, with a noticeably regressive effect on her political and philosophical development. The leaders of the movement for Unification had to look abroad for political inspiration, and her greatest philosophers in this century – Croce and Gentile – had to turn to Germany for sustenance, and were then put on the Index themselves.

The effect of the Index was most severe in Spain. The efficiency of the *cordon sanitaire* had serious consequences, synthesized neatly by Lea as 'the studious unfitting of the people for the changes in store for them'.[8] Spanish writers and intellectuals suffered a deep-rooted inferiority complex; even though the acme of the Inquisition's power coincided with the 'Golden Centuries', Spanish literature was strongly influenced. Henry Kamen writes that 'it is certain that the Inquisition in no way constricted or restrained the great cultural achievements of the sixteenth and seventeenth centuries, *provided* they kept within the limits of orthodoxy and the native traditions of Spain.'[9] Thus literature *did* flourish, but within strict confines; this explains the almost total inadaptability of the religiously inspired dramas of one of Spain's greatest writers, Calderón de la Barca, to the English stage.* Most of the great Spanish writers and artists of the time – El Greco, Ignatius of Loyola, Cervantes, St Teresa, Luis de León – were in some measure touched by the Inquisition, although the main thrust of censorship was always against speculative thought and experimental science.

Yet it is only recently that writers and artists have come to expect and demand artistic freedom. The suppression of creative activity in Spain never had the effects we have seen in the case of writers in the Soviet Union or China. The particular forms of 'pornography' that Merry del Val attacked are the products of a completely changed society, while the theological grounds for condemning free-thinking philosophers are clear

---

*Cf. the complaint of Edward Fitzgerald, who translated eight of Calderón's plays, that a literal translation could not be valid because it retained 'so much that, whether real or imagined dramatic passion, is still bombast to English ears' (*Letters and Literary Remains*, London: Macmillan, 1889, vol. i, p. 240). The deeply religious concept of 'honour' was the biggest hurdle in translating Calderón.

from the Church's point of view. As in the case of witchcraft, it seems that the violence of the reaction reflects a wrench into a different world-view, when previous values are suddenly changed. In this case the Inquisition mirrored these moments of dramatic change and thus represented a comprehensible, although not necessarily acceptable, conservatism.

The Roman Inquisition had much more influence on art than on literature, inasmuch as it governed the principles emanating from the Council of Trent. The Church's main concern was with maintaining decency and avoiding secular subjects without biblical sanction. The Inquisition was used to enforce these ideas, and to follow artistically the main thrust of the Counter-Reformation in denying the individual the right to resolve his own problems of conscience. Church architecture was standardized by Carlo Borromeo in the recommendations of his *Instructiones Fabricae et Supellectilis Ecclesiasticae* of *c.*1572, and became what is known as the Baroque; while the high standard of painting that had culminated with Michelangelo was allowed to decay. Sir Anthony Blunt explained this process:

> Artists no longer make new discoveries about the outside world. Their work is largely controlled by the Church, and, even when they are allowed a certain freedom, they seem to have lost their interest in what lies around them. Their preoccupation is no longer with the visible universe, but with developing new methods of drawing and composition. They are not breaking new ground, but rather exploiting what their predecessors had discovered for them and turning their discoveries to new purposes. They abandon the Renaissance ideals of convincing space and normal proportions, and make almost as free use as medieval artists of arbitrary construction and deliberate elongation.[10]

The process he is illustrating is the theoretical background to Mannerism, and it is exactly paralleled by what happened to Spanish literature in the seventeenth century.

Furthermore, it might be argued that this refusal on the part of artists, imposed by the Council of Trent and policed by the Inquisition, to study the 'visible universe' resulted in yet another shift away from southern Europe. It was at the end of the sixteenth century that Dutch painters visiting Rome – and one Frenchman, Poussin – developed the kind of realistic landscape that was to remain the basis of northern art until the advent of

Impressionism, but which never took root in Italy to the same extent. While Italian painters of the Baroque decorated ceilings and domes with dramatic religious scenes, the Dutch and Flemish – above all Rembrandt and Rubens – stole the primacy in art from Italy.

Scientific influence

The Church's influence on the development of scientific thought was much older than the Inquisition. The insistence of early Christian writers such as Lactanctius and Tertullian that truth is to be found in divine revelation and not in observation or reason contributed to the decline of Greek science: 'For the faithful, empirical inquiry is unnecessary, a distraction from the practice of his religion and possibly a source of dangerous heresy.'[11] The success of Christianity, and the institutionalization of religion in a way that science was never institutionalized, only enforced such views. In the early centuries of Christianity, the lead in scientific activity passed to Islam.

These attitudes were reflected in the restrictions imposed by the Mendicant Orders. In 1243, the Dominicans forbade members of their order from the study of medicine and natural philosophy, and in 1287 chemistry – in obvious reference to alchemy – was added to the list. In the latter year, Roger Bacon, one of the leading natural scientists of his time, was condemned by his own Franciscan order and imprisoned. This veto may have been the result of his persistent use of the phrase 'magical sciences' and his failure to distinguish clearly between science and magic,[12] but in any case both were frequently condemned in that century. Lynn Thorndike has shown with immense detail how magic was gradually transmuted into experimental science, but even before the publication of this work such studies as Andrew Dickson White's *History of the Warfare of Science with Theology* of 1896 had viewed the work of the Inquisition negatively in this context. On the persecution of witches, White observed: 'Of course, the atmosphere created by this persecution of magicians was deadly to any open beginnings of experimental science.'[13]

But again the full effects were felt in Italy. Thorndike shows the way in which the scientific careers of Cardano, Aldovrandi and Barozzi were inhibited by the Inquisition,[14] and long before his eventual trial and execution in 1600 Giordano Bruno came to the notice of the Inquisition. He was first tried in 1576. It is clear that these pressures, and the effectiveness of the measures taken by the Church against science in the sixteenth century, hit the centre of scientific and philosophical activity at that time. Paul F. Grendler's study of *The Roman Inquisition and the Venetian Press* illustrates how this repression of intellectual life was carried out from 1540 to 1605 in Venice.

A letter from Piero Giucciardini to Cosimo II, Grand Duke of Tuscany, written on 4 March 1616 about Galileo, indicates the situation in Rome:

> But he is vehement in his opinions, having extreme passion within and little strength and prudence to win over it: so much that these Roman skies are dangerous for him in this century in which the Prince of this city abhors belles lettres and these novelties, and cannot bear to hear these new ideas or those subtleties. Everyone seeks to adjust his brain and his nature to those of this Lord; so that those who know something and study natural sciences demonstrate their ignorance when in fact they have wit, in order not to rouse suspicions . . . [15]

This letter emphasizes the difficulties of Galileo, who was not capable of such dissembling, and provides vivid testimony of the way in which Italian writers and scientists had to "adjust their brains" to the papal wavelength.

Luigi Firpo has commented:

> Free philosophical speculation in Italy fought its decisive battle during the pontificate of Clement VIII, in the last decade of the century. It suffered the condemnation of Patrizi's *Nova Philosophia*, of Telesio's *De Rerum Natura*, and of all the works of Bruno and Campanella. It was crippled by the investigations opened against Giambattista della Porta, Col'Antonio Stigliola, and Cesare Cremonini, by the beginning of Campanella's long imprisonment, by the execution of Francesco Pucci, and by the burning of Bruno. And finally, it was completely destroyed, in spite of the heroism of its martyrs. Its last posthumous act was played out thirty years later, in the silence of Arcetri. [16]

This last name is that of the country villa in which Galileo was condemned to house arrest after his trial by the Inquisition.

Political Influence

The Inquisition was often blatantly political in its operations, as in Spain or in the Roman Inquisition in Malta, but everywhere it was established it was so to a certain extent. In setting itself up as the arbiter of morals and free thought it exercised a purely political control that surpassed the theological and pastoral concerns of the Church. Through the Index and the repression of speculative thinking it carried out an effective censorship of political ideas in those countries where the Roman Catholic faith predominated.

It is in the last analysis as a political institution that the Inquisition must be judged, since any discussion about it is necessarily conditioned by the question of whether the end justified the means employed – an essentially political demand. The Church devised the Inquisition as a weapon – one of many – in the perennial attempt to preserve itself as the central moral and political governing institution of Western Europe. Heresy was no threat until it represented a direct threat to the *temporal power* of the Church, and the most violent episodes in the history of the Inquisition occurred when the Church perceived this to be the case.

On the other hand, the Inquisition might be seen as merely the most efficiently organized system of persecution yet devised. The final charge of such historians as Henry Lea is often legal – that the Inquisition influenced judicial procedure by introducing the 'crime' of suspicion into ordinary practice, or that the accused was treated 'as one having no rights, whose guilt was assumed in advance, and from whom confession was extorted by guile or force'.[17] Yet even here political issues dominate, and it is the repression of thought and personal freedom that matters. The Inquisition was an organization that could not possibly have weathered in its original form the advance of modern theories of tolerance and democratic plurality.

There seems no doubt that the influence of the Inquisition on Western European history was mainly negative. But an institution cannot be judged morally, as an individual can be judged:

Public crimes are committed by individuals who play roles in political, military, and economic institutions. (Because religions are politically weak, crimes committed on their behalf are now rare.) Yet crimes don't seem to be fully attributable to the individual himself. Famous political monsters have moral personalities large enough to transcend the boundaries of their public roles; they take on the full weight of their deeds as personal moral property. But they are exceptional.[18]

Such 'exceptional' men were Conrad of Marburg and Peter of Verona, yet there is a great danger in assuming that moral restrictions are relaxed in the case of lesser men because the scope of their actions is not personal. Strangely, no permanent moral stigma is attached to the Church for its responsibility in the Inquisition's activity; it lurks as a vague memory. Once a certain necessity for ruthlessness is established, it becomes self-perpetuating; power must be preserved. But this raises an important question when applied to the foundation of the Inquisition in the thirteenth century: Hoffman Nickerson came near to this truth when he asked if the moral unity of Europe had been worth preserving.

This question itself presupposes another, more profound demand. Aldous Huxley, with his customary intelligence, imposed the correct terms for discussing the Inquisition when he asserted that 'The Inquisition burns and tortures in order to perpetuate a creed, a ritual and an ecclesiastico-politico-financial organization regarded as necessary to man's salvation.'[19] This perspective enables us to get under the skin of the problem: there is no doubt that the Inquisition was ruthless, but countless other similar organizations and regimes have been, and are, equally ruthless. The moral issue lies deeper still, and perhaps it cannot be approached while we remain – whether believers or not – members of an essentially Christian society, based upon the ethos of what must be considered an 'ecclesiastico-politico-financial organisation' rather than the conveniently vague and depoliticized term 'the Church'. An institution cannot be judged morally, but the ideology that created it and sustains it *can* be so judged. Pushing further for explanation or justification of the Inquisition's past, we are met with the final demand: was Christianity worth preserving?

It is only in a definitive answer to this question that final judgement on the Inquisition may be passed.

References

Chapter 1: Genesis

1 Southern, *Western Society*, p. 34.
2 Lea, *Inquisition of the Middle Ages*, vol. I, p. 58; Brooke, *Heresy*, p. 120.
3 Cf. Reviglio, *L'Inquisizione,*, pp. 12-14; and Fliche, *Histoire de l'Église*, pp. 140-46.
4 Trevor-Roper, *Witch Craze*, p. 141.
5 Quoted in Southern, op. cit., p. 17
6 Thouzellier, *Hérésie et Hérétiques*, p. 3; Nickerson, *The Inquisition*, p. 3.
7 Barraclough, *The Medieval Papacy*, p. 128; and Moore, *Origins of Heresy*, p. 22.
8 Southern, op. cit., pp. 116-17.
9 In a letter to Pope Eugene III, cited in Ladnor, *Homo Viator*, p. 247.
10 Hick, *Philosophy of Religion*, New Jersey: Prentice Hall, 1973, p. 36.
11 Cited in Morghen, *Medioevo Cristiano*, p. 227.
12 Reviglio, op. cit., p. 16.
13 Manselli, *L'Eresia del Male*, p. 237.
14 John Passmore, *The Perfectibility of Man*, London: Duckworth, 1970, p. 140.
15 Hamilton, *The Medieval Inquisition*, p. 21.
16 Moore, op. cit., p. 23.
17 Manselli, op. cit., p. 88.
18 Sumption, *The Albigensian Crusade*, p. 36.

19 *Tractatus de Haeresi*, cited in Morghen, op. cit., p. 228.
20 Lambert, *Medieval Heresy*, p. 67.
21 Thomas, *Religion and the Decline of Magic*, p. 26; Russell, *Witchcraft*, pp. 45-62; Anglo, *Evident Authority*, pp. 8-14; cf. Finucane, *Miracles and Pilgrims*.
22 Ibid, p. 28.
23 Lea, *Chapters*, p. 446.
24 Thomas, op. cit., p. 38.
25 Murray, *Piety and Impiety*, p. 92.
26 Kieckhefer, *European Witch Trials*, p. 64.
27 Murray, op. cit., pp. 93-4.
28 Morghen, op. cit., pp. 225-6.
29 Cf. Manselli, *De la 'persuasio' à la 'coercitio'*.
30 Wakefield, *Heresy, Crusade and Inquisition*, p. 82.
31 Lea, *Inq. Middle Ages*, vol. I, p. 220.
32 Lambert, op. cit., p. 71.
33 Epist. XII, 67 (5 July 1209), quoted in Fliche, op. cit., p. 19.
34 Morghen, op. cit., p. 256.
35 Hinnesbusch, *History of the Dominican Order*, p. 23.
36 Fliche, op. cit., p. 183. The Order was confirmed by Honorius's Bull *Religiosam vitam*, of 22 December, 1216.
37 Maisonneuve, *Études*, p. 269.
38 Manselli, *L'Eresia del Male*, p. 299.
39 Sumption, op cit., p. 31.
40 Hamilton, op. cit., p. 31.
41 Luchaire, *Innocent III*, p. 67

Chapter 2: Foundation

1   Lea, *Inq. Middle Ages*, vol. I, p. 310.
2   Ullmann, *A Short History of the Papacy*, p. 252.
3   Molinier, *L'Inquisition*, p. 456.
4   Lea, op. cit., vol. I, p. 359.
5   La Mantia, *Origine e Vicende*, p. 11.
6   Thouzellier, *La Répression de l'Hérésie et les Débuts de l'Inquisition*, in Fliche, op. cit., p. 301 and pp. 309-10.
7   Summarized from Thouzellier, op. cit., pp. 309-10.
8   Hamilton, op. cit., p. 38.
9   Translated from Maisonneuve, op. cit., p. 259.
10 Kaltner, *Konrad von Marburg*, pp. 58-60.
11 Cf. Hamilton, op. cit., p. 75.
12 Cf. Russell, op. cit., pp. 159-60.
13 Fliche, op. cit., p. 230.

14 Translated from Vacandard, *Étude Historique et Critique*, p. 147.
15 Thouzellier, op. cit., p. 322.
16 Hamilton, op. cit., p. 74.
17 Thouzellier, op. cit., p. 330.
18 Quoted by Haskins, *Robert le Bougre*, p. 223.
19 Ibid., pp. 224-6.
20 Thouzellier, op. cit., p. 331.
21 Hamilton, op. cit., p. 74.
22 Coulton, *Inquisition and Liberty*, pp. 129-30.
23 Haskins, op. cit., p. 195.
24 Hamilton, op. cit., p. 75.
25 Thouzellier, op. cit., p. 324.
26 Hamilton, op. cit., p. 77.
27 Cf. Fumi, *Eretici e Ribelli*.
28 Lea, *Inq. Middle Ages*, vol. II, pp. 210-11.
29 Hamilton, op. cit., p. 77.
30 Lea, op. cit., vol. II, p. 214.
31 Mariano da Alatri, Appendix to Italian translation of Fliche, op. cit., p. 693.
32 Alatri, *Inquisizione Francescana*, p. 53.
33 Ibid., p. 229.
34 Pellegrini, *L'Inquisizione Francescana*, p. 81.

Chapter 3: Manuals and Inquisitors

1 The following examples are translated from the Latin version given by Douais in *L'Inquisition: Ses Origines – Sa Procédure*, pp. 275-88.
2 Ibid., p. 154.
3 Given in Latin as Appendix A to Vacandard, *L'Inquisition*, pp. 313-22; an English translation is provided by Wakefield in *Heresy, Crusade*, pp. 250-58.
4 Wakefield argues that it was written in 1248-9 (ibid., p. 250).
5 Vacandard, op. cit., p. 313.
6 Ibid., pp. 315-16.
7 Falcone, *La Nunziatura di Malta*, p. 21.
8 Alatri, *Inquisitori Veneti*, p. 404.
9 Guidonis, *Practica*, pp. 232-3.
10 Sacchetti Sassetti,*Giovanni da Capestrano Inquisitore*, p. 336.
11 Cf. Pellegrini, op. cit., p. 82.
12 Ibid., pp. 84-5.
13 Lea, *Inq. Middle Ages*, vol. I, p. 349.
14 Lambert, *Medieval Heresy*, p. 170.

15   Wakefield, op. cit., p. 185.
16   Lea, op. cit., vol. I, p. 349.
17   Reviglio, *L'Inquisizione medioevale*, p. 44.

Chapter 4: Trial and Sentence

1   Gui, *Manuel*, ed. Mollat, vol. I, p. xlv.
2   Cf. Turberville, *Medieval Heresy*, pp. 191-2.
3   Hamilton, op. cit., p. 43.
4   Lea, op. cit., vol. I, p. 371.
5   Hamilton, op. cit., p. 42.
6   Lea, op. cit., pp. 391-3.
7   Hamilton, op. cit., p. 42.
8   Lea, op. cit., vol. I, p. 393.
9   Ibid., p. 409.
10   Hamilton, op. cit., p. 44.
11   Lea, op. cit., vol. I, p. 419.
12   In Douais, op. cit., pp. 170-1.
13   Lea, op. cit., vol. I, p. 421.
14   Cited from translation in Wakefield, op. cit., p. 210.
15   Alatri, *Una Sentenza*, p. 143.
16   Vidal, *Bullaire*, p. 44 (Vidal gives the Bull; the story is summarized
      by Guiraud, *Medieval Inquisition*, pp. 105-6.)
17   Vidal, op. cit., pp. 4-5, note 2.
18   Ibid., p. 46.
19   Ibid.
20   Guiraud, op. cit., p. 107.
21   Ibid.
22   Lea, op. cit., vol. I, p. 423.
23   Pellegrini, op. cit., p. 86.
24   Quoted in Coulton, op. cit., p. 157.
25   Gui, *Gravamina*, quoted in Lea, op. cit., vol. I, p. 424.
26   Guiraud, op. cit., p. 87.
27   Reviglio, op. cit., pp. 106-7.
28   Scott, *The History of Torture*, pp. 171-2.
29   Reviglio, op. cit., p. 106.
30   Scott, op. cit., p. 162.
31   Vidal, op. cit., p. 52.
32   Scott, op. cit., pp. 168-9.
33   Ibid., p. 181.
34   Ibid., p. 169.
35   Reviglio, op. cit., p. 107.
36   Lea, *Superstition and Force*, p. 485.

37 Hamilton, op. cit., p. 49.
38 Mollat, Introduction to Gui's *Manuel*, p. li.
39 Hamilton, op. cit., p. 49.
40 Lea, *Inq. Middle Ages*, vol. I, p. 459.
41 Hamilton, op. cit., p. 50.
42 Mollat, op. cit., pp. lvi-lvii.
43 Published in Sacchetti Sassetti, op. cit., p. 338.
44 Cf. *Processus Inquisitionis*, Vacancard, op. cit., p. 319, Peñafort's *Directory*, Douais, op. cit., p. 287.
45 Hamilton, op. cit., p. 52.
46 Alatri, *Inquisizione Francescana*, p. 235.
47 Cf. Lea, op. cit., vol. I, p. 517.
48 Alatri, op. cit., p. 237.
49 Lea, op. cit., vol. I, p. 524.
50 Mollat, op. cit., pp. lx-lxi.
51 Ibid., p. lxi.
52 Alatri, op. cit., pp. 57-8.
53 Vacandard, op. cit., table on p. 522.
54 Lea, op. cit., vol. I, p. 484.
55 Mollat, op. cit., p. liii.
56 Turberville, op. cit., p. 216.
57 Hamilton, op. cit., p. 53.
58 Guiraud, op. cit., pp. 109-10.
59 Ibid, p. 110.
60 Cf. Hamilton, op. cit., pp. 53-4.
61 Coulton, op. cit., p. 166.
62 Lea, op. cit., vol. I, p. 541.
63 Hamilton, op. cit., p. 55.
64 Lea, op. cit., vol. I, p. 552.
65 Putnam, *The Censorship of the Church of Rome*, pp. 64-76.
66 Cf. The Calendar of Witch Trials, in Kieckhefer, op. cit., pp. 108-11.

Chapter 5: The Medieval Inquisition in Italy

1 Chesterton, *The Life of St Francis of Assisi*, London: Hodder and Stoughton, 1960, p. 25.
2 Moorman, *A History of the Franciscan Order*, p. 303.
3 Hinnesbusch, *A History of the Dominican Order*, p. 57.
4 Ibid., p. 343.
5 La Mantia, *Origine e Vicende*, p. 11, n8.
6 *Pelhisson's Chronicle*, translated in Wakefield, op. cit., pp. 215-16.
7 Lea, *Inq. Middle Ages*, vol. II, p. 230.

8   Reviglio, op. cit., p. 38.
9   Lea, op. cit., vol. II, p. 245.
10 Alatri, *Inquisizione Francescana*, p. 56.
11 Ibid., p. 65, n.
12 Ibid., pp. 80-94.
13 Lea, op. cit., vol. II, p. 251.
14 Alatri, *Inquisitori Veneti*, pp. 401-2.
15 Ibid., p. 403.
16 Ibid., p. 404.
17 Quoted in D. S. Chambers, *The Imperial Age of Venice*, London: Thames and Hudson, 1970, p. 9.
18 Alatri, *Inquisitori Veneti*, p. 415.
19 Alatri, *Rileggendo*, p. 178.
20 Ibid., pp. 181-2.
21 Ibid., p. 185, n.
22 Ibid., p. 186.
23 Cox, *Mysticism*, p. 90.
24 Cohn, *The Pursuit of the Millennium*, p. 108.
25 Ibid., p. 108; Barraclough, *The Medieval Papacy*, pp. 131-2.
26 Cohn, op. cit., p. 111.
27 Ibid., p. 110.
28 Alatri, *Inquisitori Veneti*, p. 418.
29 Vidal, *Bullaire*, pp. 70-2.
30 Alatri, *Fraticellismo*, p. 313.
31 Lea, op. cit., vol. II, p. 245.
32 Cf. Pellegrini, op. cit., p. 97, n: Lea, op. cit., III, pp. 448-9.
33 Guiraud, op. cit., p. 173.
34 Russell, *Witchcraft in the Middle Ages*, p. 155.
35 Ibid., pp. 156-8.
36 Morghen, *Medioevo Cristiano*, p. 268.
37 Southern, *Western Society*, p. 133.

Chapter 6: The Medieval Inquisition in France

1   Vidal, *Bullaire*, p. xxi.
2   This account is based on Vidal, ibid., pp. iv-xxii.
3   Ibid., p. xviii.
4   Ibid., p. xxi.
5   Ibid., p. lxxx.
6   Ibid., p. 156.
7   Ibid., p. lxxxi.
8   Lambert, *Medieval Heresy*, p. 173.
9   Barber, *The Trial of the Templars*, p. 47.

10 Cf. Vidal, op. cit., p. 9.
11 Morghen, *Medioevo Cristiano*, p. 266.
12 Barber, op. cit., p. 44.
13 Ibid., pp. 58-68.
14 Partner, *The Murdered Magicians*, p. 74.
15 Barber, op. cit., pp. 157-8.
16 Lambert, op. cit., p. 173.
17 Kieckhefer, *European Witch Trials*, p. 13.
18 Cf. Russell, *Witchcraft in the Middle Ages*, pp. 197-8.
19 Cf. Reviglio, *L'Inquisizione Medioevale*, p. 49.
20 Barber, op. cit., p. 196.
21 Cheney, *The Downfall of the Templars*, p. 315.
22 Lea, *Inq. Middle Ages*, vol. III, p. 249.
23 Ibid., p. 334.
24 Thorndike, *Magic and Experimental Science*, vol. II, p. 837.
25 Lea, op. cit., p. 452.
26 Partner, op. cit., p. 54; see also pp. 46-58.
27 Fumi, *Eretici e Ribelli*, p. 7.
28 Ibid., p. 12.
29 Thorndike, op. cit., vol. II, p. 949.
30 Fumi, op. cit., p. 10.
31 E.g., by Partner, op. cit., p. 56.
32 Vidal, op. cit., p. 35
33 Ibid, pp. 35-6.
34 Ibid., p. 39.
35 Ibid., pp. 53-5.
36 Russell, op. cit., p. 173.
37 1 November, 1323 (Vidal, op. cit., p. 87).
38 23 August 1326 (ibid., pp. 113-14).
39 14 December 1326 (ibid., pp. 118-19).
40 29 May 1327 (ibid., p. 128).
41 Lea, op. cit., vol. III, p. 459.
42 Vidal, op. cit., pp. 154-5; Russell, op. cit., p. 173; Lea, op. cit., vol. III, p. 459.
43 Kieckhefer, op. cit., p. 16.
44 Calendar of Witch Trials, ibid., p. 112.
45 Leff, *Medieval Thought*, p. 256.
46 Cf. Southern, *Western Society*, p. 326 and pp. 319-31.
47 Hamilton, *Medieval Inquisition*, p. 88.
48 Cf. Cox, *Mysticism*, pp. 83-4.
49 Lambert, op. cit., pp. 176-7.
50 Ibid., p. 179.
51 Lerner, *Medieval Prophecy*, develops this argument; shorter

summaries in Lambert, op. cit., pp. 173-81 and Hamilton, op. cit., pp. 86-8.
52   Vidal, op. cit., p. 40, n11.
53   Ibid., p. 68.
54   Hamilton, op. cit., p. 87.
55   Lambert, op. cit., p. 181.
56   Scott, *The Trial of Joan of Arc*, p. 9.
57   Fabre, *Joan of Arc*, p. 249.
58   Scott, op. cit., p. 13.
59   Fabre, op. cit., p. 290.
60   Scott, op. cit., pp. 65-6.
61   Quicherat, *Procès*, I, p. 36; Barrett, *The Trial of Jeanne d'Arc*, p. 99.
62   Quicherat, op. cit., I, p. 2.
63   Pernoud, *The Retrial of Joan of Arc*, p. 1.
64   Lea, op. cit., vol. II, p. 377.
65   Quoted in Pernoud, op. cit., p. 33.
66   Ibid., p. 214.
67   Lightbody, *The Judgements of Joan*, pp. 124-5.

Chapter 7: The Decline of the Medieval Inquisition

1   Guiraud, *Medieval Inquisition*, p. 179.
2   Ibid., p. 208.
3   Lea, *Inq. Middle Ages*, vol. III, p. 190.
4   Kieckhefer, *European Witch Trials*, p. 14 and p. 111.
5   Alatri, *Fraticellismo*, p. 292.
6   Lea, op. cit., II, p. 282.
7   Ibid., p. 283.
8   Ibid., p. 269.

Chapter 8: Heresy, Sorcery and Witchcraft

1   Russell, *Witchcraft in the Middle Ages*, p. 9, n, and p. 54.
2   Ibid., p. 7.
3   Cf. Thorndike, *Magic and Experimental Science*, vol. I, pp. 506-7.
4   Ibid., vol. II, p. 602.
5   Ibid., vol. II, p. 666.
6   Ibid., vol. II, p. 554.
7   Lea, *Inq. Middle Ages*, vol. II, p. 400.
8   Ibid., vol. II, p. 422; cf. Russell, op. cit., pp. 63-100.
9   Lea, op. cit., vol. II, p. 429.
10   Ibid., p. 430.

11 Thomas, *Religion and the Decline of Magic*, p. 45.
12 Monter, Preface to *European Witchcraft*, p. viii.
13 Cf. Kieckhefer, ch. 1.
14 Ibid., p. 10 and pp. 10-26.
15 Ibid., p. 16.
16 Ibid., pp. 16-18; Cohn, *Europe's Inner Demons*, pp. 128-38.
17 Kieckhefer, op. cit., p. 113.
18 Ibid., p. 19.
19 Ibid.
20 Cf. Russell, op. cit., pp. 200-2.
21 Lea, op. cit., vol. II, p. 464.
22 Russell, op. cit., p. 203.
23 Monter, *Witchcraft in France and Switzerland*, p. 18.
24 Russell, op. cit., p. 244.
25 Ibid., pp. 245-8.
26 Ibid., p. 253.
27 Cf. Midelfort, *Witch Hunting in Southwestern Germany*, p. 17; Russell, op. cit., p. 22.
28 *Summa Theologica*, Roma: Adriano Solani, 1967, 25 vols., I, 64, 1 ad 5; II-II, 172, 5 ad 1.6.
29 Ibid., II-II, 96, 1 ad 3.
30 Ibid., e.g. at III, 46, 3 ad 3.
31 Ibid., II-II, 96, 2 (vol. 18, p. 345).
32 Midelfort, op. cit., p. 18.
33 *Summa Theologica*, II-II, 43, 7 ad 3.
34 Ibid., II-II, 33, 1; 49, 8 ad 2.
35 Lambert, op. cit., p. 140.
36 Gui, *Manuel*, ed. Mollat, pp. 19-25.
37 Horsley, *Who were the Witches?*, p. 693.
38 Russell, op. cit., p. 205.
39 Ibid., pp. 346-50.
40 Cf. Thorndike, op. cit., vol. IV., p. 313.
41 Ibid., p. 325.
42 Ibid., p. 331.
43 Turberville, *Medieval Heresy*, pp. 108-9.
44 Russell, op. cit., p. 335, n6.
45 Horsley, op. cit., p. 693.
46 Ibid., p. 712; cf. two wise women who had the Devil added to their confessions in Muraro, *La Signora del Giuoco*, pp. 156-81; Trevor-Roper, *Witch Craze*, op. cit., p. 124.
47 Kieckhefer, op. cit., pp. 88-9.
48 Cf. *Malleus Maleficarum*, p. 231.
49 Cf. Kieckhefer, op. cit., p. 90 and p. 133; Lea, op. cit., vol. III, pp. 519-34.

50 Kieckhefer, op. cit., p. 90 and p. 143.

51 Russell, op. cit., p. 230.

52 Anglo, *Evident Authority*, p. 15.

53 Russell, op. cit., p. 232 and pp. 230-34.

54 Reviglio, op. cit., p. 61.

55 Cf., for example, the account of the sixteenth-century miller Menocchio obtained by an inquisitor in Friuli, in Ginzburg, *Il Formaggio e i Vermi*, pp. 34-9.

56 Anglo, op. cit., p. 17.

57 Kieckhefer, op. cit., p. 42 and p. 103.

58 Quoted in Williams, *Witchcraft*, p. 131.

Chapter 9: The Foundation of the Spanish Inquisition: 1478

1 Turberville, *The Spanish Inquisition*, p. 101 (references are to the Italian translation, Milan: Feltrinelli, 1965).

2 Ibid., pp. 19-20.

3 Cf. Fliche, *Histoire de l'Église*, pp. 107-9,

4 Cf. Kamen, *The Spanish Inquisition*, p. 22.

5 Cf. Mocatta, *The Jews of Spain and Portugal and the Inquisition*, pp. v-vi.

6 Kamen, op. cit., p. 22. There were massacres in Aragón and Majorca in the same year.

7 Ibid., p. 32; Turberville suggests 200,000 were exiled and 50-70,000 remained; cf. Coulton, *Inquisition and Liberty*, p. 297.

8 Turberville, op. cit., p. 46.

9 Ibid., p. 47; Kamen, op. cit., p. 144.

10 Kamen, op. cit., p. 146.

11 Ibid., p. 148.

12 Ibid., p. 151.

13 Turberville, op. cit., p. 59.

14 Llorente, *Histoire Critique de l'Inquisition*, vol. I, p. 285.

15 Turberville, op. cit., pp. 67-9.

16 From Montano, *Sanctae Inquisitionis Hispanica Artes*, 1857, quoted by Darwin, *The Holy Inquisition*, pp. 20-2.

17 Kamen, op. cit., p. 164.

18 *The Manner of the Spanish Inquisition*, Ms Tanner 99, Bodleian Library; quoted by Darwin, op. cit., p. 24.

19 Llorente, op. cit., vol. I., p. 306.

20 Cf. Kamen, op. cit., p. 166.

21 Ibid., p. 165.

22 Ibid., p. 168.

23 Turberville, op. cit., pp. 73-4.

24 Kamen, op. cit., p. 169.

25 Turberville, op. cit., p. 74.
26 Kamen, op. cit., p. 171.
27 Turberville, op. cit., pp. 74-5.
28 Kamen, op. cit., p. 172.
29 Pignata, *Le avventure*, p. 9.
30 Llorente, op. cit., vol. I, p. 309.
31 In Sabatini, *Torquemada*, pp. 158-9.
32 In Kamen, op. cit., p. 174.
33 Ibid., p. 174.
34 Ibid., p. 175.
35 Turberville, op. cit., pp. 80-1.
36 Quoted in Kamen, op. cit., p. 176.
37 William Lithgow, quoted in Scott, *Torture throughout the Ages*, pp. 172-4.
38 Kamen, op. cit., p. 179.
39 Ibid., pp. 179-80.
40 Quoted in Darwin, op. cit., p. 29.
41 Kamen, op. cit., p. 181.
42 Ibid., p. 182.
43 Taken from Kamen, op. cit., p. 184.
44 Ibid., p. 187.
45 Turberville, op. cit., p. 88.
46 Kamen, op. cit., p. 187.
47 Ibid., pp. 188-9.
48 Quoted in Scott, op. cit., pp. 71-3. Kamen gives another account, pp. 191-5.
49 Cf. Reviglio, op. cit., p. 47, n.
50 Cf. Monter, *Ritual, Myth and Magic*, p. 62.

Chapter 10: Reform and the Roman Inquisition

1 Elton, *Reformation Europe*, p. 180.
2 Ibid., p. 181.
3 Cf. Daniel-Rops, *The Catholic Reformation*, pp. 21-2.
4 Ibid., p. 74.
5 Ibid., pp. 86-7.
6 Quoted in Francis Marion Crawford, *Ave Roma Immortalis*, London: Macmillan (1912), p. 348.
7 Daniel-Rops, op. cit., p. 89; Crawford, op. cit., pp. 348-56 has a good though romanticized account.
8 Putnam, *The Censorship of the Church of Rome*, p. 4; on the influence of books in early sixteenth-century Europe, see Elton, op. cit., pp. 29-34.

9 Putnam, op. cit., pp. 64-76. He gives 36 other examples before the 1559 Index.
10 Daniel-Rops, op. cit., p. 76.
11 Cf. Putnam, op. cit., pp. 182-8.
12 Cf., Lea, *Chapters*, p. 81.
13 Cf. Grendler's book *The Roman Inquisition and the Venetian Press*.
14 Putnam, op. cit., p. 26.
15 Ibid.
16 Cf. Thorndike, *Magic and Experimental Science*, vol. VI, pp. 152-5; Yates, *Giordano Bruno and the Hermetic Tradition*, pp. 341-55.
17 Firpo, *The Flowering and Withering of Speculative Philosophy*, p. 267.
18 Milton, *Areopagitica*, London: Brodie (nd), p. 33.
19 1917 *Index*, pp. 34-5.
20 Daniel-Rops, op. cit., p. 141.
21 Blunt, *Artistic Theory in Italy*, Oxford: OUP, 1962, p. 116.
22 Cf. Falcone, *La Nunziatura di Malta*, p. 9.
23 Ibid., p. 21.
24 Paschini, *Venezia e l'Inquisizione Romana*, p. 6.
25 Ibid., p. 25.
26 Pullan, *The Jews of Europe and the Inquisition of Venice*, p. 26.
27 Paschini, op. cit., pp. 117-21.
28 Pullan, op. cit., p. 313.
29 Ibid., p. 314.
30 Yates, op. cit., pp. 338-49; Thorndike, op. cit., vol. VI, pp. 428-8.
31 Holt, Elizabeth, *A Documentary History of Art*, New York: Anchor Books (1958), pp. 69-70.
32 Blunt, op. cit., p. 116.
33 Cf. Stillman Drake's *Galileo*..
34 Favaro and Lungo, *Dal Carteggio e dai Documenti*, p. 166.
35 Santillana, *The Crime of Galileo*, p. 290.
36 Favaro and Lungo, op. cit., pp. 178-9.
37 Von Gebler, *Galileo Galileii and the Roman Curia*, p. 89.
38 Favaro and Lungo, op. cit., p. 179-80.
39 Ibid., p. 233-4.
40 Ibid., p. 272.
41 Cf. Langford, *Galileo, Science and the Church*, pp. 130-1.
42 Favaro and Lungo, op. cit., p. 270.
43 Ibid., pp. 276-8.
44 Ibid., p. 292.
45 Drake, op. cit., p. 78.
46 Favaro and Lungo, op. cit., p. 319 (Francesco Niccolini to Galileo, 23 October, 1632).
47 Ibid., p. 325.
48 Von Gebler, op. cit., p. 252 and p. 263.

49 Favaro and Lungo, op. cit., p. 359.
50 Ibid., p. 443.
51 Langford, op. cit., p. 160.
52 Quoted in Redondi, *Galileo Eretico*, p. 201.
53 Redondi, op. cit., p. 204.
54 Ibid., p. 205.
55 Pignata, *Le Avventure*, pp. 15-16.
56 Ibid., p. 14.
57 Ibid., pp. 27-8.
58 Ibid., p. 74.

Chapter 11: The Witch Craze and the Inquisition

1 Norman Cohn, *The Myth of Satan and his Human Servants*, in Douglas, *Witchcraft*, p. 12; cf. Williams, *Witchcraft*, p. 177.
2 Cf. Russell, *Witchcraft in the Middle Ages*, p. 24.
3 Trevor-Roper, *Witch-Craze*, pp. 123-4.
4 Cf. Russell, op. cit., p. 249.
5 Trevor-Roper, op. cit., pp. 124-5.
6 Monter, *Witchcraft in France and Switzerland*, p. 200; Williams, op. cit., pp. 247-62.
7 Cf. Ginzburg, *I Benandanti*, p. 27, n3.
8 Turberville, *Medieval Heresy*, pp. 145-8; cf. Williams, op. cit., p. 249.
9 Williams, op. cit., p. 251.
10 Quoted from Williams, op. cit., pp. 252-3
11 Cf. Thorndike, *Magic and Experimental Science*, vol. VI, p. 514; and Trevor-Roper, op. cit., pp. 134-5.
12 Ginzburg, op. cit., p. 5.
13 Ibid., p. 4 and p. 36.
14 Ibid., p. 10.
15 Ibid., p. 15.
16 Ibid., p. 17.
17 Ibid., p. 105.
18 Ibid., p. 45.
19 Ibid., p. 156. Sion's confession is reported pp. 152-6.
20 Cf. ibid., pp. 165-6.
21 Ibid., p. 175.
22 Russell, op. cit., p. 42.
23 Quoted in Ginzburg, op. cit., p. 176.
24 Horsley, *Who Were the Witches?* pp. 689-90.
25 Ibid., p. 695.
26 Monter, op. cit., pp. 116-18, Table 6.
27 Thomas, *Religion and the Decline of Magic*, p. 520.

28   Monter, op. cit., p. 124.
29   Muraro, *La Signora del Giuoco*, p. 213.
30   Midelfort, *Witch Hunting*, pp. 180-1, Table 14.
31   Monter, op. cit., pp. 119-20, Table 7.
32   Monter, op. cit., p. 197.
33   Marwick, *Witchcraft as a Social Strain Gauge*, p. 280.
34   Midelfort, op. cit., p. 193; Trevor-Roper, op. cit., p. 142.
35   Horsley, op. cit., p. 700 and p. 705.
36   Ibid., p. 712.
37   See for instance Clark, *Inversion, Misrule and the Meaning of Witchcraft*.
38   Review in *TLS*, 23 July 1976, p. 902.
39   Horsley, op. cit., pp. 713-14.
40   Trevor-Roper, op. cit., p. 130.

Chapter 12: The Apotheosis and Decline of the Spanish Inquisition: 1558-1834

1   La Mantia, *Origine e Vicende*, p. 26.
2   Turberville, op. cit., p. 167.
3   La Mantia, op. cit., p. 36.
4   Llorente, *Histoire*, vol. I, p. 331.
5   Falcone, *La Nunziatura di Malta*, p. 45.
6   Letter quoted by La Mantia, op. cit., p. 45.
7   Ibid., pp. 208-11. Computed from his lists.
8   Turberville, op. cit., p. 168.
9   Ibid., pp. 168-9.
10   Ibid., p. 169.
11   Cf. Livermore, H. V., *A History of Portugal*, Cambridge: CUP, 1947, pp. 244-245; Turberville, op. cit., pp. 107-8.
12   Turberville, op. cit., pp. 170-1.
13   Ibid., pp. 174-5.
14   Cf. Daniel-Rops, op. cit., pp. 188-9.
15   Cf. La Mantia, op. cit., p. 92.
16   *De Justa Haereticorum Punitione*, Venice, 1599; cited in Putnam, op. cit., p. 20.
17   Llorente, op. cit., vol. I, p. 281 and p. 456.
18   Lea, *Chapters*, p. 20.
19   Ibid., p. 23; Llorente, op. cit., vol. I, p. 457.
20   Kamen, *The Spanish Inquisition*,, p. 95.
21   Ibid., p. 96; Lea, *Chapters*, pp. 62-3.
22   Lea, ibid., p. 493.
23   Llorente, op. cit., vol. I, pp. 492-3.

24 Kamen, op. cit., p. 98.
25 Croft, *Englishmen and the Spanish Inquisition*, p. 260.
26 Ibid.
27 Cf. Kamen, op. cit., p. 103.
28 Lea, op. cit., p. 80.
29 Ibid., p. 73,
30 Kamen, op. cit., p. 104.
31 Ibid., pp. 100-1.
32 Lea, op. cit., p. 81.
33 Putnam, op. cit., p. 303.
34 Kamen, op. cit., p. 108.
35 Croft, op. cit., pp. 250-1.
36 Ibid., p. 253.
37 Ibid., p. 254.
38 Ibid., pp. 257-8.
39 Ibid., p. 259.
40 Ibid., p. 260.
41 Turberville, op. cit., p. 157.
42 *An Apology for the Free and Accepted Masons*, 1738, in Oliver, *History of Masonic Persecution*, pp. 89-92.
43 Ibid., p. 91.
44 Ibid., p. 96, n19.
45 *An Examination of the Acts of the Associated Synod against Freemasons*, in Oliver, op. cit., p. 140.
46 *An Apology*, op. cit., p. 126.
47 Ibid., p. 93.
48 Ibid., p. 95.
49 The following account is taken from the edition in Oliver, op. cit.
50 Cf. Turberville, op. cit., p. 158, n.
51 Cf. Gilabert, *La Abolición*, pp. 339-340.
52 Kamen, op. cit., p. 278.
53 Ibid.
54 Translated from Gilabert, op. cit., p. 342; cf. also Turberville, op. cit., pp. 177-81.
55 Turberville, op. cit., p. 181.
56 Kamen, op. cit., p. 283.

Chapter 13: Inquisition and Index in the Twentieth Century

1 Quoted by J. R. Glorney Bolton, *Roman Century 1870-1970*, London: Hamish Hamilton, 1976, p. 156.
2 Ibid., pp. 165-6.
3 Translated from 1945 *Index*.

4 Ibid., p. vii-viii.
5 Ibid., p. ix.
6 Casati, *L'Indice dei Libri Proibiti*, pp. 27-8.
7 Quoted in Stephen Knight, *The Brotherhood: The Secret World of the Freemasons*, London: Granada, 1983, p. 252. Cf. David A. Yallop, *In God's Name*, London: Jonathan Cape (1984), pp. 175-6.

Chapter 14: Conclusion: Some Effects and Influences of the Inquisition

1 Elton, *Reformation Europe*, p. 43.
2 Cf. F. Hamlin, P. Ricketts, J. Hathaway, *Introduction à l'Étude de L'Ancien Provençal*, Geneva: Doz, 1967, pp. 13-14.
3 Jules Arnoux, *Les Troubadours et Les Félibes du Midi*, Geneva: Slatkine Reprints, 1972, p. 43 (first edition Paris, 1889).
4 Pierre Aubry, *Trouvères et Troubadours*, Geneva: Slatkine Reprints, 1974, p. 131 (first edition, Paris, 1910).
5 Cf. Hinnesbusch, *History of the Dominican Order*, p. 57.
6 Aubry, op. cit., pp. 131-2.
7 Lea, *Inq. Middle Ages*, vol. II, p. 110.
8 Lea, *Chapters*, p. 189.
9 Kamen, *The Spanish Inquisition*, p. 105.
10 Blunt, *Artistic Theory in Italy*, p. 106.
11 G. E. R. Lloyd, *Greek Science after Aristotle*, London: Chatto and Windus, 1973, p. 169.
12 Cf. Thorndike, *Magic and Experimental Science*, vol. II, p. 666.
13 White, *A History*, vol. I, p. 385.
14 Thorndike, op. cit., vol. VI, pp. 152-5.
15 Favaro and Lungo, op. cit., pp. 179-80.
16 Firpo, *The Flowering and Withering of Speculative Philosophy*, pp. 170-271.
17 Lea, *Inq. Middle Ages*, vol. I, p. 560.
18 Thomas Nagel, *Ruthlessness in Public Life*, in Stuart Hampshire (ed.), *Public and Private Morality*, Cambridge: CUP, 1978, p. 75.
19 Aldous Huxley, *The Perennial Philosophy*, London: Chatto and Windus, 1946, p. 221.

Select Bibliography

Alatri, Mariano da, 'Fraticellismo e Inquisizione nell'Italia Centrale', *Picenum Seraphicum*, Anno XI (1974), pp. 289-314.

——, 'Inquisizione francescana nell'Italia centrale nel secolo XIII', *Collectanea Franciscana*; 1. Tomus XXII, (1952), pp. 225-50; 2. Tomus XXIII, (1953), pp. 51-165.

——, 'Inquisitori Veneti del Duecento',*Collectanea Franciscana*, Tomus XXX (1960), Fasc. 4, pp. 398-419.

——, 'Una sentenza dell'inquisitore Fra Filippo da Mantova (1287)', *Collectanea Franciscana*, Tomus XXXVII (1967), Fasc. 1-2, pp. 142-4.

Allier, Raoul, *Magie et Religion*, Paris: Berger Levrault (1935).

Ambrosini, Maria Luisa, *The Secret Archives of the Vatican*, London: Eyre & Spottiswoode (1970).

Anglo, Sydney (ed.), *The Damned Art: Essays in the Literature of Witchcraft*, London: Routledge and Kegan Paul (1977).

Barber, Malcolm, *The Trial of the Templars*, Cambridge: CUP (1978).

Barraclough, Geoffrey, *The Medieval Papacy*, London: Thames and Hudson (1968).

Barrett, W. P., *The Trial of Jeanne d'Arc*, London: Routledge (1931).

Battisti, Eugenio, *L'antirinascimento*, Milan: Feltrinelli (1962).

Brooke, Christopher, 'Heresy and Religious Sentiment: 1000-1250', in *Medieval Church and Society: Collected Essays*, London: Sidgwick and Jackson (1972), pp. 139-61.

Brown, Peter M., 'I veri promotori della "rassettatura" del "Decameron" nel 1582', *Giornale storico della letteratura italiana*, CXXXIII (1956), pp. 544-572; CXXXIV (1957), pp. 314-332.

Casati, Giovanni, *L'Indice dei Libri Proibiti: Saggi e Commenti*,

Milan-Rome: Pro Familia, 3 vols. (1936).

Cauzons, Th. de, *Histoire de L'Inquisition en France*, Paris: Bloud (1909), 2 vols.

Cheney, C. R., 'The Downfall of the Templars and a Letter in their Defence', in *Medieval Texts and Studies*, Oxford: Clarendon Press (1973), pp. 314-27.

Clark, Stuart, 'Inversion, Misrule and the Meaning of Witchcraft', *Past & Present*, No. 87 (May 1980), pp. 98-127.

Cohn, Norman, *The Pursuit of the Millennium: Revolutionary Millenarians and Mystical Anarchists of the Middle Ages*, London: Secker and Warburg (1957).

——, *Europe's Inner Demons* , London: Paladin, 1976.

Coulton, George C., *Inquisition and Liberty*, Boston: Beacon Press (1938).

——, 'Historical Revision: The Inquisition up to date', *History*, vol. xxii (September 1937), pp. 153-9.

Cox, Michael, *Mysticism: The Direct Experience of God*, Wellingborough: The Aquarian Press (1983).

Craveri, Marcello, *Sante e streghe: Biografie e documenti dal XIV al XVII secolo*, Milan: Feltrinelli (1980).

Croft, Pauline, 'Englishmen and the Spanish Inquisition, 1558-1625,' *The English Historical Review*, vol. LXXXVII, no. 343 (April 1972), pp. 249-68.

Daniel-Rops, H., *The Catholic Reformation*, London: Dent (1962).

Darwin, Francis, 'The Holy Inquisition', *Church Quarterly Review*, CXXVI (1938), pp. 19-43.

Douais, C., *L'Inquisition: Ses Origines – Sa Procédure*, Paris: Librairie Plon (1906).

——, *Les Albigeois: Leurs Origines, Action de L'Église au XIIe siècle*, Paris: Poussielgue Frères (1880).

—— (ed) *Barnardus Guidonis: Practica Inquisitionis Heretice Pravitatis*, Paris: A. Picard (1886).

Douglas, Mary (ed.), *Witchcraft: Confessions and Accusations*, London: Tavistock (1970).

Drake, Stillman, *Galileo*, Oxford: OUP (1980).

Elton, G. R., *Reformation Europe: 1517-1559*, London: Fontana (1963).

Emery, Richard Wilder, *Heresy and Inquisition in Narbonne*, New York: Columbia University Press (1941).

Falcone, Pompeo, *La Nunziatura di Malta dell' Archivio Segreto della S. Sede*, Rome: Edizioni dell'Archivio Storico di Malta, (1936).

Fabre, Lucien, *Joan of Arc*, London: Odhams (1954).

Favaro, Antonio, and Del Lungo, Isidoro (eds.), *Dal Carteggio e Dai Documenti: Pagine di Vita di Galileo*, Florence: Sansoni (1968).

Fiertz, Gertrude, 'An Unusual Trial under the Inquisition at Fribourg, Switzerland, in 1399', *Speculum*, XVIII (1943), pp. 340-57.

Finucane, Ronald C., *Miracles and Pilgrims: Popular Beliefs in Medieval England*, London: Dent (1977).

Firpo, Luigi, 'The Flowering and Withering of Speculative Philosophy', in Eric Cochrane (ed.), *The Late Italian Renaissance 1525-1630*, London: Macmillan (1970), pp. 266-84.

Fliche, A., Thouzellier, C. and Azais, Y., Histoire de l'Église, vol. X: *La Chrétienté Romaine (1198-1274)*, Paris: Bloud and Gay (1950).

Fredericq, Paul, *Corpus Documentorum Inquisitionis Haereticae Pravitatis Neerlandicae*, Gent: J. Vuylsteke, and 'S. Gravenhage: Martinus Nijhoff (1906).

Fumi, Luigi, *Eretici e Ribelli nell'Umbria: Studio Storico di un Decennio (1320-1330)*, Todi: Atanòr (1916).

Gebler, Karl von, *Galileo Galilei and the Roman Curia*, London: Kegan Paul (1879).

Gilabert, Francisco Marti, *La Abolición de la Inquisición en España*, Pamplona: Ediciones Universidad de Navarra (1975).

Ginzburg, Carlo, *I Benandanti: Ricerche sulle stregoneria e sui culti agrari tra Cinquecento e Seicento*, Turin: Einaudi (1966).

——, *Il Formaggio e i Vermi: Il cosmo di un mugnaio del '500*, Turin: Einaudi (1976).

Grendler, Paul F., *The Roman Inquisition and the Venetian Press, 1540-1605*, Princeton: Princeton University Press (1977).

Grundmann, Herbert, *Religiöse Beuregungen im Mittelalter*, Hildesheim: Georg Olms (1961).

Gui, Bernard, *Manuel de l'Inquisiteur*, ed. G. Mollat, Paris: Librairie Ancienne Honoré Champion, 2 vols. (1926).

Guiraud, Jean, *The Medieval Inquisition* (tr. E. C. Messenger), London: Burns Oates and Washbourne (1929).

Guirman, Arthur, *The Great Heresy*, Jersey: Neville Spearman (1977).

Hair, P. E. H., An Irishman before the Mexican Inquisition, 1574-5, *Irish Historical Studies*, XVII, No. 67, March 1971, pp. 297-319.

Haskins, C. H., 'Robert le Bougre and the Beginnings of the Inquisition in Northern France', in Haskins, *Studies in Medieval Culture*, Oxford: Clarendon Press (1929), pp. 193-244.

Hinnesbusch, W. A., *A History of the Dominican Order: Origins and Growth to 1550*, New York: Alba House (1965).

Horsley, Richard A., 'Who Were the Witches? The Social Roles of the Accused in the European Witch Trials', *Journal of Interdisciplinary History*, IX:4 (Spring 1979), pp. 689-715.

Housley, N. J., 'Politics and Heresy in Italy: Anti-Heretical Crusades, Orders and Confraternities, 1200-1500, *Journal of Ecclesiastical History*, vol. 33, no. 2 (April 1982, pp. 193-208.

Index Librorum Prohibitorum, Romae: Typis Polyglottis Vaticanis (1917).

Index Librorum Prohibitorum, Romae: Typis Polyglottis Vaticanis (1945).

Kaltner, Balthasar, *Konrad von Marburg und die Inquisition in Deutschland*, Prague: Verlag von F. Tempsky (1882).

Kamen, Henry, *The Spanish Inquisition*, New York: New American Library (1965).

Kieckhefer, Richard, *European Witch Trials: Their Foundation in Popular and Learned Culture, 1300-1500*, London: Routledge and Kegan Paul (1976).

Kors, A. C., and Peters, E. (eds.), *Witchcraft in Europe, 1100-1700, A Documentary History*, London: Dent (1973).

Kramer, Heinrich, and Sprenger, James, *Malleus Maleficarum*, (trs. Montague Summers), London: Arrow Books, (1971).

Kristeller, Paul Oscar, *Renaissance Concepts of Man and Other Essays*, New York: Harper and Row (1972).

Ladner, Gerhart B., 'Homo Viator: Medieval Views on Alienation and Order', *Speculum*, XLII (1967), pp. 233-59.

La Mantia, Vito, *Origine e Vicende dell'Inquisizione in Sicilia*, Palermo; Sellerio (1977; Reprint of two works of 1886 and 1904).

Lambert, Malcolm, *Medieval Heresy: Popular Movements from Bogomil to Hus*, London: Edward Arnold (1977).

Langford, Jerome J., *Galileo, Science and the Church*, Ann Arbor: The University of Michigan Press (1966).

Lea, Henry Charles, *Chapters from the Religious History of Spain connected with the Inquisition*, Philadelphia: Lea Brothers (1890).

——, *Superstition and Force*, Philadelphia: Lea Brothers (1892).

——, *The History of the Inquisition of the Middle Ages*, New York: Macmillan, 3 vols (1908).

——, *A History of the Inquisition in Spain*, New York: Macmillan, 3 vols. (1906-1907).

Leff, Gordon, *Medieval Thought*, Harmondsworth: Pelican (1958).

——, 'Heresy and the Decline of the Medieval Church', *Past & Present*, no. 20 (November 1961), pp. 36-51.

——, *Heresy in the Later Middle Ages*, Manchester: The University Press, 2 vols. (1967).

Lerner, Robert E., 'Medieval Prophecy and Religious Dissent', *Past & Present*, no. 72 (August 1976), pp. 3-24.

Lightbody, Charles W., *The Judgements of Joan: Joan of Arc, a Study in Cultural History*, Cambridge, Mass. (1961).

Little, Lester K., *Religious Poverty and the Profit Economy in Medieval Europe*, London: Paul Elek (1978).

Llorca, Bernardino,. *La Inquisición Española: Estudio Critico*, Comillas:

Universidad Pontifica (1953).

Llorente, D. Jean-Antoine, *Histoire Critique de l'Inquisition d'Espagne*, Paris: Treuttel et Würtz, 4 vols. (1818; second edition).

Luchaire, Achille, *Innocent III, le Concile de Latran et la Réforme de L'Église*, Paris: Hachette (1908).

Madaule, Jacques, *Le Drame Albigeois et le Destin Français*, Paris: Bernard Grasset (1961).

Maisonneuve, Henri, *Études sur les Origines de l'Inquisition*, Paris: J. Vrin (1960; second edition).

Manselli, Raoul, *L'Eresia del Male*, Naples: Morano (1963).

——, 'De la "persuasio" à la "coercitio"', in *Le Crédo, la Morale et l'Inquisition* (Cahiers de Fanjeaux, 6), Toulouse (1971), pp. 175-9.

——, *I Fenomeni di Devianza nel Medio Evo: Le Devianza nella Società Ecclesiastica*, Turin: G. Giappichelli (1972).

Marwick, Max, 'Witchcraft as a Social Strain Gauge', in M. Marwick (ed.), *Witchcraft and Sorcery*, Harmondsworth: Penguin (1970), pp. 280-95.

Maycock, A. L., *The Inquisition: From its Establishment to the Great Schism*, London: Constable (1926).

Midelfort, H. C., Erick, *Witch Hunting in Southwestern Germany, 1562-1685*, Stanford: Stanford University Press (1972).

Mocatta, Frederic David, *The Jews of Spain and Portugal and the Inquisition*, London: Longmans, Green and Co. (1877).

Molinier, Charles, *L'Inquisition dans le Midi de la France, aux XIII et au XIV siècle*, Paris: Sandoz et Fischbacher (1880).

Monter, E. William (ed.), *European Witchcraft*, New York: John Willey (1969).

——, *Witchcraft in France and Switzerland, the Borderlands during the Reformation*, Ithaca and London: Cornell Uuniversity Press (1976).

——, *Ritual, Myth and Magic in Early Modern Europe*, Brighton: The Harvester Press (1983).

Moore, R. I., 'The Origins of Medieval Heresy', *History*, vol. 55 (1970), pp. 21-36.

Moorman, J., *A History of the Franciscan Order from its Origins to the Year 1517*, Oxford: Clarendon Press (1968).

Morghen Raffaello, *Medioevo Cristiano*, Bari: Laterza (1978; first edition, 1951).

Muchembled, Robert, 'Witchcraft, Popular Culture, and Christianity in the Sixteenth Century with Emphasis upon Flanders and Artois', in *Ritual, Religion and the Sacred* (selections from *Annales: Economies, Sociétés, Civilisations*, vol. 7), Baltimore and London: Johns Hopkins (1982).

Muraro, Luisa, *La Signora del Giuoco: Episodi della Caccia alle Streghe*, Milan: Feltrinelli (1976).

Murray, Alexander, 'Piety and Impiety in Thirteenth-Century Italy', in *Popular Belief and Practice, Studies in Church History, 8,* Cambridge: CUP (1972), pp. 83-106.

Nelli, René, *La Philosophie du Catharisme,* Paris: Payot (1978).

Nickerson, Hoffman, *The Inquisition: A Political and Military Study of its Establishment,* London: John Bale, Sons and Danielsson (1923).

O'Brien, John, *The Inquisition,* New York: Macmillan (1973).

Oliver, George (ed.), *The History of Masonic Persecution in Different Quarters of the Globe,* London: Richard Spencer (1847).

Partner, Peter, *The Murdered Magicians: The Templars and their Myth,* Oxford: OUP (1982).

Paschini, Pio, *Venezia e l'Inquisizione Romana da Giulio III a Pio IV,* Padua: Antenore (1959).

——, *Vita e Opere di Galileo Galilei,* Rome: Herder (1965; first edition, 1964: Pontificiae Academiae Scientarum scripta varia).

Pellegrini, Ludovico, 'L'Inquisizione Francescana sotto Alessandro IV (1254-1261)', *Studi Francescani,* Anno 64°, no. 4 (1967), pp. 73-100.

Perkins, C., 'The Wealth of the Knights Templar in England', American Historical Review, XV (1910), pp. 252-263.

Pernoud, Régine, *The Retrial of Joan of Arc: The Evidence at the Trial for the Rehabilitation, 1450-1456,* London: Methuen (1955).

Pignata, Giuseppe, *Le avventure di Giuseppe Pignata fuggito dalle carceri dell' Inquisizione di Roma,* Palermo: Sellerio (1980), (translated from *Les Aventures de Joseph Pignata echappé des prisons de l'Inquisition de Rome,* Cologne: Pierre Marteau, 1725).

Pullan, Brian, *The Jews of Europe and the Inquisition of Venice, 1550-1670,* Oxford: Basil Blackwell (1983).

Putnam, George Haven, *The Censorship of the Church of Rome, and its Influence upon the Production and Distribution of Literature,* New York and London: The Knickerbocker Press, 2 vols. (1906).

Quicherat, Jules, *Procès de Condamnation et de Réhabilitation de Jeanne D'Arc dite La Pucelle,* Paris: Jules Renouard, 5 vols (1841).

Redondi, Pietro, *Galileo Eretico,* Turin: Einaudi (1983).

Reinhard, J. R., 'Burning at the Stake in Medieval Law and Literature', *Speculum,* XVI (1941), p. 186-209.

Reviglio Della Venera, Carlo, *L'Inquisizione Medioevale ed il Processo Inquisitorio,* Milan: Bocca (1939); (second edition, revised and expanded, Turin: Berruti, 1951).

Riley-Smith, Jonathan, 'Crusading as an Act of Love', *History,* vol. 65, 1980, pp. 177-92.

Runciman, Steven, *The Medieval Manichee: A Study of the Christian Dualist Heresy,* Cambridge: CUP (1982: 1st Ed., 1947).

Russell, Jeffrey Burton, *Dissent and Reform in the Early Middle Ages,* Berkeley and Los Angeles: University of California Press (1965).

——, *Witchcraft in the Middle Ages*, Ithaca and London: Cornell University Press (1972).

Sabatini, Rafael, *Torquemada, and the Spanish Inquisition*, London: Stanley Paul (1913).

Sacchetti Sassetti, Angelo, 'Giovanni da Capestrano Inquisitore a Rieti', *Archivum Franciscanum Historicum*, Annus XLIX (1956), Iulius-October, Fac. III-IV, pp. 336-8.

Santillana, Giorgio de, *The Crime of Galileo*, London: Mercury Books (1961).

Scott, George Ryley, *The History of Torture Throughout the Ages*, London: Torchstream Books (1949).

Scott, W. S., *The Trial of Joan of Arc, Being the verbatim report of the proceedings from the Orléans manuscript*, London: The Folio Society (1956).

Southern, R. W., *Western Society and the Church in the Middle Ages*, Harmondsworth: Pelican (1970).

Sumption, Jonathan, *The Albigensian Crusade*, London: Faber and Faber (1978).

Thomas, Keith, *Religion and the Decline of Magic: Studies in Popular Beliefs in Sixteenth and Seventeenth-century England*, London: Weidenfeld and Nicolson (1971).

Thorndike, Lynn, *A History of Magic and Experimental Science*, London: Macmillan, 8 vols. (1923-1958).

——, 'Relations of the Inquisition to Peter of Abano and Cecco d'Ascoli', *Speculum*, I (1926), pp. 338-43.

Thouzellier, Christine, *Hérésie et Hérétiques, Vaudois, Cathares, Patarins, Albigeois*, Rome: Edizioni di Storia e Letteratura (1969).

——, *Rituel Cathare*, Paris: Éditions du Cerf (1977).

Turberville, A. S., *Medieval Heresy and the Inquisition*, London: Crosby, Lockwood, and Son (1920).

——, *The Spanish Inquisition*, London: Butterworth (1920).

Trevor-Roper, H. R., 'The European Witch-craze of the Sixteenth and Seventeenth Centuries', in M. Marwick (ed.), *Witchcraft and Sorcery*, Harmondsworth: Penguin (1970), pp. 121-50.

Ullmann, Walter, 'The Defence of the Accused in the Medieval Inquisition', *Irish Ecclesiastical Record*, LXXIII (1950), pp. 481-9.

——, *A Short History of the Papacy in the Middle Ages*, London: Methuen (1972).

Vacandard, E., *Étude Historique et Critique sur le Pouvoir Coercitif de l'Église*, Paris: Bloud (1912).

Vidal, J.-M., *Bullaire de l'Inquisition Française au XIVᵉ Siècle*, Paris: Letouzey et Ané (1913).

Wakefield, W. L., *Heresy, Crusade and Inquisition in Southern France 1100-1250*, London: George Allen and Unwin (1974).

Walker, D. P., *Spiritual and Demonic Magic: from Ficino to Campanella*, Notre Dame and London: University of Notre Dame Press (1975).

Williams, Charles, *Witchcraft*, Wellingborough: The Aquarian Press (1980; first edition, 1941).

White, Andrew Dickson, *A History of the Warfare of Science with Theology in Christendom*, New York: Dover, 2 vols. (1896).

Yates, Frances A., *Giordano Bruno and the Hermetic Tradition*, London: Routledge and Kegan Paul (1964).

Index